Is It a

BIG PROBLEM

or a

LITTLE PROBLEM?

Is It a
BIG PROBLEM
or a
LITTLE PROBLEM?

When to Worry, When Not to Worry, and What to Do

AMY EGAN, M.A., AMY FREEDMAN, M.A., CCC-SLP,

JUDI GREENBERG, M.S., OTR/L, SHARON ANDERSON, OTR/L

Illustrated by Jessica Glickman

ST. MARTIN'S GRIFFIN 🐾 NEW YORK

www.stmartins.com

Book design by AMANDA DEWEY

© Illustrations by Jessica Glickman

Library of Congress Cataloging-in-Publication Data

Is it a big problem or a little problem? : when to worry, when not to worry, and what to do / Amy Egan . . . [et al.]. — 1st ed.
p. cm.
Includes bibliographical references and index.
ISBN-13: 978-0-312-35412-1
ISBN-10: 0-312-35412-6
1. Child psychology. 2. Child development. 3. Problem children. 4. Preschool children—Psychology. I. Egan, Amy.

HQ772. I69 2007

649'. 64—dc22   2007017218

First Edition: October 2007

1 3 5 7 9 10 8 6 4 2

A Note to the Reader

All persons described in this book are fictitious, and any resemblance to real persons, living or dead, is entirely coincidental.

This book is not intended to serve as a substitute for professional advice and intervention, and is not intended to replace the advice of a pediatrician or medical professional, who should be consulted about any health care issues that may affect your child's behavior.

The information contained in this book is the product of observations made by the authors in their clinical practices, as well as their review of relevant literature in their fields of expertise. The literature at times reflects conflicting opinions and conclusions. The views expressed herein are the personal views of the authors and are not intended to reflect the views of any group or organization with which the authors are affiliated.

To Brian, David, Jay, and Wayne,
who have supported us in so many ways,
and to all of the children who have enriched
our personal and professional lives.

Contents

Part Three

. . .

WHERE CHILDREN STRUGGLE

Appendices

. . .

Acknowledgments

This book is the result of many years of collaborative effort that was due to the visionary efforts of Shari Gelman and Lillian Davis, the founders and guiding lights of the Ivymount School, a private school that has served over seven thousand students with disabilities. It was their vision, drive, intelligence, and caring that sparked the creation of the Center for Outreach in Education (CORE). In response to requests from the community for help with supporting children in typical preschools, the CORE program was founded. Since 1996, CORE has been making a difference in children's lives.

Thank you to the Ivymount staff members who have supported and encouraged our work through CORE. We would like to extend a special thanks to Jan Wintrol, Stephanie DeSibour, Lee Oppenheim, and Andrea Mullins. We feel fortunate to be part of the Ivymount School family.

We are also greatly appreciative of the school directors, teachers, and parents who have invited us into their classrooms with open minds and cooperative attitudes. We have learned much from you and we hope this book is a small way of giving back to those with whom we have worked.

From SA: I would like to thank my parents and siblings who gave me my "roots" and "wings." The values, lessons, and opportunities of my early years shaped who I am today. It is with love and appreciation that I thank my husband and best friend, Wayne. Together we have created a wonderful life filled with love, support, and mutual respect. Each phase of our lives together has brought new adventures and challenges, but best of all, knowledge, joy, and wonderful memories.

Thank you to my children, Kristin and Scott, who taught me first-hand the joys and challenges of parenthood. And a special thanks and tribute to my twin granddaughters, Sydney and Samantha, who continue to delight all with their love of life and learning. While grandparenting is a pleasure, it is truly one of life's greatest rewards to watch my children become awesome parents.

From AE: I wouldn't be where I am today without the mentoring and encouragement of teachers, administrators, and professors, or the patience and faith of parents who entrusted me with their "babies." Each in his or her own way has shaped my approach to working with children and families, and for that I am grateful.

I am also deeply appreciative to my family and close friends whose unwavering support and enthusiasm helped me get through days that didn't seem to have enough hours. To Brian, the precious gift of time you gave me by spending countless hours "flying solo" with our three young children so that I could click away at the computer is something I'll never forget. I could never have accomplished this without you: your time, your thoughts, and, most important, your daily example of being a caring, compassionate parent to our children. I am so blessed to be sharing this wild ride of parenthood with you.

From AF: I would like to thank my husband, David, for his tremendous support. With all of my heart I thank you for being my "partner in parenting." I am my best because you are by my side; I love you. Thank you to my children, Bonnie, Daniel, and Molly, who have taught me so many real-life parenting lessons. I have loved every moment we have spent together in my "mommy van" because it meant I was spending time with you. It is a joy to be your mother! Thank you to my parents, Charlotte and Gil Cushner, for encouraging me to follow my heart and always being there to support my professional and personal goals.

Finally, thank you to my in-laws, Marlene and Jerry; and to Michael, Tricy, Fred, Patricia, Jill, Michael, Marc, Sheri, Philip, Ronn, and all my nieces and nephews for putting the "fun in family!"

From JG: On a personal note, I want to thank this amazing group of women with whom I have shared this journey. It is not often that one gets the opportunity to work, create, and laugh with professionals such as Amy, Sharon, and Amy. It has been the highlight of my professional life to have worked on this book with these incredible women. I will always treasure the times we have spent writing this book and, most important, the deep friendship and bond that I feel for each of you. Thank you for this great adventure.

To my parents, Al and Clare Brown, thank you for giving me your love and for always being there for me. To my children, Rachel, Becky, and Sam, who provided us with much of the raw material for this book: you are my heart and my soul. Nothing makes me prouder and happier than being your mom. Thank you for your encouragement, support, laughter, and, most of all, your love. You have taught me what is important in life. To my best friend and husband, Jay, thank you for believing in me even when I didn't believe in myself. Thank you for supporting me, laughing with me, growing up and old with me, and, most of all, for loving me. Your passion for helping children has always inspired me to work harder and give more. I am truly blessed to be your wife.

A special thanks to Jessica Glickman for the beautiful illustrations that are just what we envisioned. To our editor at St. Martin's Press, Sheila Curry Oakes, thanks for taking a chance on us. To Djana Morris, our agent: without your faith in us, our dream would have never become a reality. Thank you!

Part One

...

THE BASICS

Prologue

Starting on the Right Foot

I t's a nagging feeling. It's a worry that keeps pushing its way into your brain at night as you lay exhausted in bed, simply wanting sleep. It's a concern that your thoughts keep turning to during the chitchat of neighborhood moms at your weekly playgroup. It's something that you hem and haw about bringing up with your pediatrician. You find yourself asking, again and again: *Is this a big problem or a little problem?* In other words, Should you worry, or should you not?

Problem behaviors come in all shapes and sizes, and at all ages and stages of development. Some are bigger than others, but all cause parents and professionals (and children) some degree of angst and stress. As members of a team of child developmental specialists, and as mothers and a grandmother, we are very familiar with these issues, and have worked with thousands of parents and professionals to help them sort out the challenges faced by young children. Our team is based in Rockville, Maryland, at the Ivymount School's Center for Outreach and Education (CORE). Our mission is to help teachers and families identify needs and implement strategies for helping young children be more successful at home and at school. The team consists of two occupational therapists, a speech and language therapist, and a behavioral specialist. We provide individualized support, resources, and strategies to help families, teachers, and, most important, children who face big and little problems. This book will do the same for you.

Differences in children's learning styles, temperaments, and personalities are a given, but when should those differences raise a red flag? What strategies might parents try on their own before getting anyone else involved in the problem-solving process? How much frustration or anxiety should a parent (or child) endure before calling in a specialist? When should a parent seek a professional opinion? And what can a frazzled parent do in the meantime, while waiting for that professional evaluation?

Let's begin with a list that sums up the most common complaints we hear from parents (and professionals) about young children. These behaviors may represent a "little" problem, easily manageable with a few specific strategies, or they may be the tip of the iceberg of a bigger problem.

---

10 Common Concerns of Parents About Their Children

1. He doesn't listen.
2. She's stubborn and always needs to have things go her way.
3. He's constantly on the go, in perpetual motion.
4. She has so many tantrums! She's so emotional!
5. He has a really hard time with changes in routine.
6. Sometimes she gets so wound up!
7. He's so clumsy and always getting hurt.
8. She can be so mean and aggressive toward other kids.
9. He's really shy and withdrawn.
10. She's such a picky eater.

These ten statements could describe almost every child, on one day or another, at some point during their early years. However, when one or more of these complaints become the norm for a child, a red flag goes up. If these glitches are pervasive and affect a child's ability to be happy, relate to others, and go about his daily life, there may be a real problem. Only further investigation will tell us whether it is a "big" problem or a "little" problem.

Most children have little problems. This book is full of strategies to help parents and other caregivers manage the little problems of early childhood. When we use these strategies to adjust the environment, modify behaviors, and give a child time to mature a bit more, little problems can resolve themselves without outside intervention. For the purposes of this book, "little" problems are those that are manageable without outside intervention. "Big" problems, on the other hand, may require the support of professionals. If our strategies and suggestions do not solve the problem, if the problem seems to be bigger than parents and teachers alone can fix, we'll point you in the right direction for further evaluation and support. Big problems will often seem much more manageable once the proper professionals are involved. A little intervention can go a long way toward keeping a big problem not-so-big!

"There's nothing out there that describes my child's issues," complained an exhausted mother recently. It is a complaint we hear frequently in our work with families of young children as well as from their teachers and child-care providers. Nice neat labels don't always describe the children we work with. They are regular children in regular schools, preschools, and child-care centers who, for a variety of reasons, are having difficulty being successful at school and/or home. Most teachers don't know what to do with these kids: they have tried everything in their bag of tricks and come up empty handed, or have come up with a plan that only works part of the time. Some of these children are even on the verge of being kicked out of preschool or child care because of their behavior.

These children may be enigmatic—happy and affectionate one minute, aggressive or stubborn as nails the next; cooperative and eager to please in one setting, but aloof or bossy in another. They appear in virtually every classroom in the country. *Aggressive, aimless, class clown, impulsive, rigid, controlling, explosive, anxious,* and *disorganized* are a few of the terms used by parents and teachers to describe such individuals.

These children don't necessarily have ADD or ADHD but may have language processing problems, or sensory processing differences. They may have difficulty understanding or remembering multistep directions. They may be extremely touch-sensitive and lash out impulsively when others come uninvited, albeit innocently, into their personal space. They may have trouble getting their body to do what their brain is directing, such as with motor-planning problems that interfere with all sorts of activities in a typical child's day. Children with any of these conditions experience constant frustration and/or assaults on their sense of self-worth. Not surprisingly, frustration and low self-esteem often leads to behavior problems.

Hitting, biting, yelling, or a thirty-minute tantrum over a Popsicle color certainly gets parents' attention, and they need to know what to do. Having a speech and language evaluation followed by speech and language therapy may address the underlying issues of auditory comprehension, but in the meantime parents need a "Band-Aid"—*practical ideas and strategies to help them get through the days*, or ideas to give the teacher that might prevent another biting incident this week.

Dealing with the immediate behavior problem is only half of the solution. The underlying cause (if there is one) needs to be identified and treated as well, so that it no longer triggers the problem behavior. This book addresses both of these needs. It takes a long-term and short-term approach to helping children become more successful in their interactions with others and in their classroom and home environment.

The chapters of part 2 delve into specific areas of development, what different or delayed development might look like, underlying causes of behaviors, strategies to support children, and explanations of why these strategies work. Sometimes, however, parents do not know what the underlying problem is—or if one exists—but *where* a child has trouble is obvious. Certain scenarios, be they birthday parties, playdates with certain friends, or trips to the store, are sure to end in tears or tantrums. For this reason, the chapters of part 3 are organized into typical parts of a child's life. Unique factors present in different environments trigger behavior problems or stress in a child. By understanding the potential stressors in different parts of a child's life, we can better prepare him for the challenge and support him throughout the experience with situation-specific strategies. Finally, the appendices provide nitty-gritty reference tools to aid in using the strategies described throughout the book.

One goal of this book is to empower parents: to remind them of their strength and influence in their young child's development. Using the resources and strategies in this book, parents can help a child experience more success and less frustration as he goes through his day, before ever stepping foot into a clinician's office.

Meet the Children

Sprinkled throughout the book are four children who are trying hard, each in his or her own way, to do what they are supposed to and still get their own needs met at the same time. They have a range of behavioral and developmental issues. Some have little problems whereas others have big problems. Through vignettes, we describe the thought processes and questions we had as we created intervention plans for them, and the strategies that helped them to be more successful in their daily lives.

Perplexing Sean

Sean has a smile that lights up a room. At two and a half, he is a delight to his parents. Still, his mom has a persistent feeling that something is not quite right. Sean has a baby brother who is six months old, and his parents can see how quickly and apparently effortlessly he appears to master early motor milestones.

In contrast, Sean sat up at nine months of age, never crawled, and began walking at seventeen months. At two and a half, his movements appear awkward and clumsy. He is only able to go up and down the stairs while holding onto an adult's hand. He is beginning to run, although his movements are more like those of a younger toddler.

Sean is generally a good eater but often overstuffs and has to be watched carefully at meals so that he does not choke. He appears to have difficulty chewing, particularly more resistive foods such as meats. He only drinks from a lidded "sippy" cup and refuses to use a cup without a lid. He has begun to hold a spoon when eating yogurt; however, he quickly tires of utensils and prefers to eat finger foods.

Sean has started to speak using single words and occasionally combines two words together. Generally he does not follow directions (e.g., "Give me your cup") or pay attention when asked questions (e.g., "Do you want your ball?"). At times he does not look at his mother when she is talking, or when he is talking to her. He simply seems oblivious to her presence. However, if his mother goes out, he greets her on her arrival home with a big hug, so she knows he is attached to her and misses her when she is gone.

Sean's father works out of the home and is a very hands-on parent. His mother works part-time at the local university. In addition, his parents hired a nanny who has been employed by the family since Sean was four months old. She is extremely devoted to Sean and his brother.

Recently, Sean started attending a Mommy and Me class. His mother began to realize that his speech and movement skills lagged behind the other children, even those who were several months younger. He has the most difficulty when the teacher calls the group together to sing songs and play with instruments. Sean refuses to sit with the other children and is only content when allowed to roam the room.

Scott, the Negotiator

At three and a half, Scott is an active, imaginative, articulate little boy. Like most older siblings, he happily bosses his two-year-old brother around and dictates their play. Most of the time, his easygoing brother is happy to comply and follow his lead.

Scott goes to a top-notch preschool five mornings a week, where his teachers report that he is cooperative, social, and full of energy. He follows the classroom routine well and is eager to try new activities. His interests ebb and flow. One month, he may be heavily into block building; and the next month, he may gravitate toward the Play-Doh table for birthday cake–making. He loves outdoor play, and on the weekends spends time at the park with his dad.

Scott's parents have demanding jobs. His father is an attorney at a law firm, while his mother, a journalist, has tried to scale back her hours at work so that she can spend more time at home with the boys. She, like most moms who work part-time outside the home, struggles to make time for everything: "quality time" with her kids and enough "face time" at work so that she stays in the loop and still receives choice assignments, and of course time for household chores and meal prep. She has the flexibility to work from home occasionally, which can be both a blessing and a curse. She also has a part-time nanny, which allows her some uninterrupted hours for work, but when she's on a deadline she often dips into her "mommy time" to finish a project.

Scott's parents frequently find themselves in debates and negotiations with him. They feel as if they've been having power struggles with him forever. They chalk it up to his being the first child and being very bright and articulate. He still throws temper tantrums, and they are not sure if this is normal. Since they work so much, they both feel they have so little time with him that they'd rather not fight. They are inclined to let him have his way unless his request seems unreasonable, such as wearing shorts to school on a thirty-degree day or going out to eat when they've already begun preparing a meal. Then they end up in a big fight that escalates into the parents yelling, Scott screaming and crying, and his younger brother becoming upset as well. (When Scott is upset, his brother usually is too, out of solidarity!) It is easy to see why Scott's parents avoid battles with him, but at the same time they often feel as if he is running the show. They don't think this is the way parenting is supposed to be, but they aren't really sure how to change things. They wonder if he may have some sort of behavior problem because he still throws tantrums and has such a hard time following directions at home.

Unpredictable David

David is a four-and-a-half-year-old boy. He was born three weeks early. From birth, David has had difficulty with regulation. That is, he vacillates from being wild and overstimulated to being quiet and thoughtful. He is known both at school and at home for being stubborn and having frequent meltdowns. David is a continual challenge to his parents and teachers.

David is less reactive to pain and touch than are most of his peers. He loves to touch, fall, and wrestle even when his siblings or peers don't want to engage in rough play. At home, David rarely follows directions. He becomes silly and runs away rather than comply. When his parents run out of patience, they usually try to pick him up, but he goes limp and falls to the floor, which irritates them even more. The most difficult thing about David is that his parents and teachers can never trust that he will follow directions when he becomes silly and wound up.

David has attended an excellent preschool program since the age of three. At school he can play with peers cooperatively, but when things don't go his way, the play quickly deteriorates, with him taking toys from other children or destroying the play setting (knocking down the block village, or pushing all the cars off the bridge). For the past two years, David's preschool teachers have had concerns about him. They share their concerns at parent-teacher conferences. David's parents are sympathetic and concerned, but they, too, are challenged by his behavior.

David's father works long hours and his mother is a busy stay-at-home mom. David has two older brothers who are in elementary school. This busy family, with three children in two schools, lessons, playdates, and so on, keeps mom and kids on the go and navigating many transitions throughout the day. Although this family does not have strict routines and schedules, the other children are able to go with the flow, whereas David is not as adaptable. He seems to have a keen sense of when things are getting stressful. At times it seems he just needs to upset the apple cart for no apparent reason. These out-of-control behaviors range from being silly and uncooperative to extreme stubbornness to a full-blown meltdown or tantrum. He is challenging because it is hard to know when he will fall apart and whether it will be a brief disruption or a major meltdown.

David's parents have the same basic philosophy of child rearing; however, both admit that at times, especially when time is short, their youngest child brings out the worst in both of them. They become angry and frustrated much more quickly as kindergarten approaches, as they are more and more uncertain about David's ability to behave appropriately there. They are increasingly anxious and feel pressure to do whatever they can to change his behavior and get him to shape up before he begins kindergarten.

"Hurricane" Danielle

Danielle is a beautiful blond-haired, blue-eyed five-year-old who was born very prematurely. She spent her first two months in a neonatal intensive care unit. At eight months of age, she seemed more like an infant. Danielle produced very few sounds and had trouble sitting up by herself. Due to her delayed development, her pediatrician recommended an early intervention program.

As Danielle approached her first birthday, with much love and attention from family, supportive friends, and professionals, she began to make gains in all areas of development. By her second birthday, she was walking and talking, with more than fifty words. At two and a half, the developmental team discharged Danielle and encouraged her mom to keep up the stimulating activities.

However, her mother felt that Danielle's activity level was more extreme than other children her age. She was always on the run and it was hard to get her to sit and listen to a story. She enjoyed getting dizzy and rocked unconsciously when watching TV. Danielle did not seem to notice when it was cold—she went out of the house without a coat and fought her mom when she tried to put on her hat and gloves. Danielle had no fear and jumped from high places without any regard for safety. She would fall or skin her knee without reacting. On the other hand, she hated to get her hair washed and cried hysterically at the sound of a hair dryer or a vacuum cleaner. She tended to make strange noises, simply for the sake of the noise.

When Danielle was three and a half, her family enrolled her in a preschool class. At this point, her mom began worrying about her child's ability to play with other children. Danielle would run up and push them, although she did it with a smile and a friendly manner. She had difficulty sitting in circle and paying attention like the other children. The teachers reported that she did not like the art projects but did enjoy the Play-Doh and the cozy corner or the housekeeping area. Teachers reported some concerns but thought, since it was her first school experience, she needed time to grow and socialize with the other children. They felt in time she would grow out of it.

Now that she is in her second year of preschool, the bar has been raised. The other children seem to be progressing but Danielle still seems to be playing like a young three-year-old. She has great ideas for play but has trouble executing the sequence of steps needed to put her ideas into action. She continues to crave movement and has a hard time sitting still in circle. She sits in the teacher's lap for support, and although she loves her friends she tends to hug them too tightly and handles toys so roughly that they often break.

Danielle is very enthusiastic; however, when she becomes excited it is extremely hard to calm her down. Her mom has difficulty with simple routines such as dressing, self-care, mealtime, and bedtime. She is feeling overwhelmed by Danielle's constant needs and by the child's ability (or inability) to meet those needs.

Smoothing the Bumpy Roads

Young children like Sean, Scott, David, and Danielle want to be successful and please adults. Children want to have friends at nursery school, go with their parents to the grocery store, enjoy birthday parties, and be able to play with peers on a playground. They want to be good, and when they are not, there is probably a reason for their behavior. They may face developmental challenges that make these regular, day-to-day experiences very difficult for them.

This book was written for the parents and professionals who want so very much to help. By sharing examples of youngsters who have experienced developmental glitches and how we worked with their families and caregivers, we lay out real-life strategies and tips for smoothing the bumpy road of early childhood. We help parents and caregivers to think about behavior differently—to think about plausible alternatives to someone's being viewed as "just stubborn," "just like his father," or "just the way she is." We lay out strategies to improve a child's behavior or comfort level in a given situation, and suggest when (if at all) to enlist the help of a professional, and how to go about mobilizing community resources. We provide information about how to tweak the environment so that the child can succeed. With this book parents, who are the foremost experts on their children, will be better able to decide once and for all, *Is this a big problem or a little problem?*—and what they should do about it. And *that* will help parents fall asleep a little easier at night.

One

A Child in His Environment

Where Nature Meets Nurture

The moment parents see their newborn baby, they are captivated. From that first lusty scream or wondrous gaze, parents and children affect each other, deeply. The lifelong dance, the give-and-take, between parent and child has begun.

Researchers describe children's development as "transactional," because of the reciprocal, progressive, and ongoing nature of the relationship between a child and his environment. From birth, infants impact their surroundings: when they cry, they get picked up; when they smile, they receive a smile in return. Toddlers, of course, perfect this dynamic: when they pitch a fit in the aisle of a grocery store, they may get the candy that had been denied previously.

A child's unique temperament and preferred learning styles influence the way he behaves. A youngster's natural strengths and weaknesses also affect his interactions with the world. Parents and other caregivers each bring their own parenting or teaching style to the table (as well as their own temperament!). Siblings throw a little spice into the mix as well. Social interactions are only one part of a child's environment. Physical surroundings and daily routines round out the other aspects of the environment in which they live. When a child's temperament and learning style interact with the teaching and parenting styles of a caregiver, the result may be a happy child and happy parent, or the child and adult may find themselves at odds with each other.

Temperament

"My three-year-old's birth was just like his life has been up to this point: intense, impatient and full of drama."

Right from the start, parents realize that their baby has a unique personality. How a child's temperament and a parent's temperament fit together and how a parent accommodates or challenges a child's temperament impacts how that child grows and develops socially, not only in the parent-child relationship but in other relationships as well.

A person's basic temperament persists throughout life; however, it becomes refined over time. An infant's temperament is made up of the way he reacts to things—how excitable he is—and his ability to calm himself. Some infants become distressed quite easily whereas others can handle the most zealous sibling's "love" with nary a flinch. Some babies drift off to sleep effortlessly yet others require elaborate combinations of rocking, patting, or bouncing. As a child matures and becomes more and more socialized, he learns to behave in ways that elicit responses and interactions from others that he finds enjoyable or comfortable. Temperament then becomes reflected in personality. A child's personality is the combination of his inborn disposition, environment, family, caregivers, and cultural or societal values.

How a child learns to live with who he is, depends, in part, on how well the parenting he receives complements his temperament. How comfortable he is with himself (and his self-esteem) is strongly affected by his environment and the people around him. This interplay is known as the "goodness of fit." When a child's temperament, environment, and interactions with the people around him are working together, then there is a "good fit" between the child and his environment. When a child's temperament, environment, and interactions do not work together, then there is a "bad fit" between the child and the world around him.

It is important for parents to understand their child's temperament as well as their own, so they can understand how their temperament, parenting style, and the home environment can influence a child and his ability to adapt to his world. Parents need to examine the temperament of each of their children individually and adapt their parenting styles to each child's needs. Some children need to be nudged and encouraged, whereas others need to be constantly reined in.

A parent may find that his own temperament conflicts with his child's temperament. For example, an outgoing, sports-oriented father may not match a shy, quiet son who enjoys being outdoors. However, they may enjoy biking or taking a hike in the park together. A quiet, serene household with two older, intellectual parents might be out of sync with their high-energy, fast-moving, spirited young boy. These parents may hire a teenager to play soccer with their child, but also make time for games of catch and cheer him on at his games. Differences in temperaments can lead to impatience and misunderstanding regarding the needs of the child, or it can offer a place for creative compromise.

Similarly, a parent's *expectations* for a child may not match his child's temperament. Expecting a calm, quiet child who doesn't like new situations to join in at a raucous birthday party without adult support, may not be realistic or fair to the child. Such an expectation may foster withdrawal or refusal if the parent insists. The same child may thrive when parents encourage a playdate with one other child, in their own home. This scenario would be more compatible with his temperament.

Parents need to create child-rearing environments that recognize each child's temperament while encouraging their children to test or explore their limits. Yes, it would be easier if that active, fast-moving child was with the sports-oriented dad, but it often doesn't work out like that. Parents need to adjust their styles to the needs of their children, and help the youngsters to learn to adapt and adjust to their environments. The vignette below describes a child who figured out how to adapt to his environment.

SAM, age 3

Sam was the youngest of three children on the way to a family outing to a large amusement park. Sam was a quiet, happy little guy who was content to play "guys" and ghost busters with his best buddy, Andrew. He was afraid of clowns, loud noise, and fast rides. He shivered in the corner when going to Chuck E. Cheese for his big sister's birthday party. Still, he wanted to join the family when they planned an outing to the big-kid amusement park. Sam's big sisters ran off with their dad to the big roller coaster, while Sam stayed with his mom. After combing the grounds, they finally found a "Yogi Bear" ride that looked un-threatening. "Yes," Sam said, "I want to go." He was clutching his mom's hand for dear life but climbed into the little car with her and off they went. He let go of her hand as the ride started to move through a dark tunnel. Sam said nothing, so his mom fig-ured he was fine. When they emerged into the sunshine she saw he had his hands covering his eyes. "Sam, are you all right?" she asked. "Yes," he replied calmly. "The lion scared me so I cov-ered my eyes. I like the ride this way." Right then, it was obvious to his mom that Sam was in very capable hands—his own.

Adaptability—how readily a child adjusts to new situations—is a trait that is tied closely to temperament. Sam demonstrated an ability to adapt to his circumstances in a way that made the experience safe and comfortable for him. Imagine moving to a new house. We expect chil-dren to find that difficult. A young child could become more tentative or more unruly or regress in some way—all reactions that would show he is struggling with the change.

A smaller change, such as replacing a child's bed, can also be hard on a slow-to-adapt toddler. Even when parents perceive the change to be positive, it can be stressful to a young child. When a child is pushed to be flexible or adaptable when he is not ready to be, behavior can deteri-orate rapidly. Often, preparation is the easiest solution. That doesn't mean that a slow-to-adapt child has to have the same bed until he goes to college. It means that we try to reduce the unexpectedness of the change.

We prepare him. We might introduce the transition by reading books about a little boy's getting a new bed. We might make a photo storybook to prepare him for the change, with real pictures of him in his old bed, buying a new bed, taking apart his old bed, and finally showing him resting or sleeping in his new bed. Children are visually oriented and are reassured by the use of visuals as well as predictability. If they can see a representation of something now or something that is expected of them, as opposed to only hearing about it, they will be less frightened.

Children are more likely to manage new challenges successfully when they feel valued and safe, which most often occurs when parents are willing to perform the "dance" of give-and-take parenting, leading and following, pushing and supporting, as they help their child adapt and grow.

What happens when children still don't manage new situations well, or their behavior doesn't improve? How much can be attributed to temperament and when might it be something more? Is he just quiet and shy or does he really not know how to join in play with others? The following chapters illustrate how to tease out things like temperament and environmental factors from more significant learning differences or delays.

Young children are works in progress. Yes, certain temperamental traits will be theirs for a lifetime, but with each year they will learn more about themselves and the best way to handle their own needs and responses. Until then, it's up to the adults in their lives to be their navigators, coaches, and always, their biggest fans.

Learning Styles

When observing young children in play groups or at preschool, it is amazing to see the differences in their personalities and styles of learning and interacting. One child is a whirlwind of activity. He is the first to climb to the top of the new jungle gym on the playground. Another child watches carefully from the sidelines when people talk. She has an incredible vocabulary. A third child is an observer—he notices everything and he loves to look at books. The fourth child is covered from head to toe with paint and is having a great time. Each of these children is engaged in play-based learning, all using different learning modes. Each child is picking up information in different ways, by looking or listening, by watching, or by experiencing. These early learning preferences or tendencies may be the mode of the moment or, if this is the child's predictable response, it may be an early indicator of her learning style.

Research shows that every child has a preferred learning style, or way of observing her surroundings and gaining new information. While everyone learns in a variety of ways, we all do best when using our preferred senses and ways of exploring the world.

Many researchers agree that there are four primary learning styles:

1. Auditory (based on hearing)
2. Kinesthetic (based on movement)
3. Tactile (based on touching and feeling)
4. Visual (based on seeing)

Certainly most children and adults use all four learning modes, but with a preference for, or more efficiency in, one or two areas.

The **Auditory** learner gains new information best by hearing it. A child may be an auditory learner if:

- He follows verbal directions easily.
- He is quick to remember the words to songs, rhymes, and stories.
- He repeats overheard phrases and comments.
- He loves to listen to books and/or music.

Here are a few ways to support the auditory learner: The more we talk, the more information he will gather. He'll enjoy hearing stories, both real and imaginary, and will like telling his own stories. A good teaching strategy for the auditory learner is to use songs and rhymes to teach new things, from colors and letters to days of week.

Kinesthetic learners like to get physically involved in learning, using their bodies to experience new places and concepts. A child may be a kinesthetic learner if:

- She pretends to be characters from a favorite book or video, acting out the stories.
- She performs an exciting motor activity over and over again.
- She loves the playground and incorporates imaginary play.

The kinesthetic learner will learn by doing. Support her learning by helping her act out stories because it will help her understand and remember her favorite books. Teach new information by creating movement games. Teach new concepts or help her remember important safety and social rules by role-playing different scenarios.

Tactile learners need to feel and touch things to understand how they work. A child may be a tactile learner if:

- She touches everything, and is especially drawn to objects with interesting shapes or textures.
- She needs to actually feel abstract concepts (e.g., to touch an ice cube to understand cold, or to feel a rock and a cotton ball to understand the concepts of hard and soft).
- She may have trouble following directions to unfamiliar tasks.

Support a tactile learner by giving her hands-on materials for play and learning. Offer her a variety of puzzles, Legos, and table games. Let her practice her shapes and letters by drawing with her finger in sand, flour, or clay.

The **Visual** learner picks up information best by seeing pictures and watching others do the activity. Signs that a child may be a visual learner:

- He is quick to recognize shapes, colors, and letters.
- He remembers how to do things that he has seen others doing.
- He loves photos, pictures, displays, TV, and videos.

You can help a visual learner by demonstrating how to do new tasks, by using charts with photos or sketches to show daily routines. Offer a child books with plenty of engaging pictures and graphics; show him educational TV and videos as a way of exploring new topics.

Using **visuals** such as objects, pictures, sketches, and print can help a visual learner learn most optimally but also help many other children learn. For example a teacher of young three-year-olds can use objects that the children can choose from to pick a song. A child picks the toy boat out of a box, hands it to the teacher, and the class sings, "Row, Row, Row Your Boat."

Visuals can help children learn rules. Parents and children can review household and safety rules given in both pictures and print. It is important that the visual information be presented where the child can easily see it and in a way that the children understand. For nonreaders, this means using pictures to support understanding.

Using pictures and print, let a preschool or young school-age child know what he needs to bring in his backpack every day to school. By hanging this on a sign on the door, he can take more responsibility for organizing his belongings for a successful school day (and eliminating the need for a parent to rush to school with emergency lunch money!).

Adults can use visuals to support learning, language, and to help children know what is expected of them. Appendix E reviews the use of visuals in greater detail. Much of this information is based on the work of speech pathologist Linda Hodgdon.

All children need to have experiences that call every learning style into play so that they can succeed in school and beyond. However, when adults help their children learn in the way that's most natural for them, they are more likely to develop the confidence needed to master all learning styles.

Natural Strengths and Weaknesses

Children are born with unique talents and capabilities, which may be unveiled during their early years of development. A parent may tap into his child's love of music by enrolling him in a music class. Or, a coordinated and fearless child may love the thrill of gymnastics and become quite adept. When youngsters experience success at something, they usually want to repeat the experience. The more they practice, the better they get, and the better they get, the more they enjoy themselves.

Conversely, when something is hard or they experience failure, they tend to avoid repeating the experience. Children's preferences for certain activities may also reflect an avoidance of other activities. The less they try to use certain skills, the less practice they get, and the less developed they become. A natural weakness may become even more pronounced because of a lack of experience.

As parents of young children recognize, development does not always proceed at an even pace. It is affected by a child's natural inclinations or tendencies toward certain activities, which are often influenced by a child's temperament and preference for quiet vs. loud, active vs. sedentary stimulation. For example, a ten-month-old who is content to sit in one place for a long period of time practicing her verbal skills may be advanced in that area while her motor skills may lag behind. Another ten-month-old may be taking first steps, crawling rapidly around the house, and pulling herself up on everything in her environment. However, she may not be as attentive to language and not have as advanced communication skills.

Each child develops at his own pace. However, because a child develops so rapidly during the first five years of life, growth in one area impacts other areas of development. A child who maneuvers his body and crawls under furniture and around his home by the end of his first year will use that knowledge at approximately three years of age when he begins to follow commands incorporating spatial concepts (e.g., "Put the shoes under the chair"). Moving his body through space allows a youngster to draw on those motor skills to develop later cognitive skills, such as an understanding of the prepositions "on" and "under."

A child who develops speech and language skills may use them to build social skills. The youngster may use language to make requests, play with peers, and to socialize with others. In this case, speech and language skill acquisition impacts social skills.

Conversely, if a child is having difficulty in one area of development, it also impacts other areas, particularly in the first five years of life. If a child who experiences tactile sensitivity chooses to play on the perimeter of the playground, away from classmates, eventually he may have difficulty playing and interacting with peers.

A child who has trouble understanding and processing language may be hesitant to approach peers, because he finds these interactions confusing. Therefore he may play alone when several families get together for a playgroup or only talk to the adults who will adjust their language in order to be understood. Eventually, the child demonstrates secondary problems interacting with peers that might have been prevented with early intervention.

When children show learning delays or differences, we can help them use their natural strengths to address, or compensate for, their weaknesses. So, a child who has trouble making friends but is very physically coordinated might do well on a sports team. His strengths or physical abilities will be highlighted and provide him with a confidence boost, while the cooperative yet structured format of team practices and games will give him the opportunity to work on his weakness—social skills.

Parenting Styles

When people find out that they are expecting a child, they immediately think about what kind of parents they will be. Will they be like their own parents, or take a decidedly different approach? They also begin to pay more attention to the parenting abilities of others and consciously imitate particular traits of those they admire.

However, what many parents do not initially realize is that although they may have some preconceived notion about how they will handle various situations, the parent who is ultimately the most successful is the one who takes into consideration the strengths and areas of need of the child. Being flexible about parenting styles will allow them the most success.

The following are some points to consider. Please note although we authors would like to think of ourselves as organized but flexible parents, we have all found ourselves, at one time or another, in all of these categories. The solutions that follow are tried-and-true strategies that we have learned through our professional work, and also from our own mistakes and successes.

The **organized but flexible parent** generally has a plan for the day. This parent makes sure that most days the child eats and naps or rests on a regular schedule. Planning careful transitions between activities is also important so that the child knows what is going to happen next. These may come in the form of a verbal warning (e.g., "Cleanup time") or visual warning (e.g., showing the child his coat and saying, "Time to go"). This parent knows when an activity is going well and should be extended, or when to cut a planned activity and bail out early. When an unexpected opportunity arises (e.g., an invitation from the neighbors to go to the zoo), this parent can determine if her child is up to the challenge. The parent has a plan, reads her child's cues well, and proceeds accordingly. Many organized but flexible parents find that they have fewer headaches if they allow the child to make some controlled choices, or **choices within parameters** (e.g., "Which long-sleeved shirt do you want?"). This also helps the child's burgeoning sense of self and independence, while giving the parent control over more important decisions.

The following profiles describe parenting styles we've all experienced at some point, and that aren't as successful for parent/child interactions.

The **disorganized parent** may multitask or begin too many projects at a time. The adult starts getting dressed, goes to wake up a preschooler, instructs him to begin his morning routine and then finishes getting dressed. Inevitably the child goes back to sleep or wanders over to the television. This parent can increase the chance of success by simply being nearby to support the child as she gets ready for school, and be there to provide help when the morning train begins to derail. Initially the parent may need to provide a great deal of assistance to the young child, but this support should be reduced over time. Finally, the parent can simply be nearby to help the child stay on task.

The **harried parent** often does not allow enough time for a specific task. Sometimes the solution involves simply thinking about the schedule and realizing how long each individual task takes. As the harried parent plows through a grueling morning schedule, the young child is literally dragged around on the adult's coattails. This translates into an irritable child who can't eat breakfast or dines in the car. Consequently, the youngster has little opportunity to work on self-help skills in the morning and does not have a quiet moment before he starts his school day. Often doing some of the morning work the night before, such as making lunches, selecting clothing, or packing bags, can take some of the pressure off both the parent and child.

The **que sera, sera parent** (Whatever will be, will be!) lives life in the moment, without a real schedule for the child. This works well when special opportunities arise, but on a regular basis this leaves some children feeling irritable, tired, and prone to frequent meltdowns. Sometimes planning out the day and sharing the plan with the child can make it go more smoothly.

The **overscheduled parent** provides nursery school and a variety of cultural and athletic opportunities. Music, dance, and soccer classes are all crammed into the day. However, this jam-packed schedule provides little opportunity for downtime, which many children need after a busy morning in a stimulating classroom. It also affords few chances to play quietly with an adult, read a book, cook with a parent, or have a playdate.

The **striving-for-perfection parent** works hard to make sure that both he and the child are at the top of their game at all times. This parent may work with the child for long periods of time on mastering the alphabet or doing fine motor tasks, yet fail to take into consideration the child's needs and areas of strength. Consequently, the child becomes frustrated and protests when the activities are introduced or forcefully pursued. This parent has more success when these tasks are broken down and presented as interesting opportunities that are provided for short periods of the day.

The striving for perfection parent tends to see that the child is especially well groomed and dressed in a matching, coordinated outfit for the school day. However, it is important to consider that the youngster, by doing her part and participating in an activity, may get the clothes dirty. Often this child is inconsolable when her dress gets grimy after a fall on the playground or gets covered with paint after art class. Sandals and party shoes make for rough going on playground equipment, which children can climb better if wearing sneakers.

The **buddy parent** is wonderful at playing and enjoys spending time with the youngster. This parent has some difficulty setting limits because he'd rather be a friend to his child. However, being able to set limits is an essential part of parenting and helps the child learn the rules and how to get along with others.

There are countless approaches to parenting, but the one that will usually work best feels instinctively right, and results in a happy and confident child.

Creating the Optimal Environment for a Child

Once you've had an opportunity to consider your child's temperament as well as your parenting style, you need a few nuts and bolts to shore up your effort to create the optimal environment in which a child may grow. Following is a short, short list of a few "best practices" to consider when living with (or working with) young children. In trying to discern whether a child has a big problem or a little problem, the first step is to set up an optimal environment, because that will give a child every possible opportunity for success. When you set up a child for success, many behavior problems will melt away. So before determining the magnitude of your child's problem, really consider to what extent these best practices are used at home and school.

Best Practice #1: Plan Thoughtful Transitions

Transition is a word that appears frequently throughout this book, because transitions are often the times when children have the most difficulty, and we see the biggest behavior problems. A transition occurs any time children are switching gears, or ending one activity and preparing to start another. Switching gears may require changes in energy level, such as when a child comes inside from playing in the yard and is expected to sit down and eat dinner. It may involve changes in whom the child is interacting with, such as when a babysitter arrives and Mom and Dad leave, or when a baby sibling wakes up from a nap and demands a parent's attention. Other typically big transitions include putting away toys, going to bed, and getting dressed, fed, and out of the house in the morning.

Transitions are difficult for children because the expectations on the child are changing: one minute it is fine to be running and yelling outside, but now he is expected to sit still and use an "inside voice" at the dinner table. Adjusting to the shift in expectations is often difficult. Similarly, when one activity is ending and another beginning, children often get hung up on the activity that is ending, and may whine or protest. A worn-out three-year-old may have trouble seeing beyond his mother's call to leave the park even though lunch and a nap would improve his mood considerably. Offering him a lunch of finger foods, which can be eaten in the stroller on the walk home from the park, may alleviate some of his distress because he now has something tangible (and hopefully desirable) on which to focus.

Difficulty with transitions can often be minimized with warnings about the pending shift, reminders of what the expectations will be for the new activity, and ample time for the child to shift gears between activities. For example, having a child wash her hands and help set the table before actually sitting down can be a nice segue between outside play and inside behavioral expectations.

Best Practice #2: Set Limits

Children need and expect us to set limits on their behavior. Yes, they push and push, but only to see where we push back, or where the line is. Children need us to be the traffic lights, organizing a big, often confusing world for them. We let them know when it is safe to go, when they are pushing the envelope, and when they have gone too far, or run a red light. Setting limits is a parent's way of teaching children how to get along in the world.

Best Practice #3: Use Simple Language

When a child is upset, he is not operating with his full mental capabilities. He cannot process, or understand, as much of what you are saying as he normally can, nor can he put together an articulate response.

The best way to talk with a child when he is upset is to use very simple, repetitive language in a calm voice. "You need a calm body," is an example of something we could say to an out-of-control preschooler who is having is tantrum. Younger children are especially sensitive to the tone or volume of their parents' voices. Yelling "Calm down!" at a child is not effective. Toddlers copy what they see, and if their parents aren't calm, they won't be able to calm down, either.

Best Practice #4: Be Consistent

Children are like little scientists, constantly probing through trial and error to see what the parents' consequence will be for various behaviors. They assess the relative importance of their parents' words and directions by the way their parents react to them when they do not follow directions. Children are experts at reading their parents, and know exactly when their parents *really* mean business. This may be a look in Mom's eye, a tone in Dad's voice, or something in their body language, but a child knows when she is close to the line and had better comply or else be at risk for a consequence.

When parents are inconsistent, or do not follow through on directions, children learn that whatever they did was effective in changing their parents' minds about something. If something works for them once in a while, like a tantrum, they are far more likely to keep trying, even in the face of repeated failures, because they know that every so often they'll hit the jackpot and Mom will give in.

Despite the best efforts, children struggle from time to time, even when you do everything the experts recommend, everything your mother (and even mother-in-law!) suggests and try to metamorphose into über-parents in the hope that you can fix your children's problems. How successful a child is with the extra support described throughout this book will give you insight about whether he is facing a big problem or a little problem. If the strategies work wonders, terrific—it was a little problem. If they don't make much appreciable difference, there may be a more complex, underlying issue that is preventing the child from being successful. When in doubt, seek a professional opinion.

Two

Play

The "Work" of Children

Learning to play is the work of children. Play helps children to understand their world and encourages them to learn how to solve problems and develop creativity. Through play, children socialize and interact with each other. Additionally physical play builds strong healthy bodies.

A time for unstructured play is time to be creative. It is something that all children need and sadly few have enough time or opportunity for this valuable learning experience. Some good examples are climbing trees, collecting bugs, playing in the stream, making roads in the dirt, or building fairy houses in the backyard.

This type of play seems to be disappearing. *If your child does not have time for any of these things, it may be time to look at his schedule and cut something out to make time for just "being a kid."*

Children's play varies at different ages. Elaine Weitzman, in *Learning Language and Loving It*, describes the types of play typically seen in toddlers and preschoolers. First, babies engage in **sensorimotor play**, where they get feedback to their senses by performing a (motor) action, such as banging pots and pans together, shaking a rattle, or knocking down a tower. They are learning that they can *affect* the world—their movements have consequences. They do not play with each other yet, though they love a rousing game of peekaboo with a parent or familiar adult.

Next, children begin to copy what they see others doing around them. This **functional play** is established in one- to two-year-olds, with some of this play continuing through three years of age. When engaging in functional play, children use items as they are intended. For example, the child may wipe a table with a sponge, brush a doll's hair with a hairbrush, or sweep the floor with a dustpan and brush. They imitate adults. Not surprisingly, favorite toys of youngsters at this age include child-size telephones, strollers, and grocery carts. Watch out for the remote— suddenly there is another member of the family determined to control the TV! Their play continues to be solitary; however, two-year-olds begin to play in parallel with each other, or share a space while doing similar activities but without directly interacting.

Two-year-olds also begin to participate in **constructive play**, which

Play is the work
of children!

continues through six years of age. For example, the child may use a big box to create a toy house, or large pillows to construct a tunnel.

Dramatic play is pretend play. The youngster may begin to participate in pretend play at three years and this culminates at six to seven years of age. Initially, the child acts out familiar scenarios, such as going to a restaurant or going to the doctor. Often, realistic props are used. As the child becomes more competent, he can use a variety of make-believe scenarios. He begins to include less realistic props in play. For example, the child may pretend that a hairbrush is a telephone or that the Play-Doh structure he has created is a cake with candles. Imaginary friends may make an appearance at this age, as well.

Among three- and four-year-olds, we see the emergence of **cooperative play** with peers. Children begin to work together in their play and eventually talk with each other about their play. Naturally, it is not always smooth sailing, so this is also the stage where adults need to be vigilant to help children use their words to solve problems with each other and take turns with desired items.

Games with rules often begin to become part of a child's play repertoire at four years of age and continue through adulthood. Five-year-olds may participate in early board or turn-taking games. Often, these games provide a structured format via which youngsters can successfully play with peers, because the rules are already set.

However, children in the pre-K to kindergarten years may spend more time creating and negotiating the rules, parameters, and roles of a play scheme than they actually spend playing. As their time concepts and abstract thinking concepts develop, they can now spend time *preparing* for imaginary events, rather than just enacting the event itself as a younger child would. They may make elaborate plans for a trip or set up a fort just so. These preparations are just as (if not more) important than the pretend trip or battle itself.

Creating the Environment

Regardless of their age, children's play may disintegrate for a number of reasons. Getting them back on track (or getting them going in the first place!) is easier when we consider the following aspects of their play.

First, consider the energy level of the activity. Children need a balance of high- and low-energy activities. When possible, meet them where they are: If they're racing around the house yelling and hollering, herd them out the door to the backyard, where their current behavior is more appropriate. As long as going outside is an option, this is a far easier way to manage the situation than trying to calm them down. Even on rainy days, they can go out—nothing is better than sanctioned splashing in mud puddles! On the other hand, if they are simply bored, they may really be asking for a little parent involvement: read a book, do a puzzle, or a crossword that would be too hard for them to do on their own.

Second, consider how much adult participation is required. Some activities require a high degree of adult supervision and involvement, whereas others do not. Try to match the activity with your own availability. In other words, don't pull out a new set of finger paints when you're about to call an old friend for a long chat! Encourage activities that they can do independently when you need them to be independent. Sometimes, they are much more likely to do such activities if they've just had a bit of undivided attention from you.

Consider the difficulty level of the activity. Some types of play or some toys are more challenging for children than are others. We don't want youngsters to encounter frustration after frustration, because then they'll be more likely to give up and resort to silly, wound-up behavior. Try to intersperse activities at which they are very competent with others that challenge them. After playing the hard game together, pull out the easy one for them to play on their own. Or, if you have time, get out the maze book to do together, but if you don't have time to play, pull out the coloring books instead.

Finally, consider the time constraints, if any. If it is a rainy day and the afternoon stretches endlessly before you, encourage your child to set up a fort or some other elaborate scheme. However, if you know that dinner will be on the table in twenty minutes, cut them off at the pass before they become engrossed in something that they won't have time to finish, and suggest an alternative activity that may be completed in a more timely fashion.

Thinking about children's play in the larger context of the rest of their day, their current mood, or your current needs and availability can help you set them up for success by matching the demands of an activity with the current resources and abilities of the child. Following are a few additional strategies for enhancing children's play.

Spicing up Playtime

- **Same old, same old:** Amazingly, adding one new toy to the mix can trigger children's play to move in a totally new direction. The addition of a new stuffed animal, a new hat or purse, or the doctor's kit, which has been buried in a bag in the closet for six months, can spur hours of new play scenarios for kids. Similarly, letting them use one or two real-life items from the kitchen can ignite your child's imagination and encourage novel types of play.
- **Location, location, location:** Change the environment to add a fun twist. Take the paper and crayons out to the deck or porch and draw pictures of the clouds. Wash the baby dolls and their clothes in the inflatable swimming pool on a hot day or in the bathtub on a rainy day. Move the chairs out of the way and throw a big sheet over the dining room table to make a "house." A secret space for kids holds all sorts of possibilities for play.
- **Rotate toys:** Keep at least half of the children's toys bagged in the attic or a closet. Every few months, rotate a few into the mix and pull a few out. This helps control the clutter in the play area as well. If something doesn't generate interest even after pulling it out several times, get rid of it. Stuffed animals may be boring individually but when kept together and pulled out

together, they create endless possibilities for veterinarian hospitals, zoos, circuses, and safari adventures.

- **Use prop boxes:** Prop boxes allow you to organize toys by theme. When pulled out, they give a child an immediate direction in which to take his play. Store boxes together but pull out one at a time. On the outside of the box, write a list of items included and those needed to complete the play theme. (Some items might be too bulky to fit in the box or might be needed around the house, so you might want to add them to the prop box only when it is in use.) Help the children get started with their play scheme and then step back and let their imaginations run wild.

  Prop box ideas include:

  ○ a birthday cake and party box with Play-Doh for a cake and party supplies

  ○ a pizza parlor with an Italian music CD, chef's hat and apron, checkered dishtowel "tablecloth," and pizza box that can also serve as the container to hold the other props

  ○ a beach trip with towels, toys, sunglasses, and even a cassette of environmental beach sounds

  ○ a pirate ship with dress-up clothes, paper towel–tube telescope, costume jewelry in a small box ("treasure!"), a map (with words or drawings, depending on the age of the children), capes (pillowcases pinned on shoulders), a stuffed monkey or bird, boots, and even cardboard swords

  ○ a camping prop box could have a dark colored sheet to drape over furniture for a tent, backpacks, toilet paper tubes taped together for binoculars, a flashlight, pillowcases or blankets for sleeping bags, a trail map, snacks, and water bottles

  ○ a firefighter prop box could include hats, rope "hoses," boots, red/orange/yellow tissue paper "fire," a firehouse bell, old cell or cordless phone "walkie-talkies," and pillows for sleeping in the fire station.

Adults and Play: An Important Partnership

Joining the child in his play is the ultimate compliment. Adult participation in play encourages the reluctant player, increases a child's feeling of self-worth, and fosters a strong bond between an adult and child. With adult involvement in play, a child may persist in an activity for longer periods of time. Adult support enhances the development of higher-level play skills. With this encouragement a child may engage in longer sequences of play, or tackle more challenging tasks. Teachers call it "scaffolding"— adults provide support to enable children to do things they wouldn't otherwise be able to do, but ultimately it is still their work, not ours.

In *Learning Language and Loving It*, Elaine Weitzman discusses three ways an adult can participate in the play. The adult and child can **parallel play.** The adult plays in close proximity to the child and comments on his/her own play, while using his own materials. This is a useful tool when engaging in functional play, where the child uses items for their real functions. For example, the adult can add comments to his own play while giving her own doll a bath.

Parallel play can also be used in constructive play. An adult, for example, can describe his own play as he builds his own structure with blocks or makes a bridge out of Legos.

Adults can also join the child by being an **active participant** in the play. In many instances, the adult takes on the role of simply being another contributor in the play and takes care not to direct the play. For example, if the child is playing restaurant, the adult can assume the role of a patron or waiter.

However, if a child is having difficulty playing with a variety of toys or has trouble engaging in play with peers, the adult may assume the role of a **play facilitator** to teach a new play skill or to encourage peer interactions. As the child becomes more proficient in the play, the adult can assume a less directive role and be more of an equal participant.

Regardless of whether you're consciously facilitating skill development or "just playing" with your child, the low-pressure, unhurried time together speaks volumes to your child about your feelings toward him. Playing together shows that you like spending time with him and that you are interested in his ideas and interests. Just as we try to read with our kids every day, try to play a little, too.

Scripting: An Important Tool

Scripts are words and phrases that a young child may be taught in different environments to help him communicate. These are generally **short** phrases and sentences that are easy to use, such as "help me," "my turn," "your turn is next," and "I'm done." Adults can model using these scripts to teach a youngster how to negotiate with peers, comment, and request help.

Adults who are engaged in play with youngsters can easily model these communicative scripts for youngsters who are having trouble interacting with peers. For example, if two youngsters are squabbling over using a particular toy, an adult can prompt one youngster to say "I'm next," instead of grabbing a desired item from a peer. Take care to phrase the words exactly as the child would say them, so that he doesn't become confused by the possessive pronoun.

When Play Is Not Fun!

Children look different in different environments. Playing in larger, more sensory rich environments tends to be challenging for some young children. Others may have difficulty in an unstructured environment, such as a park or a playground.

Whenever a child is having difficulty in a particular environment, it is helpful to observe and problem solve where the difficulty is occurring. Looking at the specific environment is important. Does it occur all the time? What specific types of play (dramatic, large motor, fine motor) is more challenging for your child? Does your child experience difficulties in other areas of development that are negatively impacting his play skills as well?

"My three-and-a-half-year-old tends to wander about the house. She really has trouble finding something to play with.

She loves her toy kitchen but tends to take all the items out
of the refrigerator and seems to have a hard time finding
something else to do in the play. How can I help her?"

Some children have difficulty getting started and then organizing and
sequencing their play. When this difficulty arises they tend to wander
the room, superficially examining items that interest them. Unfortunately children who do this on a regular basis are losing opportunities to
develop their play skills. However, many youngsters do well when given
some adult support.

Helping with Play

- **Find a quiet corner of the room where you can play together.** Turn off the TV and radio. This is particularly important with a child who appears to be distractible or who is still
  learning language.
- **Join your child in play.** Initially a child who wanders the room
  may need an adult to act as a play facilitator to help her sustain
  the play and organize and sequence it. The adult initially can
  join the child in play, which in itself can support her to play for
  longer periods of time. Do this several times a day, when you
  can, for several minutes at a time. For example, the mother of
  the child who likes to play in the kitchen corner can provide her
  little girl with a picnic basket and help her choose toy foods to
  take with her to play "picnic." Or, the adult might ask her to
  help make lemonade for her dolls using the lemons and pretend
  sugar bowl.
- **Practice and cultivate skills that can be used in play.** For example, provide real cooking opportunities for your child, which
  can then be generalized into her play. This activity will help the
  youngster organize and sequence actions, and provide real skills
  that can be used in play. Another parent whose child loved dogs
  began to spend more time with the friendly dog next door. The
  mother and child volunteered to take it for a walk, brush it, and
  feed it when the family was out for the day. Then, the child had

the routine in his head and could generalize it to his play with a toy dog.

- **As the child does more, the adult does less.** Remember, as a child is more successful in her play, the adult can do less directing the play and become more of an equal participant.

- **Help your child learn to get to completion.** This is a particularly good strategy with the child who quickly moves from activity to activity or from toy to toy. Read a simple book together that you can easily get to the end so you can say, "You're done, go play." Do a puzzle together. If your child's interest wanes as you are putting a six-piece puzzle together, put in a few pieces on your turn so that she can take the last piece and put it in as you say, "We did it. We're done!"

- **Incorporate routines to help your child organize and sequence her actions.** Children who tend to wander about in their play often have trouble with other activities requiring them to organize and sequence their actions. For example, encourage clean up at the end of a playtime. You can make it fun by setting a timer (either a freestanding one or the oven timer works well) and see how many toys she can pick up before it goes off. For a young child, begin with a very manageable goal, such as picking up three toys. Provide proximity control (be close by so they don't have an opportunity to drift over to a television or get involved in play). Once you have established this in cleanup, use this technique in play with the child who has difficulty organizing her actions (e.g., "Let's shoot five balls into the basketball hoop and then we can have a snack").

"My four-year-old plays great at home with his older siblings. When a friend from school comes over, it is a totally different story. He hogs the toys and really has trouble taking turns. Part of me wants to say, 'Forget it,' and not have classmates over, because it is such a hassle. However, I know that my child needs to learn these skills. How can I help him play with friends? And why is it so much harder for him to play with friends rather than with his brothers?"

Some children play well with their siblings. However, play with brothers and sisters is rarely an equal playing field. Older siblings often designate a younger sibling a lesser role in the play, such as the dog or the baby, and give very specific directions for how the child is to play. In other families, older siblings simply acquiesce if a problem arises and regularly give in to the younger child's demands. A youngster's peers are often not as amenable to letting one child continually have his own way.

Some of the questions that you may ask yourself when your child is having difficulty playing with peers include the following: Does he have some difficulty communicating with peers or understanding what is being asked of him? Can he follow another's lead in play? Can he get a peer's attention? Can he begin to negotiate a solution when a problem arises? Remember, many of these considerations are age dependent. One would certainly consider it to be a bigger problem if a four-and-a-half-year-old could not play with peers than if a child who just turned three had some difficulty with this. See chapter 9 for further information on peer play and playdates.

Playing with Peers

- **Practice turn taking!** At home, practice taking turns picking a desired play activity for you to do with your child. Let him pick an activity for the two of you to do together. Set a timer for when his turn is over and when you get to pick *the* activity for you to do together. Initially when it is the parent's turn to pick the desired activity, pick another favorite and make your turn shorter than your child's. Do this on a regular basis. As he gets more familiar with this, you can pick a variety of activities for your turn. You can then help your child practice taking turns with a sibling or on a playdate, as you provide support for the children to play together.
- **Work in a close partnership with your child's teacher to improve your child's social skills with peers.** How does he do at school? What activities does he enjoy the most? Where does he have the most difficulty? Who would be best to invite over for a playdate?

- **Invite a child over to have a playdate.** Keep initial playdates short. It is much better to end with the participants wanting more, rather than bickering. Set up initial playdates at a time that your child is not tired. Include him during the planning stage. Talk about what he would like to share, how to treat a guest, which toys are too hard to share so they need to be put away, and so on.
  - **Have a plan involving several activities.** Perhaps the children will create a moldable dough and then get to play with it, or make their snack together. Be prepared for all energy levels. If they are rambunctious, take them outside with a ball or bubbles. If the children need a quiet activity, bring out some Silly Putty and last Sunday's comics from the newspaper. They can take turns pushing the putty on the colored comics to make an imprint on the putty.
  - **Plan reciprocal activities that the children can do together.** Bring out a wagon and have one ride and the other pull, and then switch. Have them take turns hiding a toy in clay and the other one finding it, or take a long roll of paper and have them draw a large mural with markers or draw silhouettes of each other on large rolls of brown paper.
  - **Finally, stay close by.** It can be challenging for some children to handle altercations and a parent who is close by can often help them work out disputes before feelings get out of control. However, once the dam has burst and one (or two) children are crying, it is much harder to salvage the playdate.

"My five-year-old son loves cars. He knows the makes and can identify lots of cars on the road. He loves to draw cars, talk about cars, and read about cars. When we have a playdate, often other children are not as interested, so it is hard to find common ground."

One of the first ways to evaluate if this is a big problem or a little problem is by **assessing** if this passion is getting in the way of your child's functioning. If one exclusive interest is interfering with his participation in a variety of activities—he is generally alone, engaged in that one pursuit—it may be time to have a professional take a closer look and help broaden this youngster's interests.

It is recommended that you consult with a developmental specialist if your child demonstrates the following: Your child can only talk about one topic (such as insects, trains, or keys) and is inattentive if other subjects are brought up, has trouble maintaining a conversation with someone except when he is controlling the topic, is inattentive to spoken language, or has difficulty making eye contact with others. If the child is able to play and converse about other topics and follow another's lead in conversation, this may simply be a passion that he has a great deal of interest in.

Broadening Play Repertoires

- **Spend time playing together.** Get on the floor and play with your child. Share his play experience. Ask questions about the play and follow his lead. Then encourage your child to follow your lead in the play.

- **Add a novel twist to the play with your child and encourage him to follow your lead.** If he likes to play with a particular toy, add a twist. If your child loves to play with Fisher-Price people for example, you may show him how your person has tiny pink dots on her face, which are chicken pox! Now the play takes a different turn as the people need to call the doctor, and so on. If your child loves cars, help him build a car and then play with it. Perhaps a key piece is missing and there are clues about where you and your five-year-old can find it.

- **"Too much of a good thing is too much. . . ."** You know this is true about candy, but it can also be true for play. Encourage your child to play with a variety of toys. If some are more challenging, provide support and help so that he will explore them. Pair a more challenging activity with a desired one. For example, say, "First we will put together this puzzle and then you can play with your ——————."

"Mommy's busy" time

- **Encourage playdates with peers.** Provide support and encourage reciprocal play, such as making a picture together, throwing a ball, blowing bubbles, or washing bikes and then riding them. Provide support to ensure these experiences are successful.

"My child is a good player when I play with her. However, when I need to get dinner ready or do the laundry it is very hard to get her to play independently. Help!"

Children benefit from the pleasure of their parents' company and most love to play with adults. However, it is also important that children learn skills so they can play independently.

Promoting Independent Play

- **You (the adult) are on standby.** Sometimes children are more willing to play independently if they are close to the parent. Often, if a child can do a similar activity to a parent, she can be happy for a short period of time. For example, if your child can do some cooking with a Play-Doh set at the table while you cook or play office with her own office materials at a small desk in your office, she may be happily engaged. As children get older, they may happily match socks or spin or tear lettuce when you have to get these activities done.

- **Set up some interesting materials for your child to use for independent play.** A new set of markers or crayons can pique most any child's interest for a short while. Rotating toys can make old favorites more interesting. Or, add a novel piece to the play. Set out the stuffed animals but add a doctor's kit. Or pull out a prop box (see page 33).

- **Make your expectations realistic.** Young children will be able to occupy themselves for short periods of time. They will have more difficulty when they are tired. Set a timer for the amount of time your child should play independently, if this is hard for her. Begin with a short period of time so she will experience success.

- **Pair a less desired activity with a more desirable one.** Set a timer and tell your child that if she plays independently until the timer goes off, you can then do a favorite activity together.

Play is an essential mode of learning for children. Watching their play skills develop in conjunction with their language and motor skills is one of the joys of parenting young children. Their free use of imagination and their ability to become so deeply engrossed in a pretend play scheme is both amusing and precious. Before long they'll be consumed with books, computers, sports, and phone calls, so enjoy this rich phase of their lives while it lasts!

Part Two

. . .

UNDERSTANDING DEVELOPMENT

Three

Social Emotional Development and Managing Behavior

*Nuturing Relationships,
Fostering Independence, and
Weathering the Storms*

In this chapter, we talk about how to take a screaming, raging little ball of dynamite and shape him into a usually civilized, independent, thoughtful, empathetic little guy. In other words, how you'll shape his behavior and navigate the stormy seas of emotional development in these early years.

Top Tips for Changing Behaviors

"I don't even know where to start. Suzy's a very spirited, willful kid who has a hard time following directions. If I get tired or distracted by one of the other kids, I then have a hard time setting consistent limits with her."

Some families do not know where to start with their children's behavior. There may be so many concerning behaviors or so many times, daily, where the children seem out of control that it is all just overwhelming. Suzy is a four-and-a-half-year-old who has difficulty controlling her energy level. One minute she's wild and wound up, but the next minute she's calm and mellow. Her family is always on the go and has difficulty accommodating her unpredictability, impulsiveness, and stubbornness.

Use a Triage Approach

Safety is your top priority. For now, let the rude or inappropriate stuff go by the wayside. Aggressive behaviors, running away in parking lots, or any behavior that could endanger your child or others should be addressed first. Focus your energy there and don't sweat the smaller stuff.

Although she doesn't follow directions, sit for mealtimes, or play well with her sister, Suzy's parents decided to focus on correcting her "game" of running away from them in the child-care parking lot. When other behaviors occurred, they stuck to their old methods of verbally reprimanding her, redirecting her, or just doing things for her.

Have Clear Expectations

Be clear about what you hope to achieve. Eliminating tantrums is a vague, broad goal that will be difficult to meet. Choose a goal that is specific, definable, and achievable. For example, aim to reduce the frequency of yelling and food-throwing during dinner, from daily to once a week.

Set realistic expectations that are appropriate for your child's age. It is realistic to expect a preschooler to fall asleep on his own, but it is unrealistic to expect that he will never wake up (or wake you up) in the middle of the night. Similarly, it is very difficult for most toddlers to sit quietly for the duration of a religious service. They may be more likely to do so if they have things to occupy them, such as books, crayons, or the contents of Mommy's purse.

Suzy's parents were confident that, at four and a half, she should be able to control her impulsivity enough to get to the car while holding an adult's hand. This was a realistic goal and was a single event in the day, so they could focus their energy on it rather than trying to solve all of her issues at once. They could also brainstorm with her teachers about strategies and focus on being consistent with Suzy.

Break Goals into Small Manageable Steps

By breaking down your goal into smaller parts, both you and your child will experience success and see progress more quickly. There are two approaches to follow. The first, **behavior shaping,** occurs when you reinforce closer and closer approximations of your end goal. When a child is learning to use his words, he might first yell, "Mine!" when he wants something. A few months later, we teach him to say, "My turn," and then "My turn next," and eventually, "May I have a turn when you're finished?" or "In five minutes it'll be my turn okay?"

The second way to break down a goal is called **chaining.** To use this technique, break a larger task into little steps, teach them one at a time, and "chain" each new step to the ones already learned. For example, hand washing or putting on shoes requires a number of sequential steps. By learning one step at a time, children experience small successes and bits of independence more quickly, although they may still need help with other parts of the task. A preschooler can proudly put on his shoes, though he may not be able to tie them for a few more years. Or, he may be able to wash his hands independently but need a reminder to turn off the water (and stop playing in it!).

Timing Is Everything!

Some skills, like bathroom independence, require a certain degree of biological readiness. Just as babies begin to walk at different ages, children begin to use the toilet at different ages. Without some indicators of readiness, you may be setting up yourself and your child for months of frustration. Similarly, when a child starts climbing out of her crib, it may be a good time to make the transition to a regular bed.

Other timing considerations include family or life events. You may capitalize on timing by leaving the pacifier at home when you go on vacation for two weeks. Without the familiar environmental triggers to remind your child of his need for the pacifier, he may learn how to soothe himself in other ways. Once you're back home, he won't need the pacifier because he's got these other new self-soothing skills. Conversely, the arrival of a new baby might *not* be the best time to start potty training because your toddler's life (and your own) have just been turned upside down. Stress levels are up, hours of sleep are down. Everyone is coping with a new routine and a new life. Once everyone settles down, think about toilet training again.

Suzy's family found that she remained calmer and more cooperative when they picked her up from child care at the same time every day. This consistency enabled the staff to prepare her for pick up (and ensure that she did not begin an activity that she wouldn't have time to finish).

Individualize Goals for Your Child

You are the expert on your child and know how he responds in new situations. Consider his temperament and personality when deciding how to teach him a new skill or how to transition him from point A to point B. Will he respond better to a cold-turkey technique or to a gradual shift? Some families take the crib down on the same day that the bed goes up, whereas others have both set up over a number of weeks or months so that the child can make the transition at his own pace.

Use Frequent Positive Reinforcement

Positive reinforcement is any response that increases the likelihood that a behavior will be repeated. For example, generate enthusiasm for potty training by letting a child pick out some "big-girl undies" at the store, or by checking out children's library books on the topic. Talking about (or observing) how big kids do things often provides incentive for a young child to work on a new skill. Other, more concrete forms of positive reinforcement, such as earning special privileges, snacks, or stars on a chart can be effective, too, assuming the child is old enough to remember why he is receiving the special treat or old enough to understand what the stickers on the chart represent.

When Suzy walked calmly to the car with her mother, she'd immediately receive a favorite snack in the car on the way home. This immediate response to the target behavior (walking to the car) was effective because Suzy loved the snack and she received it right away, so there wasn't time for her to act up in some other way before getting her reward.

Giving Meaningful Praise

- **Be specific.** Let your children know exactly what they did well. "Thanks for putting those away so carefully!"
- **Think about touch.** Some kids love a hug or spin but others find that uncomfortable.
- **Think about volume.** Public praise, so others hear, too, may be extra reinforcing or it may be calling unwanted attention to a child. Whispering praise is often very effective.
- **Immediate praise is good.** The less time that passes between the target behavior and the reinforcement, the more likely the child will be to link the two in his mind.
- **Consider nonverbal winks, smiles, or a thumbs up.**

Repetition, Repetition, Repetition!!!
Consistency, Consistency, Consistency!!!

Repetition and consistency are crucial to establishing and reinforcing behavior. Routines help children know what to expect and what is expected of them. They can anticipate what comes next, and that knowledge gives them a feeling of security. They don't need to worry or nag about when something will occur because they *know* when it will occur. For example, bedtime problems are reduced for many children by instituting an almost ritualistic routine that may include singing the same song, reading the same book, taking the same number of drinks in the bathroom, or saying good night in the exact same way. Young children need to practice these routines, or new skills, over and over and over again.

Similarly, consistency is important because it provides children with predictable responses to their behaviors. They are like scientists: They will try something over and over to see if they get the same result each time. Think about a toddler touching the stove. Each time he does it, his parent yells, "No!" and pulls him away. He may try this over and over and, when he's convinced that he'll get the same response each time (and it is not a desirable response), he'll quit. Temper tantrums are similar: Once a child realizes that they don't get him what he wants, the frequency of tantrums drops significantly. However, if the child receives an inconsistent response, or his tantrums *sometimes* get him what he wants, he'll be much more tenacious in trying over and over.

Suzy's teachers gave her her picture book every day about five minutes before her mother picked her up. She'd read it over and over again. They'd talk with her about how she was expected to behave and what she'd get in the car if she walked calmly through the parking lot. Her mother, to her credit, gave her the same consequence each time she ran away. She gave her a quick, firm reprimand, made her go back to the building with her and walk back to the car properly, and provided no snack on the way home. Suzy typically had setbacks after school vacations, but all in all her running in the parking lot decreased markedly over a few months, as her mom continued to provide consistent consequences to her behavior.

Two Steps Forward, One Step Back

When setbacks occur, and they will, it is important to handle them in stride and not to become discouraged. Your child will see how you react and take his cues from you. If your response to his "accident" is matter-of-fact and you emphasize your confidence that next time he'll remember to use the toilet, he'll think about it in the same way. Alternatively, if you become upset with him and dwell on his "failure," he'll feel badly about himself and become discouraged about his abilities, too.

Children thrive with a routine and they become stressed without it. Expect setbacks or regression when there is a big change, such as a school vacation, a new baby, a new house, or even a bad cold. They are coping—reverting back to what they know really well (e.g., diapers!) and putting the new, tougher big kid stuff on hold for a while.

The ABCs of Behavior

Remembering your ABCs—**antecedents** trigger **behaviors**, and behaviors have **consequences**—can help you more effectively shape your child's behavior.

As Scott's mom hustled through the grocery store, the three-and-a-half-year-old's whiny requests became more insistent with each passing aisle. Her patient answers became more terse and tight lipped until the situation climaxed with Scott's stubbornly planting himself on the floor in the middle of the cereal aisle, refusing to budge until she agreed to buy him his preferred sugar cereal. About this time, Scott's two-year-old brother in the cart had finished off his bag of crackers and was also whining. Score one for Scott the Negotiator: Mom agreed to one box of sugary cereal and made a beeline for the checkout line.

In retrospect, it is easy to see the storm brewing. But in the heat of the moment, it is easier to simply react to your child's inappropriate behavior by giving in and hoping to get out of the situation (e.g., grocery store) as quickly as possible. Later, when you're calm, you may replay the incident, trying to figure out how it could have been resolved differently and what you might do next time to prevent the scenario from occurring again. Try to look for the causes and effects of your children's behavior, or technically speaking, the antecedents and consequences.

The first step is to define the problem behavior. You need a very clear idea of what behavior you're targeting for change, and in what situations. Rather than talking about reducing tantrums, decide what the observable behavior is that you'd like to eliminate: yelling? screaming? hitting? kicking? This helps ensure that all the adults are on the same page. In Scott's case, reducing his whining at the store is a much more manageable goal than eliminating the whining altogether. Ideally, everyone who interacts with the child in the target situation will share the same goal for behavior change and therefore act consistently with the child.

With a clearly defined behavior in mind, analyze the antecedents and consequences. Antecedents, in some cases, are quite predictable even if they are unavoidable. For example, when a child is hungry, tired, or sick, she may become more ornery, sassy, prone to fighting with siblings, or more inclined to throw a tantrum when she doesn't get her way immediately. That doesn't make these behaviors acceptable, but at least they are somewhat predictable and understandable so we can try to nip them in the bud. You may spend more snuggle-time with a sick child and less time preparing dinner (don't feel guilty if you've memorized the number for pizza delivery!). You may whip up a snack for hungry children upon walking in the door, before even going to the bathroom or changing out of work clothes. Similarly, before a playdate with a child who loves trains as much as your son, you might let him choose one or two favorites to put away, if you think sharing them will be too difficult. Before a long drive, insist your child use the bathroom to prevent an accident in the car. Or, before going to a sit-down restaurant, you might throw crayons and paper in your purse, because your children are more likely to *behave appropriately* if they don't get bored.

Effective parents are always thinking several steps ahead of the current moment so that they can lay the groundwork for smooth sailing by anticipating their children's needs and reactions and being ready for them. These preventative steps we take remove the triggers, or antecedents, to certain undesirable behaviors. Without the triggers, the behaviors don't occur as frequently, if at all.

One father takes his son up to his room with him upon coming home from work and asks him about his day while changing out of his suit. This strategic "quality time" has the added benefit of physically separating a tired three-year-old from his equally tired five-year-old sister. Previously, the father went upstairs alone but usually was half-dressed when the yelling and fighting began in the family room below, requiring him to go downstairs, annoyed, to referee the fight and give the children his full attention. Their fighting got them the attention they craved, but it was negative attention. Now, the little boy gets his father's attention immediately, and without coming to blows with his sister in the process. His sister appreciates having her little brother out of her hair at that point in the evening. Being a bit older and of calmer disposition than he, she's content to wait until bedtime for uninterrupted one-on-one time with her father. *The key is that the father is able to give them what they want before they resort to inappropriate behavior to get it.*

In Scott's case, he hasn't seen his mom all day, and the first thing she does after work is drag him off to the store, where he is expected to walk along rather patiently with the cart, surrounded by food he is not supposed to touch while his mother comes and goes, giving him only a fraction of her attention. When he whines—aha! she responds to him! She may give him her undivided attention for a moment or two (granted not too happily but that's okay—as far as he's concerned it's better than nothing!). Then, when he *really* acts out and throws himself on the floor, she actually gives him what he wants: a brand of cereal that she hardly ever succumbs to buying for him! So what is the antecedent, or trigger? Possibly seeing food that he can't have, or only getting part of mom's attention when he'd really, really like more of it, and/or being generally bored. The consequence for his whining and sit-in at the cereal display is attention (albeit angry) from Mom yet ultimately receiving a box of his favorite cereal. This is positive reinforcement of an undesirable action!

With regard to behavior, positive does not always equal good. A **positive consequence** simply means that the behavior is more likely to occur again. A **negative consequence** decreases the likelihood that the behavior will occur again. In this case, Scott is more likely to whine and plant himself on the floor of the store next time because it worked for him this time.

Functions of Behavior: Why Children Do What They Do

Without understanding the **function** of the behavior, it is impossible to make an effective plan for reducing the problem behavior. In *Severe Behavior Problem* Mark Durand identifies four broad functions of behavior: getting attention, getting something like food or a toy, escaping a situation, and doing something because it feels good or relieves stress (e.g., chewing gum). Remember that people, and especially children, are tenacious: They will get their needs met by hook or by crook. So, if you squash one behavior, another will crop up. It is your job to influence that new "replacement" behavior to be sure that it is more socially appropriate than is the old problem behavior.

Children do all sorts of annoying things to get adults' **attention**. Scott was whining, at least in part, because he wanted his mother to respond: He hadn't seen her all day and he wanted to spend some time with her. She'd give him her attention momentarily, which shows that the whining worked.

Other possible attention-getting behaviors (both appropriate and inappropriate):

- Picking a fight with a sibling the moment Mom gets on the phone or computer
- Interrupting a conversation to say something
- Tantrums, crying, yelling
- Intentionally breaking a rule to get an adult to come over quickly to intervene
- Raising a hand in school
- Saying "Excuse me" while others are talking
- Making eye contact
- Tapping someone on the shoulder

Additionally, Scott wanted a box of cereal, something **tangible.** Ultimately, he got that as well, which shows that his impromptu sit-in was an effective behavior. Receiving almost anything tangible can be reinforcing, from food or drinks to toys. A toddler may bite a peer on the hand, which causes the peer to drop the toy, and then the toddler picks it up. An older child knows to use words and ask for a turn. Such a request, especially at preschool, is honored because the staff is very tuned in to making sure that children receive positive reinforcement for using their words. Preschool teachers pride themselves on teaching children that children's words have power, and are ultimately more effective than being physically aggressive to get needs met.

Possibly, Scott was whining because he was bored and didn't want to be at the store: He wanted to **escape** the situation he was in. After the sit-in, his mom promptly headed for the checkout line and they left. Again, his whining received positive reinforcement in that it got him what he wanted. Children may become aggressive when they are uncomfortable—it is a sure-fire way to get an adult to intervene and remove them from the situation. Time-outs are often inadvertently reinforcing, when the function of the behavior is to escape a situation. If a child who is bored or uncomfortable acts out and is put in time-out, this may be giving the child exactly what he wants. Children who become easily overwhelmed or overstimulated in large groups or loud situations may do something—cry, fight, yell—to get themselves removed from the group. As they learn how to cope better, they begin to use more socially appropriate ways to escape a situation, such as saying, "I need a break," or asking, "May I go get a drink of water?"

Finally, children may do things simply because the action feels good. A toddler who plays with her food may not be trying to get attention or be removed from the table, she may simply like the feel of squishing mashed potatoes through her fingers. Similarly, children often love to run because it feels good, and they don't distinguish between appropriate and inappropriate places for running. Sometimes they are escaping a situation or intentionally running in a hallway to get attention, but often they do it because it is intrinsically fun.

Making a Behavior Plan

Identifying the behavior, its antecedents or triggers, its consequences, and its function, gives us all the information we need to make a behavior plan. This plan should outline three things: (1) how the environment can be adjusted to prevent the behavior from occurring (i.e., remove triggers); (2) how positive reinforcement will be used to teach a more appropriate replacement behavior; and (3) what the negative consequences will be when the target behavior does occur.

First, look at the antecedents—what happened before the behavior and determine if there are any ways to modify the environment to prevent a similar situation from happening. Parents need to go to the grocery store, and often the children must come along. Assuming Scott's mom couldn't do her shopping before coming home, there are several things she could have done to make it less difficult. First, she could have spent some time playing with the boys at home before going off to the store. She could prepare Scott by laying out her expectations before even stepping into the store. Along with those expectations, she might make little goals and rewards for him. For example, "Watch for aisle eight. That will be halfway, and you can have a snack when we get there if you're being a helpful shopper and remembering to use your big-boy voice." This gives him a concrete visual cue to watch for, so that he knows a snack will definitely be forthcoming, and it gives him a behavioral expectation phrased in an information-giving format: Be helpful and use a big-boy voice. This is preferable to a negatively phrased instruction, such as "Don't

Behavior Plan

Target Behavior: _Scott is whiny and uncooperative at the grocery store. Goal: reduce whining and nagging and be helpful; use "big-boy voice!"_

Antecedents: _(Triggers) Mom's attention is focused on her grocery list instead of on Scott. He's hungry, surrounded by food. Probably bored, too._

Consequences: _Gets attention from Mom (briefly) and sometimes a box of cereal—just so he'll quiet down._

Function: _He wants Mom's attention definitely. May also want tangible cereal, or to leave the store (escape) because he is bored._

****

Environmental Adjustments: _Give him positive attention (play!) before going to the store. Make a plan with Scott before going in: At what point will he get a snack for good behavior—"big-boy" voice & helping Mom?_

Replacement Behavior: _He'll get attention by helping Mom pick out groceries; a snack (tangible) at a certain point; and he'll be less bored if he's helping._

Positive Reinforcement Strategies: _Praise, snack, allowed to make limited choices about what to buy_

Consequences (Negative Reinforcement for Target Behavior): _Withhold attention/eye contact (ignore him!) if he whines, no cereal/snack if he's not being helpful and using a "big-boy" voice_ whine," which tells him what *not* to do but doesn't tell him what *to* do. Additionally, this would allow her to give him the snack before the whining starts in, so that she's not accidentally reinforcing the whining. Scott's mom also incorporated some of the tips for navigating the grocery store with kids, in chapter 12, to decrease the likelihood of Scott's whining.

Next, she thought about an appropriate replacement behavior for the whining and sitting on the floor. How else could Scott get his needs met? He wants attention, cereal, and probably to be done with the store altogether! If he actively helps to put things in the cart, he'll be getting more attention. If he cooperates initially, he'll get a snack halfway through the store and probably another little bit of positive attention for doing so well up to that point. Mom may want to hold out until closer to the end of the trip for the cereal but, again, make it contingent on his good behavior. The more Mom can include him, the less bored he'll become and the more willing he'll be to help if he sees it gets results: Maybe she'll let him pick out a few other things, too, just for being a helpful shopper.

Finally, Mom needs to follow through with negative consequences so Scott learns that his whining will not get him what he wants. She needs to be sure that the punishment fits the crime; in other words, that the consequence will not inadvertently reinforce the behavior. So, if Scott wants attention, she should remind him that she can only understand his big-boy voice, and withhold eye contact (if possible) until he uses an appropriate tone of voice. Then, she should clearly give him her attention to reinforce his big-boy voice. If the cereal is what he wants, she should give him a very clear goal to meet before he can have it. It should be a realistic, manageable goal, because she doesn't want to set him up for failure. She should also take into consideration the fact that he hasn't seen her all day, and it is late in the day, so he is likely tired, too.

Cheat Sheet for Negative Consequences

- If a child wants attention, withhold it. Turn your back to him, avert your gaze, leave the room, pretend you don't hear him, ignore him, or put him in time-out.
- If a child wants something tangible, don't give it to him until he asks politely, behaves appropriately, waits for a turn, and so on.

- If a child wants to escape a situation, do not let him leave until he asks appropriately or participates in some appropriate way, with assistance if necessary.
- If a child does something unacceptable because it feels good, find a more socially appropriate way to get the same need met. For example, have him chew gum instead of fingernails, hair, or his shirt collar. Instead of his playing in the sink or water fountain, tell him to get a wet paper towel or sponge and wash the tables, or let him wash toys—undoubtedly they need it!

Time-Out

"Time-out" refers to time away from positive reinforcement. It can be used effectively when the activity from which the child is being removed is actually fun or desirable. As mentioned earlier, if a child is trying to escape a situation, time-out is *not* an appropriate response, because it is giving him what he wants—a way out.

It should be noted that sending a child to his room to take a break or collect himself is an appropriate and effective strategy for helping some youngsters who are having trouble behaving appropriately. This is not quite a time-out but it is another effective strategy for managing behavior. Sending a child to his room to chill out or calm down when he is whining, bickering with siblings, or behaving in a silly, wound-up way may curtail even worse behavior. This child responds well to, and may even be relieved by, an enforced opportunity to be alone in his room. Playing alone is calming and organizing for him, and may be just the ticket to helping him get back on track, behaviorally.

However, it is important to consider your child's individual disposition because for some, this same directive will escalate a situation into an intense battle of wills. For these children, any form of time-out or mandatory alone time feels extremely punitive, will be strongly resisted, and should be used judiciously by caregivers.

Having a child take a break when he's wound up or sending him to sit on a step for a time-out when he's hit his brother, for example, might both be effective strategies for managing a child's behavior, but they should be used under different circumstances.

The reason for being sent to time-out should be very clear to the child. Prioritize your target behaviors and only use time-out for the most egregious, so that the youngster doesn't spend all day in time-out.

During a time-out, a child may have a desired toy taken away for a period of time, or he may be removed from the immediate area but stay nearby, in a chair in a corner for example, or he may be in a quiet area, such as a different room. A neutral location with few distractions or dangers is ideal, so that the adult doesn't have to interact with the child after sending him to time-out. A key part of time-out is withholding attention from the child, and this is more likely to happen if the child cannot do dangerous or destructive things that require adult intervention. Additionally, a child's bedroom often has toys or books that would be enjoyable to the child, so this is not necessarily a good option.

When sending a child to time-out, speak as little as possible and avoid getting into negotiations or discussion. In a firm but neutral voice say, "No biting! Go to time-out!" A neutral voice is better than an angry voice because it gives the child less attention, less of a reaction to his behavior. Similarly, showing exasperation or strong facial expressions also gives the child more attention. Remember, from a child's perspective, negative attention from a parent is better than no attention. So try to avoid giving negative attention during time-out.

After the initial directive to go to time-out, interact as little as is safely possible. Ignore all annoying behaviors and only intervene when there is danger.

Typically, time-out lasts for as many minutes as the child is old, so a three-year-old receives a three-minute time-out. The time-out should go into effect as soon as possible after the behavior occurs so that the child understands that it is the consequence for his behavior. Ideally, a timer ringing signifies the end of time-out. At that point, if the child is calm, consider asking the child if he knows why he was sent to time-out, and talk about how he could have handled the situation differently.

When the timer rings, tell him that the time-out is over. If he is still very upset, encourage him to take some deep breaths to calm down, or tell him he needs a calm body before he rejoins the group or activity.

If he repeats the target behavior, start the time-out all over again. Just because a child is calm during time-out doesn't necessarily mean that time-out is working—after all, the time-out was implemented because of some other bad behavior that occurred. Watch over the long term to see if the targeted behavior decreases.

Time-out is not just a neutral break, it is a negative consequence. Before resorting to this, try the strategies listed previously, such as eliminating the "triggers" of the behavior (prevention), and teaching and rewarding a more appropriate behavior that accomplishes the same thing for a child. In other words, time-out should be a last resort and may be used when these other techniques have first been tried yet the behavior still persists.

Time-out can be very traumatic for a child so, when he's not in time-out, be sure to beef up your loving and warm interactions together. Make his "time-in" fun and positive. If time-out from positive reinforcement is going to be effective, that "time-in" must be good and rewarding!

Big Problem or Little Problem: What Does "Normal" Look Like?

Tantrums

"Her tantrums can be so violent—she throws herself on the floor and even bangs her head sometimes . . . is this normal?"

Young children express themselves in a variety of ways. Toddlers especially are just beginning to learn how to control their emotions. They don't have many words to describe how they feel, so their body language reflects how they are feeling inside. Violent temper tantrums may simply reflect the very strong emotional storm raging inside a child. His extremely strong feelings need an extremely strong outlet. A toddler may bang his head on the floor or run into a wall or do other things that hurt himself. He may seem surprised when it hurts, and cry all the harder. He is clearly not in control of his body at the moment. Occasionally, a tantrum may be so severe or long that he vomits.

Handling Tantrums

The most important thing to do when a child is having a tantrum is not give him undue attention for such behavior: If he gets attention, he's likely to repeat the behavior or escalate to an even more extreme behavior, intentionally. Banging his head may have been an accident the first time but, if it gets a big reaction, he may do it on purpose the next time. A neutral, matter-of-fact response is best.

Some children prefer to be left alone (in a safe place) where they can calm themselves down and have some time to themselves. Others respond well to a big, long bear hug, the child equivalent of swaddling. Babies often calm when swaddled in blankets because their bodies are contained and they feel that deep pressure everywhere. Some young children respond to the same sort of experience. Holding a child close and tightly may help her calm down. Other children simply need to wear themselves out and would do well to run as hard as they can out in the yard until exhaustion overtakes them.

All these are perfectly acceptable, "normal" responses to a child who is out of control. They are not punishments but ways to help a child get back on an even keel. These strategies help them learn how to calm themselves and regulate their bodies. As they grow into four- and five-year-olds, they may begin to recognize when they are stressed out (or you may point it out to them) and opt to go straight outside or go to their room to get themselves together before a situation escalates to a tantrum.

Little PROBLEMS:

Children typically outgrow frequent tantrums by age four or so. They learn to use words to express themselves, to negotiate, wait, and tolerate not getting exactly what they want when they want it. Of course, being tired, hungry, or sick can weaken the emotional reserves of any child to the point that he has a meltdown and falls apart crying over something that wouldn't normally set him off. Life changes such as a new school, new sibling, or new babysitter can also make otherwise resilient children more emotionally fragile and prone to meltdowns.

An important consideration is a child's temperament. A child who was an "easy" baby and generally in control of his emotions may rarely have a tantrum. So when he does, it might be a clue that something is wrong (e.g., he's coming down with a cold). Conversely, children who were fussy babies may continue to have difficulty regulating themselves well into childhood and beyond. Tantrums may occur daily or several times per day. This is not an insurmountable problem but one that you may need to take special care to help them learn how to cope with. You may need to make a point of identifying when they are becoming stressed and showing them how to manage. ("You're breathing really fast right now. Let's try to take a deep breath together." Put a hand on your chest so he can see it rise and fall, and try to copy you.) Additionally, parents should develop their own coping methods for dealing with a child who resorts to tantrums frequently.

Coping with Frequent Tantrums

- **Remember they are not personal!** A child's tantrums are not about you, they are about his inability to cope with the current situation. Tell yourself, "Boy, it must be exhausting to be him!" In other words, if you're stressed out just watching him, imagine how he feels. That may help replace your stress or even resentment toward him with a tiny bit of empathy.
- **Focus on regulating your own breath and try to think before you speak.** Use as few words as possible because a child who is this emotional cannot process much of what you're saying. Appearing calm may or may not help your child to calm down, but undoubtedly appearing upset and yelling will escalate his behavior.
- **Take your own break.** When he's driving you crazy, it can be extremely helpful to escape to your own room or the bathroom, shut the door, and sit for five minutes. He may be banging on the other side of it, but at least you are separated. Take a few minutes for yourself, clear your head, and make a plan for what to do next.
- **If a tantrum occurs in the car, pull into a gas station and fill up your tank.** One wise mother of several young children said her most peaceful moments some days occurred at the gas

tank: The children were all buckled in their car seats, in the car, while she was blessedly out of the car—pumping gas for several quiet, uninterrupted minutes.

- **Sometimes it is helpful, in a quiet moment, to think about the qualities you love about your child.** Compliment and praise your child when he is behaving well and let him know how much you love him. Point out the unique qualities that he possesses. Build up your reserve of "warm fuzzies," because every tantrum can be so depleting and frustrating for both of you. In the calm times, let him know that you have confidence in him and that you know he's trying hard to control himself.

BIG PROBLEMS:

Under certain circumstances, tantrums may signal a bigger problem. If they are interfering with a child's friendships or school experience, additional evaluation may be warranted. When the frequency, duration, or severity of a child's tantrums seems extreme, keep a journal for a week or two to track when, why, and for how long they occur. Note the specific behavior during the tantrum (yelling, crying, throwing things, banging head, biting, vomiting, etc.). Once you've got some data, talk to your pediatrician. Hopefully, the data will reveal patterns that could be helpful in correcting the problem. For example, if tantrums typically happen during a certain kind of task or in a particular environment, there might be a way that you can tweak things so that the trigger isn't as prominent. Review the previous section and appendix F.

The "Uptight" Child

"He's so tightly wound and he gets angry so easily. It's like he never relaxes. Is this just his personality or should I be concerned?"

Some children are really intense, whereas others are more laid back. Some children thrive in a crowd while others prefer more time to themselves. There is no right or wrong way to be so long as a child is generally happy, learning, making friends, and feeling good about himself. When we say a child is "tense," what do we mean? Frequent clenched fists or teeth? Quick movements and or quick verbal responses? A scowl on his face? Easily frustrated with toys or games? Quick to dismiss others? Is it more of a physical presentation, or a manner of interacting with people or objects? The answers to these questions give us clues as to why a child may seem tense.

You need to figure out whether the cause of a child's tension is something external or internal. That is, is there something in the environment that is stressing him out or is it more global, about how he interacts with the whole environment. When trying to determine whether this is a big or a little problem, consider timing. Has the child always been tightly wound or was he a happy-go-lucky toddler who became increasingly tense once he started preschool? Has the tension only been present since some specific event, such as a new baby or a car accident? Or has he always seemed uncomfortable in his skin? Is he only tense at child care?

Little PROBLEMS:

When behaviors only occur in a particular environment, look at what is unique about that setting that could be stressful. Preschool and home tend to be very different experiences for a child, so if he seems more relaxed in one than the other, talk with the teacher about what strategies might be working in one environment that could be used more in the other. Even group size *can* be modified in a child care or school setting by ensuring that part of the day is spent in small groups or in individual work or play. Additionally, large group times like recess can be made to feel smaller (and less stressful) when there are activities that one or two children can do together like coloring, jumping rope, or blowing bubbles.

Conversely, if a child thrives at school but seems stressed out at home, consider implementing more consistent routines at home and give ample warning before transitions. Have expectations of your children as teachers do at school, and support them to meet those expectations.

Some children thrive in their routine (school and home) but, when anything is altered, they become stressed. A vacation, a visiting relative, or the hype of various holidays can make some children tense and shorten their already short fuse! As an infant, one typically developing boy would become physically ill (fever, upset stomach) whenever the family traveled but he'd miraculously heal as soon as they returned home. As a preschooler, he didn't become sick but he was very tense and serious, slow to laugh and quick to cry while away on vacation. This was inconvenient for the family, but did not qualify as a big problem that needed intervention. Instead, his parents tried to bring the familiar with them. They did not wash his blankie for several days prior to a trip (so that it would smell like home), they packed the night-light from his room, they encouraged him to help pick books and a few toys to bring, and they learned not to bother packing brand-new clothes because he would totally reject them anyway. He simply functioned better away from home if he had lots of familiar reminders.

BIG PROBLEMS:

When a child's tension level seems to increase, you need to consider what has changed that might have been the trigger. With each year, classroom expectations rise for how children behave, how they interact and play with each other, how much language they understand, how they express themselves, and how much they do for themselves. A child who seemed fine in her toddler class may seem like a different kid in the three-year-old class, not necessarily because of the teacher's personality but rather the increased demands. A child senses when she is having trouble, when everyone else seems to be understanding directions or doing tasks with ease that are very difficult for her. Somehow, the group has moved on without her, and she's working as hard as she can but barely keeping up. As a result, she may have more behavior problems and outbursts (which are noticeable) or she may internalize her stress and stay "below the radar" where her difficulties are less noticeable. She may seem less happy, less playful than in the past, more tense and serious. This is an important development for parents to discuss with teachers, as parents may notice subtle behavior changes before teachers. If the teacher identifies possible developmental problems, she may alert the parents to a need for further assessment by a speech and language pathologist, occupational therapist, or other learning specialist.

Sometimes, there is no obvious developmental glitch or obvious stressor in a child's life, yet he still seems angry or anxious. An evaluation by a child psychologist or pediatric psychiatrist can be very beneficial for exploring the roots of a child's stress and helping him learn how to cope. Such mental health professionals can be extremely helpful when a child is coping with an identifiable stressor as well—a traumatic event, for example, or a life change such as divorce.

Mental health problems such as anxiety disorders, depression, oppositional defiant disorder, mood disorders, attention deficit, and hyperactivity disorders require diagnosis by a pediatric specialist, such as a developmental pediatrician, pediatric psychiatrist, or child psychologist. Teasing out what is appropriate vs. inappropriate behavior is very difficult, and very dependent on the age of a child. Only a qualified pediatric medical or mental health professional can make such a determination.

A mental health issue can be considered a big problem when it interferes with a child's daily functioning over time: his ability to eat, sleep, play, make friends, participate in activities, or complete schoolwork, for instance. One-time unusual behavior is not typically cause for alarm. Monitor the child over a period of time to see if a concerning behavior resolves itself or becomes more impairing for a child.

Separation Anxiety

"He won't go to anyone else. I'm glad he's attached to me but I'm a little concerned that he cries whenever anyone else cares for him."

Virtually all children experience separation anxiety. It typically peaks during toddlerhood and wanes as their language and memory improve.

Once they understand that their parents are definitely coming back, their anxiety generally decreases. When they can express themselves with words and get information with words (like a reassurance that Mommy always comes back), they are better able to cope with separation.

Dealing with Separation Anxiety

Children take their cues from adults. If parents are anxious, children sense this and assume that there must be something not quite right about the situation, and therefore become more fearful and clingy. Although parents may feel a bit anxious the first (or second or umpteenth) time they leave their child, it is important that they show confidence in his ability to cope with the situation. Children respond to the expectations set for them. If you assume the evening with a babysitter will be a disaster, and you convey your concerns or worries directly or indirectly to your children, chances are good that they will fulfill your expectations and have a rough night. Conversely, if you express confidence, odds are better that they'll have a smooth time.

Most children who become upset when parents leave are able to calm down shortly thereafter. It is important for children to form attachments with other adults, and one way this happens is when that other adult has the opportunity to calm and soothe the child. The child realizes someone other than his parents can make him feel better and he begins to trust her, realize he can be okay with her, and maybe even have fun with her. This transition will only happen successfully when the parent really leaves (without wavering or coming back for one more quick hug!).

Leaving a Child with a Babysitter

1. Be sure he is familiar with the caregiver. Go to the house together for a playdate or have the person over for a visit beforehand.

2. Prepare him ahead of time by explaining what will happen, when, and for how long. Focus on concrete details when possible, such as what he'll have for dinner. Have him pick out a game he wants to play with her or choose pajamas he wants to wear. The fact that you're leaving is a nonnegotiable, but what he does while you're gone is an area that he's got some control over.

3. Do something to make the event special, like renting a new DVD for the evening, or bringing a special snack to share with the playdate host.

4. Suggest that he draw you a picture or build something to show you when you return, and tell him how excited you'll be to see it.

5. If the child is leaving home, have her bring something familiar, such as a favorite doll or photo of the family.

6. Exude confidence in her ability to handle time without you.

7. Be swift in your departure. When you decide it is time to go, give a quick hug and kiss then go out the door. Do not prolong separating. Going back for one more kiss could be more than he could bear and you may inadvertently open the floodgates.

8. Remember that even a kicking and screaming toddler whom your sweet teenaged babysitter has to pry off you will likely calm down within a few minutes of your departure. Have faith!

9. If you anticipate a rough separation, prepare the caregiver with such strategies as favorite activities, toys, songs, videos, and food.

Little PROBLEMS:

Toddlers are famous for doing things like standing at the door until their parents arrive, refusing to play, or for crying themselves to sleep when they realize that Mommy or Daddy is not going to put them to bed that night. As with tantrums, some toddlers exhibit very strong separation anxiety. Use the same caregivers repeatedly so that they form a bond, and their anxiety should lessen as they become more familiar with the person. They may not look forward to the babysitter's coming, but they should tolerate her without a huge tantrum and hours of tears.

As their language improves, young children may try to negotiate the terms of the babysitting ("Only if we can order pizza!"), or make clear their unhappiness with the situation ("But I don't want you to leave! I want you to stay here, Mommy!"). This is typical, and you can easily ride it out.

Sometimes a child experiences a resurgence of separation anxiety, typically when other changes occur, such as the arrival of a new baby, houseguest, or absence of the other parent on a business trip. Monitor his behavior, because it should abate after life resumes some normalcy.

BIG PROBLEMS:

As with tantrums, if you feel that a child's reaction is too severe, ask yourself a few questions. Does the anxiety crop up whenever you leave her with anyone (including her other parent, school, etc.), or is it just a particular caregiver? If it is just one person and the behavior has been persistent, you might consider finding another caregiver or avoiding leaving the child alone with that person for a few months. Does it occur more when you're leaving her at another person's house vs. your own? Some children do well in another house because there are different toys and activities while other children prefer the familiarity of their own surroundings. Does she otherwise seem to be well adjusted, in terms of friendships with other children and relationships with other adults? If she has friends whom she talks and plays with, teachers with whom she has a good rapport, and grandparents or other adults of whom she is fond and speaks well of, then her anxiety will likely resolve itself.

On the other hand, if the separation anxiety seems to be accompanied by other behavioral changes, a professional evaluation may be a good idea. For example, if a child develops separation anxiety while also becoming angrier, moodier, or more fearful, talk to your pediatrician about seeing a pediatric psychiatrist or child psychologist.

If a young child stops going to people with whom he's had a previously good relationship, and also seems to become more withdrawn, use less language, or stop playing in ways that are typical for him, call your pediatrician.

The Child Who Doesn't Talk at School:

"My daughter has stopped talking at school. She won't say why. It is frustrating to me because as soon as she gets in the car, she talks just fine. Is she trying to get attention? How do we get her to start talking again?"

Selective mutism refers to a child who speaks freely in some environments where she feels safe and secure, such as home, but is rendered virtually silent in other environments perceived to be socially challenging, such as school. Selective mutism is generally thought to be a childhood anxiety disorder. There *may* be additional contributing factors, such as a language processing problem or a motor planning problem. A child may be stressed from feeling like she is on "sensory overload." Whatever the cause, she is experiencing anxiety, and the way she responds is to become mute. Some children experience this to a lesser degree and speak some, but considerably less, in school. Difficulty speaking in a particular environment can negatively impact her developing social skills and self-esteem. Other children tend to treat a mute child as younger than she really is. A child who is selectively mute will have real difficulty communicating basic needs in this environment, such as the need for a bathroom break or a drink of water. In addition, teachers may have difficulty ascertaining academic levels with a child who doesn't speak in school.

Some children who do not speak in a social or school setting for a month or more but speak without difficulty at home may go on to be diagnosed with having selective mutism. Communication difficulties, such as stuttering, must be ruled out, as well as other disorders, such as autism. A significant number of children with selective mutism also come from a bilingual home environment.

Addressing Selective Mutism

- **Take the child to a mental health professional, such as a pediatric psychologist or child psychiatrist.** Anxiety is a key component to this behavior. Early identification and referral to a professional is essential. Professionals generally agree that the sooner selective mutism and its underlying anxiety are addressed, the easier it is to remediate and the better the prognosis. The initial testing may include an audiological (hearing) evaluation, testing to rule out learning disabilities, and a complete speech and language evaluation. Ideally, the professional will work with the family as well as consider the teacher and classroom environment.

- **Be patient! This is not a manipulative behavior.** A child must be really, really stressed out if she's become selectively mute. She is *not* just trying to get attention. Encourage nonverbal communication, such as pointing, gesturing, and nodding or shaking her head.

- **Work closely with the teacher to ensure that the child has a vital, active role in the classroom.** Being the teacher's helper is a good idea because it keeps the child close to the teacher, which may be comforting to the child, and gives her numerous opportunities to interact directly with her peers (by passing out lunches, papers, and so on).

- **Use a team approach.** Parents, teacher, mental health provider, and other specialists such as an occupational therapist, speech and language pathologist, or pediatrician, who may be involved need to work together to support the child.

BIG PROBLEM OR Little PROBLEM:

Intervention is critical for her to be able to talk again and function outside the home. In the meantime, work closely with her teachers and other professionals, and be patient. Try not to pressure her—she's already coping with a level of stress that has made her somewhat dysfunctional in school. Give her as much love and support as you can during this difficult time.

Toddlerlike Behavior

"She'll just walk up and take a toy away from another child or knock down a block tower that another child is building. She doesn't seem to care how she affects other people."

Toddlers (new walkers through roughly two years old) only see the world in terms of themselves. They have little regard for others beyond how they are affected by them. They have not developed sense of empathy, so it is difficult for them to understand others' reactions to things or to take someone else's perspective into consideration. Two-year-olds have no qualms about walking right up to another child and taking away a toy or pushing him aside so that they can get to a desired activity. Sharing is very difficult at this age because toddlers just cannot fathom that someone else would want a toy that they want. Additionally, toddlers' emerging language skills don't provide them with the tools they need to interact with each other, so they resort to physical actions. A common, albeit antisocial, way to join a friend in play at this age is to knock down his building, or color on his drawing. The toddler is then confused by the other child's reaction of rage or tears. Teachers and parents work hard to teach turn-taking, using words, and other basic social skills to twos and young threes.

By three and a half years of age, children are beginning to control their impulses a bit more, remembering to use their words (at least initially), and understanding that their actions have consequences. By five years of age, children should be adept at negotiating with each other, solving problems, remembering and reminding each other of class rules, calling to an adult when they need help, and empathizing with each other when feelings are hurt.

Nurturing Prosocial Behavior

- **When possible, have multiples of toys for toddlers.** This is a preventative strategy that will allow you to spend time doing things besides refereeing fights over toys.
- **Set a timer for turn-taking.** Seeing time pass on a clock helps children wait because they know their turn is coming. Also, it

takes the burden off you: You're not the one saying time's up, the timer is "saying" it.

- **Be there.** When two toddlers are together, resign yourself to the fact that you really need to spend almost 100 percent of your time with them, on the floor. It is simply beyond them, at age two, to play well together for any length of time.
- **Help toddlers learn impulse control.** Show them how to count to three before knocking down a tower. "Ready? One, two, three!"
- **Model simple language for them.** Speak exactly the way they'd repeat it: "Say 'My turn!'"
- **Give older children "toddler-free" time.** They need to build or spread out their play when they don't have to worry about the toddler destroying their work. The toddler's naptime is good for this, as is time when the toddler stays in another room.

Little PROBLEMS:

A child's age is the clearest indicator of whether his egocentric behavior is a little or a big problem. If a two- or three-year-old child has strong attachments to the main people in his life, his language is blossoming, he is curious about the world around him, and he plays in a variety of ways, his impulsivity and egocentricity should steadily decrease with time.

BIG PROBLEMS:

If a toddler's egocentricity is accompanied by other developmental differences, such as language delays, limited play repertoire, repetitive behaviors, or a rigid insistence on routines, seek further evaluation through your pediatrician. Similarly, if a child of four or five years still seems to have no empathy for others, or recognition that he affects others, a closer evaluation may be warranted.

Autism is a pervasive developmental disorder, or **PDD**. PDDs are characterized by delays or differences in several areas: social skills, communication skills, and stereotypical or repetitive patterns of behavior, interests, or activities. This is a spectrum disorder, which means that the symptoms and characteristics can present in a wide variety of combinations from mild to severe.

Signs that a child may have a pervasive developmental disorder such as autism include: social problems that may include a lack of interest in other children, difficulty with the back-and-forth nature of interactions, lack of awareness of others in the environment, lack of eye contact, lack of spontaneous language, and difficulty using nonverbal gestures such as pointing or following an adult's pointing at something. Children with pervasive developmental disorders often adhere to impractical routines or rituals, exhibit repetitive behaviors such as opening and closing doors, flapping their arms, rocking, jumping, tiptoeing, or twirling objects in front of their eyes. Their play skills are greatly impaired and often consist of lining up objects by color or category. Pretend play and social play may not develop during the preschool years, but aggression, self-injury, or hyperactivity may become more prominent.

As discussed throughout this book, there are numerous reasons for delays or differences in language acquisition. However, when a language delay or difference is seen in combination with the delays or differences described above, there may be a much bigger problem at hand.

As with concerns about other potentially big problems, talk to your pediatrician promptly. A comprehensive evaluation performed by a multidisciplinary team should be undertaken to identify autism or other significant developmental delays. This team may include a psychologist, neurologist, child psychiatrist, speech pathologist, or occupational therapist in addition to a developmental pediatrician. Parent advocacy and collaboration with medical specialists is essential. Early intervention services are *critical* for children diagnosed with a pervasive developmental disorder such as autism. For more information, see appendix H.

Four

Speech and Language Development

Can We Talk?????

"What are the normal stages of speech and language development?"

"My child can hear; why can't she listen and follow directions?"

"How can I help my child learn to socialize and use language to talk to adults and play with peers?"

"What about stuttering? How do I know if my child needs help or will outgrow this?"

Parents may hear some common terminology when learning about speech and language development. **Auditory comprehension** refers to what a child understands. It includes **receptive language,** which is a child's understanding of words, commands, question forms, prepositions and concepts. Auditory comprehension includes a youngster's listening abilities. The child must be able to hear the message, as well as pay attention to speech in a noisy background, discriminate between two similar sounds and remember what is said.

Expressive language refers to a youngster's ability to communicate using vocabulary, sentence length, and sentence structure. Expressive language includes **articulation skills,** which are how a child forms speech sounds. Expressive language also encompasses **pragmatic skills,** the ability to produce language for a variety of purposes. Children need to use their language skills to comment, to greet others, protest, exclaim, pay attention when someone is talking, and take conversational turns.

A **speech-language pathologist** (also called a **speech pathologist** or speech therapist) is trained to identify, evaluate, and treat children and adults with a variety of communication disorders. In most U.S. states, a speech-language pathologist must hold a master's degree in this field. An **audiologist** is a professional in hearing science and is trained to evaluate hearing and treat hearing disorders.

Feeding and articulation skills are enmeshed. The way children use their lips and tongue for drinking and eating provides practice for developing later higher-level movements for more complex sounds. Articulation difficulties can result in a child's feeling frustrated. A child with significant difficulty pronouncing sounds may have a hard time being understood by others, which can result in some secondary difficulties communicating with peers and even adults. If the child lashes out in frustration when he is not understood, behavioral difficulties may also emerge. Each area of development impacts and is impacted by the other areas (speech, language, motor, sensory, and social-emotional).

General Speech and Language Milestones

What's Normal?

Although there is a range of normal development, knowing general speech and language milestones can serve as a guideline for parent expectations. Remember, some children tend to develop a little more rapidly in one area or another; for example, the early walker may not be an early talker.

One-Year-Olds
- Look for a parent when asked, "Where is Daddy?" or "Where is Mommy?"

The Evolution of Language

- Follow a highly familiar command, "Wave bye-bye"
- Say first word approximations
- Use gestures (e.g., "Up," "All done," "Bye")
- Jargon (string sounds together while varying the pitch, so it sounds as if the child is talking even if a parent cannot make out a word)

Two-Year-Olds
- Can follow a variety of simple commands
- Begin to answer yes-and-no questions
- Can answer "what" and "where" questions
- May have a vocabulary of fifty words at the beginning of the second year, with rapid vocabulary growth to two hundred words by the end of the second year
- Use words to label items in the environment (e.g., "dog," "cup")
- Begin to put two or even three words together
- Speech may not be understood by strangers

Three-Year-Olds
- Can identify one color correctly
- Demonstrate understanding of the concepts "big" versus "little"
- Demonstrate understanding of the prepositions *in, on,* and *under*

- Answer "who," "why," and "how many" questions
- Produce three- to four-word phrases
- Approximately 75 percent of speech is intelligible to strangers by the end of the third year.
- Express feelings, such as "I don't like that!"
- By the end of the third year, follow two-part commands (e.g., "Put the ball on the floor and clap your hands")

Four-Year-Olds

- Identify and name a variety of colors
- Produce four- to five-word sentences
- Can tell a story
- Speech is understood by others approximately 90 percent of the time.
- Use regular past tense (e.g., "He walked home")
- Begin to participate in verbal pretend games
- By the end of the fourth year, can follow a three-part command (e.g., "Put the book on the floor, give me the doll, and open the door")

Five-Year-Olds

- Understand time concepts such as "before" and "after"; "first," "second," and "last"
- Understand "when" questions
- Produce five- to six-word sentences
- Produce irregular past tense correctly ("I went to the store")
- Have developed most of the sounds in the speech sound repertoire, although may still have difficulty with one or two sounds or consonant blends (such as tr or sl blends)
- Listen attentively to a short story and answers several questions about it
- Participate in long conversations with others

Six- to Eight-Year-Olds

- Sentence length and complexity continues to increase.
- Have generally acquired all speech sounds by the eighth year

- Understand "how often" question form
- Can adapt the politeness of how they speak to their communication partner; for example, they speak differently to a teacher versus to a peer
- Retell stories with greater detail in an organized manner

Signs that May Indicate a Child Should See a Speech-Language Pathologist or Child Development Specialist

(adapted from *Childhood Speech, Language and Listening Problems*)

- A child does not imitate gestures or sounds
- A child produces a limited number of speech sounds
- A child whose speech is significantly more delayed than peers
- A child who produces speech that draws attention to how he is making the sounds rather that to what he is trying to say
- A child who does not make eye contact
- A child who has difficulty communicating and appears frustrated
- A preschooler who communicates with gestures and single words rather than sentences
- A preschooler whose grammar is significantly delayed as compared with that of peers
- A child who is inattentive to speech and language, and who does not appear to hear you
- A preschool child who follows directions only after watching what others do
- A preschooler or school-age child who does not appear interested in playing with peers

Auditory Comprehension

She Can Hear; Why Doesn't She Understand?

Emily is an active five-year-old in her last year of preschool. During the first parent-teacher conference, her teachers reported that she has trouble following directions in the busy classroom. At times, she is inattentive when instructions are given. At other times, once her attention has been gained, she doesn't appear to understand the instructions. Instead, she often looks at what her classmates are doing and then imitates their actions. She has difficulty responding appropriately to questions.

Emily may be experiencing difficulties with her auditory comprehension of language. This can be complicated by a variety of factors. Some children have trouble with auditory comprehension because they have difficulty paying attention to the most important auditory information (such as a teacher asking a question). They have trouble tuning out extraneous distractions in the environment. Some youngsters seem acutely aware of barely audible sounds, such as the hum of a light or the sound of birds outside, and this can make them unavailable for classroom instruction. At home, there are many environmental noises that may make it difficult for a child to attend to a verbal request. The most notable home distraction is the television (which many children believe is their primary focus and that a parent's voice is a secondary distraction)!

Children who have auditory comprehension challenges may have difficulty with auditory discrimination. **Auditory discrimination** is the ability to discern between two different auditory stimuli. A child may have trouble distinguishing between two similar sounds in a word. For the early-school-age child, this will negatively impact his ability to read and to understand instructions.

Other youngsters have difficulty with **auditory memory** skills.

These students have problems recalling such auditory information as numbers, words, or instructions. Some demonstrate challenges with word retrieval. They may have problems recalling and being able to produce a specific word or phrase.

Many children with auditory comprehension difficulties exhibit a variety of behaviors. This may include poor attending skills, particularly in a busy environment (such as a classroom). These youngsters often appear to have a short attention span and to lack motivation. Others may respond inconsistently to auditory instruction and at times answer questions inappropriately. Children with these difficulties may have trouble understanding material and be negative about learning. They may demonstrate a slow or delayed response to an instruction or a question.

Some children find it challenging to answer various question forms (e.g., who, what, where, when, why) correctly. Some youngsters show confusion when faced with temporal words, such as "before" or "after." Other children have trouble recalling and sequencing events in order. Some find understanding spatial concepts (such as "under," "in back of") challenging, particularly when these phrases are embedded in longer sentences.

Children with auditory processing challenges can appear irritable. Adults who have experienced this problem have reported that it is like driving along in the car, listening to a preferred radio station that is a little bit out of range. You may persevere because you really want to listen to that particular ball game or news program. Eventually it becomes so difficult that you give up and find a new station. Our children may work hard to listen to auditory information but, if it becomes too challenging, they eventually fatigue and shut down.

Parents and teachers who are concerned that a child is experiencing auditory comprehension difficulties should seek an evaluation from a speech-language pathologist. The child can be tested to see if her abilities fall within the range of age expectations or if she requires language therapy to facilitate these skills.

Whether a child has difficulty with auditory discrimination, auditory memory, comprehension of questions, or difficulty with following instructions, there are ways to support him at home and at school.

Enhancing Auditory Comprehension

YOU HAVE TO HEAR TO RECEIVE

Parents who have any concerns about their child's speech, language, and listening abilities should schedule their child for a complete audiological evaluation with an audiologist to assess the youngster's hearing. Optimal hearing is an essential part of understanding and producing language. Many children have chronic difficulties with middle ear fluid and frequent ear infections. Fluctuating fluid in their middle ears makes them respond inconsistently and at times appear to be noncompliant. An audiologist will also make referrals to the child's physician for medical follow-up as needed.

Competing noise in a busy classroom or home can make focusing on language challenging for some children. Eliminate sound-producing environmental distractions, such as the stereo or television, when you are talking with and playing with children. Although you may be providing wonderful language stimulation, some children may be focusing primarily on the Barney "I Love You" song that is playing on the tape. Remember young children are still learning language, so provide opportunities where they can hear it clearly.

SLOW DOWN YOUR SPEECH!

A basic, yet highly effective strategy to facilitate understanding of language in young children is to simply slow down your rate of speech, giving the child more time to receive and process the information. Pause at punctuation, such as commas and periods, to give the youngster more processing time and also let him know that you are not communicating one huge, incomprehensible thought. The child learns that the information can be broken down into more manageable units. Practice using this slightly slower rate when reading and singing to the child. Another valuable strategy is to put yourself at eye level with the child as you speak at a slow, normal rate. This will help him look at you while you talk.

BEGIN AT THE BEGINNING: BREAK DOWN LARGER GOALS

"I just had this nagging feeling that something wasn't right. It was in the back of my mind or I would wake up in the middle of the night thinking, well, really worrying, about it. The more time I spent with friends who had children who were the same age, the more I realized that Sean's development in several areas was lagging behind his peers. My husband and I made an appointment to discuss our concerns with our pediatrician, who then made arrangements for Sean to have a full developmental evaluation. Sean demonstrated difficulties with motor, speech, and language and social development. We enrolled him in a therapeutic nursery school program, where he received therapy to develop his skills. Best of all, the therapists in the program are a great resource to me and now I know what I can do to help him. I feel like a weight has been lifted off my shoulders."

When Sean began his therapeutic nursery school program, he did not follow single-part commands. A speech-language pathologist showed his mother how to work on following some single-part instructions within the context of familiar routines. They began with having Sean throw his trash away following a meal. He was told simply, "Throw trash away." He was provided with cues as needed, such as handing him his napkin and having the trash can close by. Sean's parents and the staff of his therapeutic nursery school program practiced this several times a day, which helped the youngster understand what was expected. They praised Sean for following the direction, saying, "Good helping!" or "Good listening."

As your child participates more, back off and provide fewer cues. For example, you may reduce use of gestures. As the youngster continues to successfully follow the command, you can put necessary props farther away. As the child becomes more successful with following commands within a routine, you may introduce an unfamiliar one-step direction and eventually two-part commands.

LESS IS MORE: USE FEWER WORDS

To help the child who is having difficulty processing information such as question forms and commands, once again, begin at a level that she can experience some success. Initially use fewer words and more actions, and be sure to pair words with actions. This is particularly essential in a busy environment. It is more challenging to follow instructions in a busy classroom rather than in the child's home.

FINGER CUE

"First, hang up coat. Next. . ."

A finger-cueing strategy is an important tool to help adults break information into smaller, more manageable units. The child is given a great deal of information from listening to your request and looking at your face. Break down the instructions by counting on your fingers. Alternatively you can point to each finger as you give the next step of the instruction. This is a useful cue to repeat instructions or to give a series of related instructions (e.g., "First, hang up your coat. Next, sit down. . . .")

A finger-cueing strategy can also help a child who is having difficulty with word retrieval. For example, if you are talking about the animals you saw at the zoo you can finger-cue which items were already mentioned. This allows processing time and the child can visualize other items in that particular category. For those children who need a little more assistance, you can add a sound cue to help remember a particular animal, or give a definition to spark remembering a key item.

A PICTURE IS WORTH A THOUSAND WORDS:
USE VISUALS TO SUPPORT AUDITORY LEARNING

Speech is fleeting. One says something and then the auditory signal is gone. Using pictures whenever possible can help the child focus on what you are saying, particularly when a new topic is introduced. Pictures can help a child who is not having success, understand what is expected.

Using pictures and photographs in the classroom can help children attend longer and be more available for auditory learning. For the older preschooler and young school-age child, pictures, photographs, or simple drawings with stick figures can be added to printed words, to ensure understanding of the material. Often, using pictures and these other visuals helps slow down your rate of presentation and divide the information into more manageable units that a child can understand.

THINKING TIME

Many children with auditory comprehension challenges have difficulty answering questions. In a busy classroom, or even at home while eating dinner with siblings, they don't often get time to process the questions posed to them. Other children may yell out the answer before they have time to process the question. To remedy this, introduce the concept of "thinking time" to all the children and help them practice this. Use a signal that you want them to think for a moment, such as tying on a thinking cap or pointing your index finger to your forehead, before you call on someone for an answer. Use a gesture to remind the other children not to blurt out a thought, such as an index finger pointing to your lips. Reinforce this response by saying, "Good waiting" or "Good thinking!" to the child who waited to respond. Even if the youngster with auditory comprehension difficulties is not ready to reply to a question, at least the child will have more opportunity to process it.

Speech and Expressive Language Skills

No One Understands My Child's Speech!

"My three-and-a-half-year-old child talks all the time; however, nobody but me can understand her. She is social and very chatty but everyone looks at me to interpret what she is saying. She's starting to get frustrated. I have noticed recently that she has become more reluctant to approach her friends because, if they don't understand her, they go find another child who is easier to communicate and play with. This is really starting to feel like a big problem. Where do I go for help?"

Use the general speech and language milestones (see pages 76–79) to decide if a child is having a bigger speech problem requiring intervention or a little one, which she may outgrow. Ask yourself, "Does my child's speech differ significantly from that of other children his or her age? Does my child appear frustrated? Are my child's speech and/or language difficulties causing her to have a more difficult time at school or playing with peers?"

In the vignette depicted above, this three-and-a-half-year-old is having a difficult time being understood. She is feeling that she cannot talk to peers because they won't understand her, and is becoming frustrated by her unsuccessful communication attempts. She appears to have a "big problem," requiring professional intervention. A speech and language evaluation would give the speech pathologist a chance to listen carefully to this youngster's speech and language, and to compare it to the skills of others her age. After the evaluation determines whether the child requires speech and/or language therapy, the speech-language pathologist (sometimes called a speech therapist) would begin speech therapy. The speech pathologist would determine appropriate goals for this youngster to work on to successfully develop her speech sounds. The therapist will often incorporate games and play into the session and give parents ideas for follow-up activities to continue to improve speech at home. (See appendix G.)

"My two-and-a-half-year-old, Lauren, is a generally happy but silent child. She understands what is said to her and can follow a variety of one- to two-part commands. However, her first words have been very slow in coming. When her mother and I realized this, we vowed to spend more time practicing talking with her and asking her to imitate words. This doesn't seem to have had any measurable effect in helping her develop any more vocabulary, but has pushed all of our frustration levels through the roof. What should we do?"

This family made an appointment for an evaluation with a speech-language pathologist, and the child was promptly enrolled in speech therapy two times per week. An appointment was also made for a complete audiological (hearing) test to rule out any hearing or middle ear difficulties.

Lauren was diagnosed with **verbal apraxia**. No weakness of the oral musculature was found. Instead she appeared to have difficulty organizing, sequencing, grading, and controlling the movements needed to produce sounds and words. Children with verbal apraxia, also sometimes known as dyspraxia, have difficulty imitating sounds and they are often limited in the type and amount of sounds they can make. This can limit their ability to communicate and socialize with peers, particularly in a nursery school classroom. Sometimes children have verbal apraxia alone, or they may have additional difficulties imitating motor sequences (motor apraxia); these later youngsters may appear to be clumsy. (See chapter 6.)

One of the hallmarks of apraxia is inconsistent errors. Words may pop out of the child's mouth but, when she tries to repeat them, she can't get the sounds out, particularly upon request.

Once Lauren began speech therapy, her parents and therapists made a list of words that she said on a regular basis and also noted which words that popped out occasionally. They worked together not only to add words to her vocabulary but also to increase the number of opportunities for her to use words in her existing vocabulary. For example, she approximated the names of her parents by saying "Ma" for Mom and "De" for Dad. Her parents made a family photo album that Lauren looked at frequently as she named her family. They also began playing hide-and-seek with her after dinner. One parent would hide while the other would help Lauren search, calling out for the other parent. Soon she was using her vocabulary much more frequently.

Lauren was encouraged to practice making sounds by blowing a variety of whistles and kazoos. This helped her learn to coordinate respiration (using her vocal cords in conjunction with her mouth and nose) to make sounds. She enjoyed these games immensely. Her parents also got her a tape recorder and recorded Lauren making sounds. After a short time, she was able to reproduce some sounds. When her parents played back the tapes, she imitated herself. Soon she could imitate her parents if they said words from her existing vocabulary. Imitating new words was still too challenging for her.

Lauren's parents were also trained to identify when their daughter was the most vocal. Was it easier when she was swinging on a swing or roughhousing with her dad? Was she a little more vocal when relaxing in her bath or when happily playing with her dolls? By observing this, they could create more opportunities for Lauren to use her sounds. They also learned to respond to her utterances. For example, if she said, "Da?" when playing, they might name the item for her or respond verbally, rather than asking her to use a word that was too difficult for her to say. When Lauren's parents received speech and language goals that were broken down into smaller, more manageable pieces, they were able to see progress in their daughter's speech development.

"My child doesn't use irregular past tense. He says he 'goed' to the store, 'drinked' his milk, and so on. Is this a problem that requires a speech-language pathologist?"

Whether this is a problem or not really depends on the child's age. A four-year-old who says that she "goed" to the store is simply applying a grammatical rule that she has learned. This rule states that you add an *ed* to the end of a word to denote past tense. A child who says "goed" has not yet learned the exceptions to the "add an *ed* rule." With a four-year-old or younger child, provide an indirect correction. When the child tells you, "We goed to the store," simply reply, "Yes, we went to the store. Remember what we bought?" Providing an indirect correction lets the child hear the correct grammatical form but allows you to respond to your child's message without his feeling criticized.

Five- and six-year-olds begin to learn the exceptions to this rule. If your early-school-age child demonstrates many grammatical errors, she may benefit from a speech and language evaluation. If your five-year-old's speech is generally grammatically correct, simply use an indirect correction when your child is talking to you and she will catch on. However, if you like you can set a timer for five minutes a day of talking practice. Make it fun! During this time, practice some of those irregular past tense verbs. For example, pour your child a tiny cup of juice and say, "Drink the juice." Then ask, "What did you do? You *drank* the juice." Practice several times. Tell your child to throw a Koosh ball. Ask him what he did and model the phrase, "You *threw* the ball." You can do the same with the verbs *go/went*. Outside of this practice session use an indirect correction to keep your child talking!

Speech Development and the Bilingual Child

"Our child is learning two languages. How do I help him? Who do I go to for help if I think my child is having trouble learning two languages?"

In the book *Dual Language Development and Disorders*, authors Fred Genesee, Johanne Paradis, and Martha Crago discuss several ways that we introduce children to a second language. In some families, both languages are introduced at the same time from infancy. This is referred to as **simultaneous bilingualism.** Many families use the "one person, one language" method to help children sort out each language. The mother, for example, may speak only English to the child, whereas the father speaks to his youngster only in Spanish.

Other children may learn one language at home and later, after the age of three, often at school, learn a second language, or the dominant language of their region. These children are referred to as **second language learners**. In the United States, many children learn English this way, during their first exposure to child care or preschool.

In *Learning Language and Loving It,* Elaine Weitzman discusses three stages that children who are exposed to simultaneous bilingualism go through.

In Simultaneous Bilingualism
1. Young children mix words from both languages and use them together.
2. From approximately 2.5 years, the children begin to separate out the languages. Many of these children learn scripts or phrases that can be used in a variety of contexts.
3. A dominant language evolves when one language is used more than the other. Most children have established both languages

including sentence structure, grammar, and vocabulary by 7 years of age (Elaine Weitzman, 1992, 201).

Bilingualism with Second Language Learners

In *Dual Language Development and Disorders*, the authors cite a 1997 study by P. O. Tabors that describes stages that second-language learners may go through:

1. The child may try to speak the native language at school.
2. Once realizing that this language is not understood, the child may become nonverbal in the classroom as they take in the second language.
3. The child then begins to speak in single words and short phrases. Often those first phrases are scripts of highly familiar phrases used in the classroom.
4. The child begins to construct novel phrases (Fred Genesee et al., 2004, 119–20).

There is variability in the rate of language development in children who are second-language learners. Some children show significant skill acquisition in one year, yet others may need two years or longer to acquire a second language. Often, children continue to make grammatical errors as they develop the second language.

Certainly a child's individual personality traits and innate language abilities will influence rate of language acquisition, as will the quality of the language exposure and the amount of time exposed to the new language.

Supporting Language Development in Bilingual Homes

- Provide quality opportunities to hear and use language skills. Play and read with your child.
- Use visuals whenever you can. Take photos of outings and family members. Get postcards from a trip, which can be used to discuss where you went and what you did. (See appendix E.)

- Closely monitor hearing, particularly if your child does not always appear attentive to sounds and speech or has frequent colds or ear infections.
- Use a slow, normal rate of speech and simple, grammatically correct sentences as you talk to your child about what you are doing.
- Limit environmental distractions such as background music, television, and radio, since it is hard to attend to a second language in a noisy environment.
- Ask your child's teacher if you can come in and take pictures of your youngster and activities, as well as of classmates and teachers. This will help your child learn names of classmates and to feel like a member of the classroom.
- Ask the teacher to help your child find ways to participate nonverbally until your youngster feels more comfortable with the second language. Perhaps you can suggest that the teacher may be able to pair him with a peer to blow bubbles, paint, or participate in cooking and art projects.

If You Think Your Child Is Having Difficulties Developing Two Languages

Consult with a speech pathologist who has expertise with children who are learning dual languages. Ideally, look for a speech pathologist who speaks both languages that your child speaks. If the youngster is thought to have speech or language difficulties, the intervention is optimally provided in his dominant language. It is thought that if a child has firmly established language skills, it will assist in developing a second language. Also get an audiological evaluation (hearing test and typanogram, to see if there is fluid in the ears) if you suspect him of having difficulties developing language.

Helping Children Develop Speech Skills

Vocal play is a great way to help a child develop and practice a variety of sounds. Toddlers and preschoolers benefit from a variety of sound play opportunities. Make sure you are facing your child for these activities. Add novel props to your play by using two toy telephones, which you can pick up to talk to each other. Bring out toy microphones and tape recorders. You can also use a recorder to make tapes of your child talking, singing, and retelling favorite stories. Your youngster will love to play them back!

Singing songs with your child also helps him develop breath control for speech. Sing simple songs at a slightly slower rate. This gives your child more opportunities to sing some of the words. Make up silly songs to practice sound production. Two-year-olds, for example, love the "No" song, which consists of singing *no* to a simple tune. Incorporate songs into your routines. For instance, sing a cleanup song as you put toys away.

Reinforcing all speech attempts encourages your child to keep talking. For example, a child may say "Tat!" when he sees a cat. The adult responds, "Yes, cat!" This provides the child with an adult model, but at the same time responds to the message the child was conveying. It is called an "indirect correction" because it gives the child an adult model of a target word, but doesn't make the youngster feel criticized, particularly if it is a sound that your child simply hasn't mastered yet. Best of all, it keeps him talking! Children who are always directly corrected (e.g., "Not tat, say cat") will eventually get frustrated, try less often to talk to you, or find someone else less critical of them to communicate with.

"I saw a wabbit."   "I saw a rabbit, too."

Eating and Drinking Help Develop Articulation Skills

"My toddler and preschooler always use 'sippy' cups. My kids love them, and besides, sometimes they are really messy with a cup without a lid. Will these cups really get in the way of their speech development?"

The way youngsters use their lips and tongue for eating and drinking impacts how they use them for speech development. Skills developed initially for eating can significantly impact a child's development of speech sounds. A child who eats a variety of age-appropriate foods and textures will be also practicing some of the movements used to develop higher-level sounds.

A toddler is able to actively use his lips to help him drink from a lidless cup and then use his tongue to bring the liquid up and back for swallowing. A toddler or preschooler who drinks from a spouted cup or bottle does not actively draw the liquid into his mouth using smaller lip movements. Instead, he will pour the liquid into his mouth and move his tongue in an immature, forward-and-backward suckling pattern. He will not practice the up-and-down tongue movements that facilitate development of more difficult speech sounds such as *s, r,* and *l.* Older toddlers and preschoolers who use pacifiers may also have difficulty producing the more sophisticated mouth movements needed for later speech sound development. Also, the more time a toddler or preschooler has a pacifier in his mouth, the less opportunity she has to practice producing speech and using his developing communication skills.

Teaching Children How to Drink from a Lidless Cup
- Before you take away a spouted cup, you must make sure your child has good cup drinking skills. Provide lots of opportunities to practice.
- If your child is having difficulty managing the lidless cup, you can practice initially by drinking a thicker liquid, such as a yogurt shake or fruit nectar, since they come out more slowly and are easier to manage.

- Make it fun! Your young child can practice drinking from a cup without a lid while you have a tea party. Or you can shop together for a special lidless cup, which in itself is a treat.
- You can also encourage your child to drink from a straw, which also provides practice using more mature mouth patterns. You can purchase cups with a lid that has a hole to be used with a bendable straw. This also keeps spills to a minimum.
- If your child has some difficulty giving up a sippy cup, remember that it is hard to change behavior and persevere. By giving the youngster opportunities to drink from a lidless cup, you are laying the foundation for higher-level speech skills.

Add Movement to Speech and Language Activities

Children often become more vocal when they move their bodies. A toddler may be most talkative when pushing a toy lawn mower or swinging at the playground. Playground experiences also help a young child develop vocabulary, particularly verbs and adverbs.

Create obstacle courses for a youngster to teach him new concepts, such as the use of prepositions (e.g., "under," "on"). As he moves through the obstacle course, talk about what he is doing by stressing the prepositions and using them in short phrases.

Combine motor and language activities by having the child act out familiar nursery rhymes. "Jack Be Nimble," "Humpty Dumpty," and "Jack and Jill" are easily acted out and will delight your youngster.

Use Books and Pictures

Introduce books and pictures to facilitate speech and language development. Young children often enjoy homemade photo albums portraying family members or a special event. Talking about a trip to the zoo or birthday party while looking at pictures depicting the event helps children practice using more complicated grammar, stringing together longer sentences, and learning how to tell a story. Younger children respond better when the albums use larger photos (at least 5 x 7-inch prints). Children enjoy reading these homemade books again and again, and the repetition helps to develop vocabulary.

Youngsters often like to read songbooks. Favorites may include the Raffi series or *The Wheels on the Bus* by Ellen Appleby. Pause at punctuation to give the child ample time to process the language. Pause at a key juncture of the song and let her fill in a word.

Read books that contain a redundant refrain. The more a child is able to participate in a story, the more likely she is to be interested in it. A young child, or one with speech and language difficulties, may have trouble participating in the story if the words are constantly changing. Choose stories like *Dear Zoo* by Rod Campbell and *Brown Bear, Brown Bear, What Do You See?* by Eric Carle. The redundancy of the refrains also helps a child understand the story.

Books can also provide the link to developing both language and play skills. Reading a familiar story such as "The Three Bears" and then acting it out gives your child an opportunity to sequence her language and play. Knowing the story line helps to organize your youngster's play and gives lots of opportunities to practice using language.

Develop Speech and Language During Daily Routines

Children who are just beginning to understand and use language benefit from incorporating communication opportunities into their daily routines. Meals, cleanup, play, and bath times allow him to practice using his speech. For the child who is just beginning to talk or has difficulty producing intelligible speech, model key phrases during these routines. These may include, "My turn," "I'm done," or "I need help."

Be playful! For example, sing the cleanup song as you both slowly put toys away. Next, you and your child may sing it quickly as you rapidly put items on the shelves. Varying the routine and making it fun will focus your child's attention on this task and teach vocabulary simultaneously.

Be forgetful! During familiar routines, "forget" a key piece of an activity. For example, place a cup of pudding in front of your toddler and sit down next to him expectantly. He may then exclaim, "No spoon" or listen intently as you say it. Or, hand your preschooler a small pitcher of juice but momentarily "forget" the cup. Creating a situation where he needs to ask for something specific is another way of developing your child's speech within daily routines.

By creating communication opportunities within the course of your child's day, you will be amazed at the results!

Developing Social Language and Communication Skills: Pragmatics

Interaction and play with peers are essential for social, emotional, and communication development in the preschool years. Some children effortlessly acquire the ability to play and socialize with peers. For others, this is a laborious process that requires adult facilitation and support.

Three-year-olds tend to be adult oriented and start to take conversational turns with a parent or teacher. However, after the age of three and a half, most children are more interested in playing and interacting with peers, and they begin to be able to have short conversations and communicate with adults and classmates. Most start to develop more cooperative play. By age five, children are using language to create elaborate play scenarios and interact with peers for extended play times.

Young children want to be able to socialize and play with friends. However, for some, this is a daunting task. Social success is more difficult for those who have limited communication abilities, less advanced motor skills, developmental delays, and/or difficulty organizing and sequencing play or sensory integration challenges.

Prerequisites for Socialization and Play

The following skills enable a youngster's ability to socialize and play with peers:

- Get a peer's attention.
- Communicate with friends.
- Follow a request.
- Negotiate a conflict.
- Take turns.

- Pay attention to the play scenario.
- Be a leader in play.
- Follow another's lead.
- Organize and sequence the play.
- Be flexible about developing a play scenario.

Young children are still developing these skills, whereas older children have more of them in place. When a child is experiencing difficulty connecting with peers, it is essential to take time to carefully watch the interaction. Observe how she enters play and interacts with peers. What are her strengths and what do adults do to support her play? The adults in a young child's life can provide important encouragement and be instrumental in helping her learn how to communicate and socialize with peers.

Communicating with Peers

TEACH REQUESTING
Snack and playtimes often provide opportunities to help a youngster learn how to request what she wants and needs. For example, by putting a little juice in a cup and waiting, a parent or teacher gives a child more opportunities to request what she wants and practice using her vocabulary words. Similarly, by blowing a bubble or two and waiting, the adult provides more speech and language opportunities. This is particularly important for the child who is just beginning to communicate.

Older preschoolers and early-school-age children can work on requesting when adults pair them to make a snack for a friend. They can, with adult facilitation, ice and decorate a cupcake, or make a fruit salad or a sandwich for another youngster. This involves communicating with peers to make wants and needs known. Some children need to do this in a structured context repeatedly before they can generalize this skill to unstructured play.

SCRIPTS AGAIN
Earlier in the chapter, we talked about teaching children to use key phrases, particularly if their speech attempts are unclear, or they are just

learning to put words together. These scripts, words such as "I need help," "I want ___," and "Your turn is next" are also useful to help children use their language to negotiate with peers, comment, and request help. For example, if two youngsters are squabbling about the use of a particular toy, an adult can prompt one preschooler to say, "I'm next," instead of grabbing the desired item from a peer.

BE A PLAYER

Both parents and teachers of young children can support social interaction by taking part in preschoolers' play. Get on the child's eye level and be a participant. Some young children may need to experience success while playing with an adult partner before they are able to generalize these skills to playing with peers. Play with an adult helps to develop social and communication skills, and youngsters are often then able to sustain the play for longer periods of time. With adult support, a child may be able to come up with novel ideas or learn to organize and sequence his language and play.

TEACH TURN-TAKING

Have your child pick a play activity. Afterward, choose another game or activity and encourage him to follow your lead. At first this may be difficult for the preschooler or young school-age child who finds turn taking a challenge. Initially, the adult may pick another favorite activity of the child and have a shorter turn. You may want to use a timer to support the child's switching gears and to facilitate turn taking. Eventually, this can also be generalized to play with other family members and finally with friends. Turn taking skills are essential for socializing with peers.

HAVE YOUR CHILD GET TO KNOW PRESCHOOL CLASSMATES

Some children need specific help to learn the names of their teachers as well as classmates. Talk to the teachers about taking individual pictures of classmates and staff so that you can put them in a photo album. Look at the pictures at home with your child, and name the people in the photos. This skill can be used to teach "calling a friend's name" to get a classmate's attention at school. Practice this both at home and in the classroom.

HAVE PLAYDATES WITH FRIENDS FROM SCHOOL

Some children find their first classroom experiences intimidating and stressful. Parents can help a child have a successful school experience by inviting a classmate over for a playdate. Younger classmates can be invited with a parent. It is much easier for the children to get to know each other in a one-to-one setting rather than a larger group. These playdates will provide the youngster with early social skills that the child can then generalize into the preschool classroom. After all, there is nothing in a classroom that is more inviting than a child your youngster calls "friend."

Let's Hear Your Voice: Could There Be a Problem?

"Four-and-a-half-year-old David has vacillating behavior. One minute, he is a whirling ball of energy and overstimulated; the next, he appears quiet and thoughtful. In unstructured activities, such as at the playground, he often runs around wildly and screams and yells to his friends to catch him. His voice is often raspy and hoarse, and teachers and parents are becoming concerned."

David's frequent yelling can be detrimental to his vocal cords and should be evaluated by a physician. Many times parents first discuss this with their child's pediatrician, who then makes a referral for a pediatric ear, nose, and throat physician (**otolaryngologist**). This doctor has special equipment that can be used to take a closer look at how the vocal cords are functioning and what may be causing the patient's difficulty. Sometimes allergies, gastroesophogeal reflux, viruses, a growth such as nodules (small blisters), or even polyps can form on the cords, causing voice disorders. The physician will devise a remediation program and may then make a recommendation for follow-up treatment with a speech-language pathologist specializing in voice disorders. For example, speech pathologists often develop strategies to help children reduce chronic yelling which is not good for their vocal cords.

Big problems that require consultation with a physician include:

- Constant yelling or throat clearing
- A hoarse, gravelly, or raspy voice
- A child who frequently uses a voice that is too high or too low

Reducing Yelling and Screaming

- Make it visual! Discuss optimal loudness levels with your child. Make a visual gauge out of poster board with an arrow that shows three levels: quiet, conversational, and too loud. Use this gauge to show your child what level of loudness he is using.
- Place your hands together and ask your youngster to pretend that these hands are your vocal cords or voice box. Show how they are supposed to gently open and close as your child talks. Then have your child clap hands together as hard as he can several times. Explain when a child does that with his vocal cords, it hurts them just as his hands sting when he claps them too hard. Explain that if we yell or scream too much, sometimes the vocal cords get blisters on them. Then they can't close easily and the voice sounds hoarse.
- Practice what you preach! Model using an optimal loudness level. Practice going to find family members rather than yelling for them. Practice taking turns talking at mealtimes rather than talking over each other.
- Place a "happy face" sticker on your children's lunch boxes or bags, or use a fun rubber stamp on their hands, to remind them to keep their voice happy by not screaming in the lunchroom or on the playground.
- Make sure your child's teachers also know your optimal voice plan. Everyone should work together to support your youngster

on these goals. We generally believe that teaching one child voice modulation will also benefit the others. These strategies can be used with all the children in your child's class.

- Reinforce your child when he uses his "healthy voice." Give specific praise ("You went to find your sister; you didn't yell!"). Praise specifically and often.
- Encourage your child to drink plenty of water.

Stuttering

For a young child, talking is a lot like learning to ride a bike. Just as the new biker initially rides for a short distance, the toddler coasts for a short distance, producing little phrases of two or three words. As the rider then begins to go for longer stretches, the preschooler begins to produce longer phrases and sentences. The cyclist starts to explore novel terrains; the young child begins to use communication skills across different environments—at home, then school, or on a playdate. Both the rider and the preschool child may experience some bumps along the route. For the preschooler, these may appear as hesitations or repetitions on the road to fluency.

As adults, we know that all speakers experience some disfluency in their speech. These may come in the form of repetitions, hesitations, or revisions. The young child who is experiencing rapid growth in speech and language skills, is prone to produce some of the same patterns of disfluent speech. Disfluency is often seen in children between the ages of two and a half to five years of age. For some youngsters, it may be due to difficulties coordinating breath control with organizing thoughts and producing more complex utterances. These disfluencies often appear as phrase repetitions (e.g., "I want, I want my blanket"), revisions ("I want two—three cookies!"), or interjections ("I need my blanket, I mean my pillow").

Stuttering may be defined as disfluencies that involve repetition of a word or part of a word (e.g., "Bababy"), sound prolongation (e.g., "Mmmmore"), or a blockage of a word the child is trying to say. If stuttering occurs frequently, the child may need the help of a speech-language pathologist to help him speak more fluently.

What Causes Stuttering?

Many speech pathologists believe that there is more than one cause for stuttering. Some children may have a genetic predisposition to stutter, as stuttering does run in some families. Stuttering occurs more in boys than girls. Some children may stutter due to difficulties coordinating breath control with organizing what they want to say, particularly as their phrases and sentences get longer and more grammatically complex. Experts are in agreement that parents do not cause their child's stuttering.

How Can Parents Promote Fluent Speech?

Children are more likely to stutter when they are feeling tired, stressed, or rushed. The following strategies can be incorporated into your day to facilitate fluent speech.

ESTABLISH REGULAR ROUTINES

Children benefit from a schedule and regular routines in their home and school day because it helps them to know what to expect. Establish regular bedtimes and mealtimes. Use meals as a time when the family comes together and enjoys one another's company. Turn off the radio or television while you eat, since it is a distraction to try to talk over the background noise.

PROVIDE CAREFUL TRANSITIONS

Hurrying or rushing young children makes them feel out of control and more likely to produce disfluent speech. Provide careful transitions and adequate time to get dressed and ready to go to preschool. You may want to incorporate using a picture schedule to help a child break down a larger task (e.g., getting ready) into smaller, more manageable pieces. For example, you can take pictures of your morning routine. This may include photos of the steps to getting ready including waking up, getting dressed, and brushing teeth. Attach Velcro to the back of the pictures and mount them on sturdy cardboard. As your child completes one activity, he can then look and see what he needs to do next. (See appendix E.)

PRACTICE TAKING TURNS TALKING

Throughout the day, practice taking turns talking with your child and other family members. Encourage everybody to listen without interrupting as each person talks. To not have to struggle to get and maintain others' attention helps decrease pressure to communicate for the child who is experiencing stuttering. Turn taking can also be practiced during play. Praise your children throughout the day when you catch them waiting their turn.

LIMIT DEMAND SPEECH

A major goal for a child who is experiencing a period of stuttering is to decrease the incidences of stuttering and increase opportunities to produce fluent speech. When a child is stuttering, it is crucial to avoid asking her specific questions, because it puts pressure on the youngster, making it more likely that her response will be stuttered.

Refraining from direct questions is difficult for most parents. For example, when a child is picked up from nursery school, parents who are eager to catch up with the child ask, "What did you do at school today?" Resist the urge to ask. Instead, get down on your child's eye level and say, "I am happy to see you!" Wait and listen for what information your child will offer you and comment on what she offers. Comment on the project your child is carrying (e.g., "Wow, pretty colors").

Also, avoid asking your child to recite for relatives ("Lynn learned a poem at school. Tell Grandma."). Avoid telling a child who may be stuttering to say please or thank-you, as this is another form of "demand speech." Instead, model using these phrases to teach her manners.

BE A GOOD COMMUNICATION PARTNER

Get down on your child's level and speak at a slow, normal rate of speech with your child. If he asks you a question, pause briefly before responding. This teaches him that adults also need to gather their thoughts before responding. Use shorter sentences and follow your child's lead in conversation. Speech pathologists have found that finishing a child's sentence or giving such advice as, "Slow down and take a deep breath," is *not* conducive to promoting fluent speech. Instead, it puts pressure on the child. The best way to promote smooth, fluent speech is by being a good communicative partner yourself. This often takes some practice!

REQUEST THE PLEASURE OF YOUR CHILD'S COMPANY

Play together! Color a picture, build a tower, put together a puzzle, blow bubbles, throw a ball back and forth, or play age-appropriate board games. Let your child know that you enjoy playing and spending time with him.

Together, read songbooks or enjoy books with a repeating refrain. (Reading books with your youngster is an excellent way that you can practice modeling a slow, normal rate of speech). When reading, remember to pause at punctuation, so your child hears the sentences and phrases as smaller units.

Turn off the radio and sing in the car with your child. You may find that if you sing the songs at a slightly slower rate, he will be able to sing more of the song with you.

Look together at pictures, loose photos, or photo albums. You may want to keep a box of photos that you and your child can look at together. By talking about them with your child, you are providing a relaxing activity where you can demonstrate slower speech.

SEEK HELP FROM THE EXPERTS

If you think your child is stuttering, seek professional help from a speech-language pathologist. Look for a speech pathologist who has expertise with stuttering and works with young children. Make sure the professional holds a Certificate of Clinical Competence from the American Speech-Language-Hearing Association (ASHA). The speech pathologist will first obtain valuable information from you about the types of disfluencies you are seeing in your child. Parents can provide important information about how often and under what circumstances their youngster produces disfluent speech. The speech therapist may then schedule an evaluation to determine how best to help your child.

Remember, your child may encounter some bumps along the road to fluent speech. However, there are strategies you can use to help, and professionals ready to help you.

A Final Word on Developing
Communication Skills . . .

Some children develop speech and language abilities quite easily; others need either some "big" or "little" strategies to develop these skills. Parents and teachers provide invaluable support and can help considerably by helping children put in the pieces as they develop their communication abilities.

Five

Motor Development

Developing Strong Bodies and
Coordinated Movements

Motor Development Is the Cornerstone of All Development

Motor development is the foundation for all other development because movement is essential to the development of children's body image and their ability to respond to their surroundings. Through movement at all levels (rolling, crawling, and walking), children learn about the environment, themselves, and many of the concepts which are important for higher-level learning. By moving their bodies around obstacles in their path, young children learn about spatial concepts such as up, down, in, out, on, off, over, and under. They learn by doing, and eventually the responses become automatic. Children's ability to move in their environment also has an impact on their social development. In all stages of childhood, they interact with peers on a motor level. Independence requires the ability to move and allows youngsters to make choices, to separate from a parent and return, as well as experience a broader range of activities and learning experiences.

Gross motor refers to development and functional use of large muscle groups that account for balance, stability, and mobility. Standing, walking, running, and skipping are examples of gross motor skills. **Fine**

motor development (the development of the smaller muscles of the body, such as the arms, hands, eyes, and mouth) is dependent on a good gross motor foundation. Children must be able to assume and maintain an upright posture without using hands for support to free their hands to explore and manipulate objects and tools. The small muscles of the eyes are equally important for helping children perceive and understand the world around them. The most precise muscles are in the mouth and critical for eating and speaking.

Unless there is a neurological, orthopedic, or other developmental disability, all children learn to hold up their heads, reach, sit, stand, and walk. This automatic progression of motor milestones, most of which occurs in the first year of life, provides the foundation for all future motor milestones. Basic motor skills are followed by skilled motor development: the ability to run, jump, climb stairs, and negotiate playground equipment.

Gross Motor Development

Perpetual Motion Machines

Children, by their very nature, are active even before they are born. Every mother can relate to those kicks, stretches, and even somersaults that are so frequent during pregnancy. From the moment of birth, babies become movement machines. Each squirm, wiggle, and stretch may appear to be random; however, these actions are the forerunner to more purposeful movement. This reflexive movement is preparing a baby to become an energetic, mobile, independent person.

During the first year, a child progresses from being pinned to the earth by gravity to being able to stand up and move to explore and interact with his environment. This developmental sequence encompasses a succession of smaller movements that establish the foundation for higher-level movement. Each milestone, or "building block," is dependent on the previous one and lays the groundwork for those that follow. If one of these building blocks is missed or not fully developed, it may manifest as a problem with quality of movement or inability to easily acquire specific skilled movements, such as running, jumping, skipping, and pedaling a tricycle.

While basic motor milestones are automatic, they also typically have an orderly timetable. However, it is the variances in this timetable that cause many parents, especially first-time parents, to be concerned. They ask why the nine-month-old next door is walking when their fourteen-month-old is not, or why Cousin Henry can ride his trike and same-age Susie cannot.

The variance in motor milestones depends on a variety of factors: genetics, temperament, and environment. Often, when parents express a concern about slow motor development, they are quick to admit that they walked late or all the boys in their family were slow in motor development. Contributing factors in motor delay may include a child's having been in an orphanage for the first year(s) of life, or prematurity. Preemies' motor skills most often reflect their age, corrected for prematurity. Early developmental delays often translate to nothing more than a timetable delay, and subsequently these motor skills catch up. If there is a glitch, it may show itself as a delay in skill development; avoidance of motor exploration; fear of movement; clumsiness, with frequent falls, or in general; and/or less ability than peers. If a child's motor development is lacking or lagging, it could be a basic motor problem. A basic motor problem would be difficulty with stability, mobility, and/or balance. If the basic motor ability is okay but there is a problem with skilled motor development such as skipping, riding a trike, or catching a ball, the problem could be motor planning, which is a more sensory-based skill. (See chapter 6.)

Most children fall within the normal range for early motor development (birth to thirty-six months), some children are on a slower timetable, and still others have atypical motor development. When concerned about a child's motor development, first consider the child's age and the specific activity with which he's having trouble.

The following list of red flags in motor development can help a parent decide whether or not to seek professional advice. A red flag does not necessarily mean a big problem, but it is a call to stop and look closer.

BIG PROBLEM OR Little PROBLEM:

- Not walking by eighteen months
- Inability to independently move from one position to another

- Significant difference in motor function and use of one side of the body vs. the other
- Not alternating feet on stairs by age four
- Frequent tripping and/or falling past age three
- Fear of movement
- Avoidance of motor play

On the Go

"My son is a whirlwind of movement. He's very accident prone and won't slow down enough to be safe and do things well."

Most children are "motor driven." They develop or learn new skills and then practice those skills over and over again. Picture the child who has just learned to pump on the swing, or one who learned to jump down from a low height; he wants to do more and more. Children build on their motor skills by taking any and every opportunity to use new skills. Motor skills can be enhanced with experience opportunities.

Many young children can be fearless and unaware of their limitations. This, combined with a high level of motor activity, can result in "getting in" or moving faster than their motor abilities allow. Careful supervision and the choice of safe play areas can go a long way toward keeping children safe. Eventually most children's judgment will catch up to their motor abilities. Certainly some children continue to be risk takers. For some that leads to a tendency to be accident prone and for others it leads to a high drive for motor activity and excellence in performance.

Skilled Movement

"My three-year-old still runs like a penguin."

"I dread the stairs; my four-year-old daughter clings to the stair railing and still needs to put both feet on each step. She is so slow and unsure of herself."

By the age of two, most children have all the physical abilities needed for motor development. Higher-level motor skills are simply a refinement

One child's flight of stairs is another child's Mount Everest.

and combination of these basic abilities. Some children have a greater degree of natural coordination and motor skill than do others. For example, Olympic athletes have innate motor talent combined with the discipline to practice and refine their skills. Even though your child may not be on the fast track to highly skilled or competitive sports, all children benefit from opportunities to practice physical skills and have fun with motor play. The following strategies are geared toward children between the ages of two and five years.

Building Gross Motor Skills

- **Begin to eliminate the stroller, except for long distances.** Expect and encourage children to walk. Make walking fun by observing nature, singing songs, and using the environment to add variety to your movement. Try jumping over cracks, walking along low retaining walls, and so on. When your little one gets tired, let her ride on your shoulders, a position that provides an excellent opportunity for her to work on upper-body balance and control.

- **A family walk, before or after dinner, benefits everyone.** In addition to the obvious physical rewards, this is an excellent time for talking with family members and practicing social skills as you greet friends and neighbors. Chart how far you walk each day; it can be an incentive to walk a little farther each time.
- **Make use of backyards, community playgrounds, and nature's playgrounds.** Children love to climb on rocks and over tree branches, step across streams, or jump off logs. Teach youngsters to wear sneakers or hiking shoes when they are out in nature.
- **Plan for physical playtime at least twice a day.** What child wouldn't relish the opportunity to jump in mud puddles and build "dams" along the edge of a street during a rain shower? (Keep them inside during electrical storms.) For indoor play, use common household objects to make obstacle courses. There are many good exercise and aerobics videos for children. Most community centers have set times for indoor play, and many shopping malls and fast-food restaurants have indoor play areas as well.
- **By age three, all children should have a tricycle or other riding toy with pedals.** Teach safety, use a helmet, and explain riding rules. Many children are ready to start with their first two-wheel bicycle by age four or five; training wheels can ensure success until the child has the coordination, balance, and judgment to ride independently.
- **Play ball.** Use a simple playground ball to practice catching, bouncing, throwing, and kicking. Using a beanbag or beach ball for throwing and catching can slow down the action and help your child be more successful. From the beginning, a child should learn to keep his eye on the ball.
- **Encourage your child to engage in challenging motor play.** Emphasize safety but gently urge your child to try the next step, such as trying the higher slide, climbing higher, or swinging higher. The best encouragement is a physical spot or light assist.

If a child needs more help than this, or if she can't reach a piece of equipment, maybe she should try it at a later date when her size and skill match up to the activity. Encourage your child but remember not to push her to take risks that she is not ready for.

- **Provide a balance between active physical play and sedentary play.** In this age of electronics, it is easy for children to opt for TV, computer, or video games, leaving little time left for active play.

- **Consider lessons or organized physical play.** By the age of four or five, many children are ready for swimming lessons, martial arts, gymnastics, dance, and a host of other physical team or individual activities. Don't push lessons unless your youngster expresses an interest, and remember it is important not to overschedule a young child. Lessons should be fun and taught by instructors who specialize in and have knowledge about the physical development and risk factors in young children.

- **Join a team.** An introduction to team sports, at this age, should focus on fun and learning basic skills, not on winning and losing. Look for a sports organization and coach with a fun, fitness, and basic skill philosophy. Consider getting involved yourself. It is a great opportunity to be involved in your child's enlarging environment. You will be rewarded with exercise, an opportunity to sharpen your sports skills, and a chance to work with children.

"She is always falling and seems weaker and less coordinated than other children her age."

THE PROBLEM:

Ever since Mary was a baby, her parents have noticed that she was slower in motor development than other children her same age. She didn't sit until she was ten months, or crawl until thirteen months. They were really worried when she didn't begin to walk until eighteen months. Other than this slow motor start, everything else that she did was always before her age mates. She used her hands well and was quite a talker.

At age four, Mary always has scrapes and bruises on her legs from frequent falls. She loves the playground, but has difficulty keeping up with the other children, and her parents worry that she will fall on stairs or from high equipment. All the other kids get on their tricycles without giving it a thought. Mary never quite remembers how to get on and off her tricycle. She is still tentative on the stairs, placing both feet on each step when going up and down stairs, and needing to hold the railing when going down. Her preschool teacher says that she has difficulty sitting cross-legged on the floor during circle and story time. Mary prefers to "W" sit. In ballet class, she is the first child to tire and one of the least coordinated.

Detective Work:

- Is there anything significant in Mary's birth history?
- Has her vision been checked?
- Is she fearful of movement or heights?
- Does she seem to have difficulty figuring out how to move her body to do certain motor activities?
- Has there been progress in the quality of her movement or are things getting worse?

Analysis of the Problem:

Most likely, this is a little problem that will need some intervention at this early age in order to prevent any secondary social or self-confidence issues.

Plan of Action:

Start by playing detective to see if this is simply motor immaturity or more of a sensory processing difficulty. Unusual fear or difficulty in figuring out how to move may indicate a sensory processing problem. If Mary has the ideas and knows how to do the activity but is just delayed with the motor action or awkward in the execution of the movement, it is most likely immature motor development. If there has been a deterioration of skills, this may be a bigger problem and it is imperative to seek medical advice immediately.

The underlying cause of Mary's motor delays will determine the best course of action. If it seems that her motor differences are related to sensory differences, the recommendation would be to see an **occupational therapist** for assessment and subsequent treatment if recommended. If it seems that her motor differences are caused more by a delay or immaturity of gross motor skills, the recommendation would be to a **physical therapist** for assessment and treatment if recommended.

Mary needs lots of opportunities to practice her motor skills, at home and at the playground. This will require some thoughtful planning on the part of her parents and teachers to make this fun and to ensure her safety. Walking along the landscape timbers that often border a sidewalk or playground is an excellent way to enhance balance. This lends itself well to a game of "Follow the Leader." Follow-the-leader games can incorporate a variety of motor skills such as hopping, jumping, turning, and other movements. Riding a tricycle is a great activity for building lower-body strength. When the family is not in a hurry and the stairs are empty, Mary should practice going up and down to build her skill and confidence. It is better to have her hold the rail and alternate feet, than be independent while still having to place both feet on the same stair. As she gains control, her need for support can be decreased. Practice is important, but so is spontaneous movement; never force or push Mary to do something that she is unable to do.

After a month of incorporating structured motor play several times a day, Mary was falling less frequently, riding her tricycle independently, and, much to her delight, able to stand on one foot during ballet class. She was doing better on the stairs, but still relied on the handrail. A daily family walk soon became a favorite time for everyone, and Mary enjoyed seeing if they could go a little farther each day. To be on the safe side, her parents had her evaluated by a pediatric physical therapist who recommended short-term treatment. Mary has now advanced from physical therapy to a community movement/gymnastic class, which she loves.

Using Movement to Improve Functioning Through the Day

Motor activities contribute so much more than just movement! Did you know . . .

- A walk around the block or ten minutes at the playground can go a long way toward setting up an active child for a good day at school (improved attention and better ability to participate in more sedentary activities).
- Frequent movement breaks reset a child's arousal system and help that child to remain at that "just right" level of activity and attention.
- "Heavy work" involving large muscles of the body can help calm an over aroused child.
- One hour daily of vigorous physical activity is recommended for children, as well as adults. Some children get this through recess, movement classes, and playground time; however, many children engage in more social and sedentary activities at these times.
- On a car trip, frequent stops (at least every two hours) for a stretch and movement break can avoid that dreaded cabin fever that develops when children are in close quarters for too long.
- If you have a child that doesn't seem to enjoy physical exercise (he may be the one who really needs it the most), provide the exercise in a game or dramatic play theme, (e.g., community hero theme, treasure hunt).
- Physical therapy or carefully selected movement classes or lessons can build a stronger motor base in your young child.

Fine Motor Development

Hands that Work!

The motor system of the human body is incredibly complex. In fact, it is our brain and hand function that separates us from other primates. The integrity and efficiency of this system depends on bone structure, muscles, joints, tendons, and nerves. Together, these components lead to strength, tone, and range of motion to produce the ability to move with purpose. The most skilled part of this complex system is the *hand*.

How Hands Work

"Fine motor development" refers to the development of the small muscles of the body. Good fine motor development is dependent on good basic large motor control. Fine motor development is necessary to be able to use arms and hands functionally. Critical to good hand use is the ability to coordinate both sides of the body. This is called **bilateral coordination**: using both hands together (both hands doing the same thing, e.g., rolling the ball or carrying a large object); using one hand as the doer and the other as the stabilized/helper hand (e.g., holding the bowl while scooping Cheerios or stabilizing the paper while you draw or color), and then the most complex action, where each hand is coordinated, but doing something different (e.g., using the scissors and guiding the paper for effective cutting, playing a musical instrument, or driving a car with a standard transmission.)

Hand Function

The human arm and hand are an amazing duo with the ability to reach, grasp, and manipulate with strength, precision, and gradation. We rely on hand function for activities of daily living, written communication, job related skills, play, hobbies, and sports. There is very little that we do each day that does not require coordinated use of the hands.

Even the simple act of reaching for a cup of coffee requires an enormous amount of motor coordination:

First, you need to position your arm to reach with your hand in a supinated (thumbs-up) position. Reach too far and you will knock the cup over; too short of a reach and you will not get to the cup. Position your thumb and forefinger to grasp the cup handle, supporting under the handle with your middle finger. Adjust your grasp: too light and you will drop the cup; too tight and it will be uncomfortable. To take a sip of the coffee, you must bend your elbow to get the cup up to your mouth. But you can't take that first sip until you rotate your wrist sufficiently until the rim of the cup reaches your mouth (too close and you'll have coffee down the front of your shirt; too far away and you won't get any).

Picking up a mug of coffee involved just one hand; imagine your child preparing to use scissors, which requires both hands working together: one to hold and move the paper, and the other to manipulate and guide the scissors. Both the coffee and the scissors activity require the dominant hand to operate with the little finger side of the hand for stability and the thumb side with the mobility.

Have you ever noticed that when you are doing a skilled/hard fine-motor task, you often have your tongue out? This is called an **overflow movement**; children do this often and it is an indicator that the task is hard and more than just the hands are working. Another overflow movement in young children is the mirroring of the other hand. These are normal responses until a task becomes automatic or easier.

Eye-Hand Coordination

Many hand functions are guided by vision but can be accomplished without looking. However, the most complex hand function, tool use, is not only guided by vision but its efficiency depends on coordination between the eyes and the hands. When you think of tools, you probably think of the more adult tools such as hammers, screwdrivers, saws, and so on. But you use many tools every day, such as silverware, pencils and pens, scissors, and toothbrushes. The tools of childhood are crayons, markers, glue sticks, scissors, and paintbrushes. Certainly, the most complex tool use by a young child occurs when he learns to write. This complex task combines tool use, vision, precision grasp, cognition, and motor memory. No wonder writing is often difficult and causes concern of parents and teachers when a child refuses or is unable to learn to write!

Helping with Fine Motor Issues

"My child is a real klutz; he is always breaking his crayons and small toys."

Whether this is a problem depends on your child's age and his intention. If the toys are appropriate for his age and he is not purposely taking them apart or misusing them, it is possible that he may have difficulty adjusting his movements and is holding, squeezing, or pushing the items too hard. It is also possible that your child may have difficulty with motor planning. (See chapter 6.)

WHAT TO DO

Provide your child with toys that are well constructed and virtually indestructible. Toys with fewer pieces and parts can offer greater play success. Magic markers are a good alternative to crayons that break easily. If this is a persistent problem, consider contacting an occupational therapist for an evaluation.

"My son is very clever in finding ways to avoid the arts and crafts projects at preschool, but he is great with blocks and Legos. Is this typical or an indicator of something?"

Young boys are more apt to avoid fine motor and arts and crafts activities at school than girls. The reason for this is twofold; their fine motor and visual motor skills usually develop later than girls' and they are generally more interested in construction and active play. Other reasons children avoid these activities are sensitivities to messy materials such as glue, difficulty with such activities because of immature bilateral (use of both hands together) skills for cutting and project assembly, disinterest, or fear of failure.

WHAT TO DO

Be clever and embed these activities into other preferred play (e.g., making and cutting out stop signs for the race track, or making tickets for the class circus). Talk with your child's preschool teacher about the possibility of expecting your child (better yet, all the children) to engage in every available activity twice a week. This will provide your youngster with much-needed practice opportunities. Who knows? He may really start to enjoy this kind of activity once he gets started. Consider that there may be a sensory component to his avoidance. (See chapter 6). If that is the case, it will be important to modify the activity. For instance, if he doesn't like to get his hands dirty, try using a brush or a sponge on a handle for finger painting. If touch sensitivities are interfering in his ability to participate in school and are affecting his daily routine, consider talking with an occupational therapist to determine if your child may benefit from an evaluation.

Learning to Write Their Names

"Will he be ready for kindergarten? He can't write his name and he has no interest in learning."

"He can write his name, but all the letters are reversed. It is a mirror image."

Many parents of three-, four-, and five-year-old children are concerned about handwriting and it is no wonder, because there is such a range of interest and ability at this age. Some three-year-olds and many four-year-olds can already write their names while others show no interest. Some avoid all activities that involve paper and writing tools. It is important to give your child opportunities to work with crayons and markers before she has any formal writing instruction. By kindergarten, some formal instruction in handwriting will begin. For many children, this will just be refinement and review, whereas others will soon acquire this skill and a few will struggle with learning to form letters. Some children never reverse letters or start their name on the right side of the paper; however many do, and this is considered normal for children just learning to write, especially those who begin without any formal instruction. To get that child back on track, put a green line (start) on the left side of the paper and a red (stop) line on the right side. When the child starts in the right place, the letters proceed in an orderly manner. Most children learn to write their name in uppercase letters because these are easier to form than lowercase letters and not as easily reversed. Teach your child that all uppercase letters start at the top and go down. If she persists in starting on the right side of the paper and reversing letters after instruction and practice, she may need to be evaluated by a handwriting specialist.

"She holds her markers and crayons with all five fingers wrapped around them."

Very young children lack the hand stability to hold crayons or markers with anything other than a fisted grasp. By age three, they should be holding the writing tool in a **supinated** (thumbs-up) position between the thumb and fingers. The ideal grasp is one where only three fingers are on the shaft of the crayon, with the ring and little finger **flexed** (closed) to provide a stable hand. Many children do not have the stability in their fingers to hold the crayon securely, hence the reason for using the fourth and or fifth finger. It is often helpful to assist your child in achieving this thumbs-up grasp. If she has difficulty achieving or maintaining this grasp, her hands may not be developed well enough for this specialized tool use.

Prewriting Skills

Even the very youngest children reach for a pen to "write." Sometimes it is on the walls or another inopportune place, but nonetheless the interest is there because they want to imitate what they see adults and older children doing. Help your child develop the readiness skills to use such tools as crayons, markers, pencils, paintbrushes, and scissors. The basic skills needed to be successful with tool use are: the ability to coordinate eyes and hands; the ability to use both hands together, one as the doer and the other as the helper or stabilizer; isolated finger use; strength and coordination for an adaptive grasp; and visual perception.

Remember that it isn't necessary to actually be drawing or writing to work on the components of hand development necessary for handwriting. Playing with small toys and items that fit together is good for strengthening the small muscles of the hands and fingers. Holding multiple objects in one hand and releasing them one at a time is a great activity for developing in-hand manipulation skills. Give your child a handful of raisins or other preferred food items and have him eat one at a time without using his other hand. Stabilizing a toy, or holding a toy in one hand while operating it with the other hand, develops the bilateral coordination that is needed for being able to stabilize a piece of paper while your child draws or writes.

Keep it fun! It is always more enjoyable to draw if the lines will become a railroad track on which to drive the toy train. Or your child can make decorations by cutting strips of paper to make a paper chain. Coloring animal cutouts will be fun if they are to become part of the circus decorations.

Use chalk and paint and paintbrushes, not just crayons and markers. Work on the vertical by using large pieces of paper taped to the wall, an easel or chalkboard. Working on the vertical plane allows for large strokes and it facilitates good wrist extension.

Draw and color with your child in what is referred to as "guided drawing." Rather than the adult's making the first drawing and leaving the child hesitant to try because he knows that he can't do as well, start by having the child draw a circle, then say, "That looks like a head," and ask the child to make the eyes. You then add a nose, ask child to make the mouth, then wonder out loud if the head will have straight or curly hair. Wait for your child's response and action. If he hesitates, ask if the hair should be curly or straight and add hair in a primitive fashion. Then make an oval for the body, ask your child to add arms, then legs, and, depending on the age of your child, the two of you can do fingers, clothing, and so on. Embellish the picture by triggering your child to draw more, in response to your guidance. Ask such questions as "I wonder if it is winter or summer, daytime, or nighttime?" Let your child decide. Weather elements can be added, such as rain or snow; time of day, by sun or moon and stars. Then add a primitive tree, or flowers for summer, and let the child continue with this embellishment. Continue this process as long as your child is interested and an active participant. Make a fuss over the finished product and display the results in a prominent place. You can take this a step further by having your youngster describe or tell a story about the picture and you write the story down. As he realizes that he can draw something, you will see more interest and more experimentation. Be sure to have various types of paper, markers, colored pencils, pencils, and pens readily accessible.

Learning to Write

Grasping the pencil, approximately one inch above the point, with the thumb and index finger, is the preferred way to hold a pencil. The shaft of the pencil should rest on the web of skin between the thumb and index finger, the middle finger should be behind the pencil shaft at the same level of the thumb, and the index finger should provide the counter pressure to secure the pencil. This is the classic **tripod grasp**. An efficient grasp results in the thumb and index finger forming a circle or oval. While writing, the wrist should be slightly extended, with the lateral (little finger) side of the hand resting on the writing surface. Initially, a child will use a static tripod or other functional grasp, meaning that the whole hand moves in the writing process. This will soon evolve into a dynamic grasp, where the fingers move independently from the whole hand. A dynamic grasp is necessary for writing to be efficient and automatic.

Be a writing model for your child. Let your child see you writing. Share handwritten material with your child: a note or grocery list; a letter from Grandma, holiday greeting cards with signatures, a handwritten schedule of the day, journals, and so on. As soon as your child can read, use your handwriting as a way of connecting with her. Leave notes for her. All children feel special when they find a "love note" from Mom or Dad in their lunch box. Long before your child can write, let her dictate letters and stories to you, which you write for her and reread together.

"He doesn't have hand dominance and uses both hands interchangeably. Should we encourage his ambidexterity or be concerned?"

THE PROBLEM:

Four-year-old Jason has not established hand dominance and his parents are concerned that this may be connected to his disinterest and poor performance in all coloring, prewriting, and other preschool fine motor activities. He is a very active boy and interested in sports. He seems equally good with either hand or foot. From the time he was a baby, Jason always used his hands interchangeably for play and eating, and it seemed to be an asset. Now his family wants to know how to help him establish dominance: Should they intervene or just let nature take its course?

Detective Work:

- Is Jason's lack of hand dominance pervasive through all activities or just tool use?
- Does he cross midline with his hands?
- Does he know his right hand from his left?
- Does it seem like he uses both hands *equally*, or is one used more than the other?
- Does he exhibit signs of other sensory processing differences?

Analysis of the Problem:

This is most likely a little problem or possibly not a problem at all. Many children show a hand preference by age one; they continue to interchange hand usage in play, but usually one hand is more dexterous than the other. However, some experts feel that hand dominance is not fully established until age six. If that is the case, Jason may just not be ready for more specialized hand work. Some four-year-old boys are not ready for skilled motor activities even while many peers are already writing their names and using scissors to cut shapes. These activities require consistent use of the same hand if a child is to succeed. Children are expected to cut, paste, draw, and begin to write in kindergarten, so this could become more of a problem next year. Continued, lack of hand dominance may demonstrate that Jason has a mild sensory processing disorder.

Plan of Action:

Take the pressure off your child and don't push, but encourage lots of other hand play, such as Legos to help build small hand muscles. Entice him to use a scissors or markers as a part of another play theme, such as making a menu for a restaurant, cutting green paper to make play money, or a making a map for the matchbox cars. If he has a tendency to use one hand more than the other, help him position the tools (scissors, markers) in that hand. Encourage and engineer play that requires him to reach or move his arms across his midline. Consult an occupational therapist for an evaluation and possible treatment. Jason's family found it helpful to buy him a watch to wear on his most preferred hand, to remind him that it was his eating and writing hand.

A Place to Write

Provide your child with a desk or workspace that has a surface large enough to accommodate large paper and projects and is at an appropriate height to work while standing or sitting. The chair should be sized to your child. A chair is a good fit when the hips, knees, and ankles bend at approximately 90 degrees and the child's feet are flat on the floor or resting on a footrest. The table height should be approximately halfway between the child's waist and his armpits. A good workspace is well lit, with lighting that does not cast shadows. For a preschooler, a child-size play table can double as a desk. Once your child begins to have homework, he should have a designated workspace. Many children do their homework at the kitchen table, but they should still have a desk or workspace in their own room for encouraging a distraction-free area for homework, art, and other school or hobby projects.

Handwriting Struggles

There are many reasons that a child may have difficulty learning to write. A child may have immature hand development or increased or decreased muscle tone that makes efficient grasp and the needed isolated finger and hand movement difficult or impossible. She may have a visual perception problem that affects what she sees or how she sees it (e.g., letter reversals or significant difficulty with spacing and adherence to lines). A few children are truly dysgraphic (unable to copy, write, or translate words or thoughts onto paper).

Not all children are on the same developmental level. It is important to know when your child is simply not ready, when she lacks the prerequisite skills, or whether she is experiencing other problems with handwriting. By age six, most children should be able to hold a pencil with a functional writing grasp and print their name, and be actively involved in learning to print letters. Many children do this at a much earlier age, and those who are avoiding or unable to experience relative success by age five to six, may benefit from assessment and help from a specialist, such as an occupational therapist.

The Computer, a Learning Tool, but How Much Is Too Much?

In this age of technology, everyone needs to learn to use a computer. At the prewriting and early writing stage of development, the computer can be a valuable tool for developing visual perceptual skills through educational games and programs. Although the computer is fun and can be used as a learning tool, most young children should be engaged in more social sensory motor play than spending time at the computer or watching TV.

The Visual Connection

"He has 20/20 vision, but he doesn't use his eyes effectively."

Good fine-motor function, most specifically visual-motor, is dependent on the coordination of the eyes and hands. There are three components of vision that have a direct effect on how we use our eyes and hands; **visual acuity, visual function,** and **visual perception.**

1. **Visual acuity** refers to how well our eyes focus and see objects both near and far. This is where the term 20/20 vision is used. Eyesight described as 20/20 is the ability to see clearly at twenty feet. This is considered perfect acuity with no need for glasses or contacts to correct for either near or far vision. Your child could have a visual acuity problem if he:
   • Consistently leans too close to his play or books
   • Rubs his eyes
   • Eyes tire easily
   • Tilts his head
   • Sits too close to TV or a computer monitor
   • Needs to sit in front of room to see the chalk or white board
   • Has difficulty seeing in the distance

   Problems with visual acuity can be diagnosed by an ophthalmologist or an optometrist. The correction for young children is usually glasses. Some children need to wear glasses all the time and others may only need them for close work.

2. **Visual function** consists of visual tracking, binocularity (team of the two eyes), convergence, and sustained focus.

   Visual tracking is how your eyes move to see; there are three types of eye movements: saccadic, fixation, and pursuit.

   Saccadic movements allow the eye to jump smoothly and precisely from one object to another, such as from looking from one picture to another or one word to another; or in the case of a preschooler, from one friend to another during a circle activity. Your child might have a problem with saccadic movement if she:
   • Appears inattentive
   • Loses attention during activities requiring use of vision
   • Has difficulty reading

Fixation allows the eyes to fixate on one spot or target long enough to make sense of what is seen; for example, a picture in a book, a shape, letter, or word, or to sustain eye contact with another person or object.

Your child might have a problem with fixation if she:

- Looks away from the target object or person
- Appears disinterested
- Does not enjoy books
- Has trouble reading

Pursuit allows the eyes to track a moving object, such as a ball or a person walking across the room. A child may have difficulties with pursuit if she:

- Has difficulty catching a ball
- Has difficulty keeping eyes on a moving target

Binocularity, or eye teaming, is the ability to use both eyes together with accuracy and efficiency. When this does not happen, people consciously or unconsciously suppress one eye to eliminate double vision or other problems associated with eye teaming. This can have serious consequences for learning. It is said that the efficiency of the visual system drops from 80 percent when both eyes are used to only 20 percent with one eye.

If your child may have difficulty using both eyes together, she may:

- Tilt her head or cover one eye
- Complain of lines blurring and words jumping on page
- Have difficulty judging spatial relationships, may bump into things
- Have trouble learning to ride bike
- Sit in awkward positions

A problem with eye teaming may cause learning and/or behavioral problems. A child with eye teaming problems will probably have difficulty reading. Another common problem is the inability to stay on task.

Whenever a child has difficulty with gross or fine motor development, the visual system should also be evaluated carefully. In some cases, a correction or remediation in one or more components of the visual system could alleviate the motor problem.

3. Visual Perception

"My child insists that all the clowns on the page are the same, when one is clearly different!"

Visual perception is the ability of the brain to understand and make sense of what the eyes see by recognition, insight, and interpretation, and, based on this understanding and interpretation, the ability to express the meaning verbally or with motor actions.

Some children can see well and have good hand skills but still struggle with arts and crafts, drawing, prewriting, and assembly of toys. If this is the case, one must consider a visual perceptual problem. This child may need **practice** opportunities, visual exercises, or an evaluation by an occupational therapist and /or optometrist. In most cases, the youngster will learn to compensate for a mild visual perceptual problem. The greatest functional effect may be on reading and writing. To become an efficient reader or writer, a child needs to have visual discrimination to be able to see the sameness or difference in letters. Visual memory is necessary to remember the shape of letters that are similar or can be reversed. All components of visual perception are used in reading and writing.

The 7 Most Common Components to Visual Perception
1. **Visual discrimination:** the ability to see sameness or difference. A child with difficulty in this area may not be able to find the horse that is the same from a row of four horses where one horse is identical to the model and the other three have slight

differences, such as a braided tail, a saddle, and longer ears. Another version would be to find the one picture that is not the same or different. A row of ice-cream cones may look identical except that one of the cones has a different texture.

2. **Visual memory:** the ability to hold an image in one's head and remember it. A good example of this is to show a child a picture of a solitary rabbit, remove the picture, and then present another picture with five different animals (including the rabbit) of all about the same size, and ask your child to point to the one that she saw on the first picture.

3. **Visual spatial relationships:** the ability to identify when an object or one part of an object is going in a different direction than the others. For example, a row of teacups all face the same direction (handle pointing the same way) but for one that is facing the other direction.

4. **Visual form constancy:** the ability to recognize and identify the same shape, even if there is a size difference or the shape is rotated, reversed, or hidden among other forms.

5. **Visual sequential memory:** the ability to remember a series of forms from multiple series of forms, only one of which is exactly the same.

6. **Figure ground:** the ability to find an object or a picture of an object against a busy background. A common example of this is the adult or child who cannot find a box of crayons in the art drawer. The crayons are in plain sight in a drawer filled with paper, scissors, pencils, markers, and tape. A favorite activity that requires figure ground perception is a workbook or coloring page where common objects are interspersed on the picture in unusual places and the child needs to find them. Kids love this type of activity, which sharpens their visual perception and helps them be better observers.

7. **Visual closure:** the ability to recognize a form although it is incomplete or partially obscured. An example of this might be one's ability to know that a circular line composing only three-quarters of a circle would be a circle if it were completed along the same path. This ability is important because you are often

in situations where you do not have the complete picture and your brain needs to fill in the details. Imagine reading a book, and there is a hole in the page with portions of several letters of a word missing; as an adult, you will probably be able to reconstruct that word.

Enhancement of Visual Perception

All children love to play games and do simple puzzles, so seek out puzzles, mazes, geometric design sets, work sheets, and other similar activities, to practice and enhance visual perception. Many children's video games also tap areas of visual perception.

Intervention for Visual Perceptual Deficits

If you suspect that your child may have a visual perceptual problem, first rule out a primary vision or visual functioning problem and then make an appointment with an occupational therapist for visual perceptual testing. Visual perceptual deficits may affect a child's ability to learn to read or to be an efficient reader.

BIG PROBLEM OR Little PROBLEM:

There is a wide range of abilities in motor skills, from the klutz who has difficulty with most skilled movement to the Olympic athlete with awesome skills. Whether any difference in motor development is a big problem or a little one depends on how it affects a person's daily life—for young children, that is play and learning.

If you suspect that your child may have a delay or problem with motor function, you will want to bring this to the attention of your pediatrician. Be sure to relate specifics and examples of your concerns. Referrals may be made to a physical therapist for gross motor issues and to an occupational therapist for fine motor, visual motor, and visual perceptual problems. Referral should be made to ophthalmologist or optometrist for suspected problems with visual acuity or visual function.

Six

Sensory Processing

Making Sense of Your Senses

Nothing Feels Right!

"Danielle is having another bad day. We overslept and had to rush to get dressed. Of course, Danielle wanted to wear her favorite outfit, which was dirty. She 'pitched a fit' and finally took the clothes out of the laundry basket and put them on. I didn't have time to argue with her. Next, she was upset about new socks that had a ridge in the toe; she screamed as if someone was hitting her. I finally gave up and let her go to school without socks. We arrived at school late and a classmate was playing with her favorite toy, so she threw herself on the floor and could not be consoled. The teachers assured me she would be all right but I felt horrible leaving her. . . . What am I doing wrong? What is wrong with her?"

If this sounds familiar, take heart—this type of behavior is not an uncommon phenomenon and it is estimated to occur in approximately 10 to 15 percent of all children. Danielle is not misbehaving; she is experiencing a sensory processing disorder. Sensory processing (also known as sensory integration) is a theory developed more than forty years ago by Dr. Jean Ayres, an occupational therapist with advanced training in neurosciences and educational psychology. Dr. Ayres defines sensory processing as "the neurological process that organizes sensations from one's own body and the environment and makes it possible to use the body effectively within the environment" (Ayres, 1972, 11.) The theory is used to explain the relationship between the brain and behavior, and attempts to explain why individuals respond in a certain way to sensory input and how that input affects behavior. The first five senses are the ones we are most commonly familiar with: tactile (touch), auditory (sound), vision (sight), gustatory (taste), and olfactory (smell). In addition, there are two powerful sensory systems that also impact behavior: the vestibular (movement and balance) and proprioception (joint/muscle). The **vestibular** sense provides information about where the head and body are in space and in relation to gravity. The **proprioceptive** sense provides information about where body parts are and what they are doing. All of our responses, actions, and behaviors are a reaction to some input that has come from the outside environment, from within our own bodies, our memories, or our conscious thought.

Sometimes, a seemingly unrelated quirk or demands may have an underlying cause, such as a sensory processing disorder that can manifest itself in a myriad of ways. Understanding sensory processing may better help parents and teachers to recognize a common thread that runs through the challenges in a child's day.

BIG PROBLEM OR Little PROBLEM?

If a child's sensory processing differences are so great that they prevent him from playing in a variety of ways, developing friendships with peers, or following instructions in a classroom, he probably has a big problem that should be evaluated by a professional, such as a pediatric occupational therapist who is trained to recognize and treat sensory disorders.

On the other hand, if a child can get what his sensory system needs—get his "fix," so to speak—and then move on and function adequately, his sensory issues constitute a little problem. This child probably does not need intervention but would greatly benefit from observant, responsive parents, teachers, and caregivers. For example, a parent might realize, for everyone's best interest, she must allow her child to run around outside, prior to being expected to sit quietly and calmly for a period of time, such as in church or at holiday dinners.

How Does It Work?

Sensory integration theory states that, when information or input comes into your senses and travels through the central nervous system, it is organized, sorted, and interpreted, and then a response is made. You are usually not conscious of this process because it happens automatically.

There are sensory receptors within the body, which receive information both from within and from the external environment. Specific receptors stimulate electrical and chemical reactions, which relay information to the sensory systems within the central nervous system. Sensory areas direct the information to the appropriate areas of the brain, where it is analyzed. A perception or an understanding is formulated from the incoming sensory information. Perceived information is sent to the motor areas of the brain, telling the brain when and how the body should respond to the sensory information. Command messages are sent to the muscles and organs so they know how to respond. The body makes a motor response based on that information. These actions provide new sensory data in the form of feedback to the brain, where further analysis and refinement occurs. The success of initial responses gives the brain information to adjust and readjust the responses accordingly.

Sensory Processing/Disorder (SID)

We all have sensory differences, some people are terrified of roller coasters, whereas others travel miles to go on the fastest and highest. Some people can't stand tags on their clothes, yet others don't notice them. Nobody has a perfect sensory system; we all have our own quirks, whether we are aware of them or not. Children also have their own idiosyncrasies or individual differences. The difference between quirks and sensory processing disorders is that the latter interfere with daily life. If a child's sensory difficulties are interfering with his functioning, he needs intervention. The child with sensory processing disorder processes sensory information inefficiently, demanding effort and attention with no guarantee of accuracy. When this occurs, the goals he strives for are not easily attained.

Smooth sensory processing enables all the impulses to flow easily and reach their destination quickly. Sensory processing disorder can be likened to a traffic jam in the brain. Some bits of sensory information get tied up in traffic, and certain parts of the brain do not get the sensory information needed to function properly. The ability to attend to a task depends on the ability to inhibit, or screen out, nonessential sensory information such as background noises or visual distractions. The child with sensory integration disorder may frequently respond to or register irrelevant sensory information and is then considered distractible, hyperactive, or uninhibited. These children are always on alert and constantly asking about or orienting to sensory input that others ignore (e.g., a refrigerator motor, heater fan, distant airplane, and other background noises or distractions.

When Danielle screams and throws a tantrum because the socks are offensive to her tactile system, she is experiencing real distress due to inadequate processing of the tactile information. Her tantrum could easily be misunderstood and labeled an "emotional problem," rather than a response to her tactile sensitivity. She misinterprets the sensory input caused by the seam in her sock and her reaction is to fight or flee the situation.

Some children may fail to register some forms of sensory input and are unresponsive to important stimuli. For example, a child who falls down and skins his knee but doesn't realize he is bleeding isn't reacting appropriately to sensory input.

Signs of Possible Sensory Processing Disorder
- Overly sensitive to touch, movement, sights, or sounds
- Underreactive to touch, movement, sights, or sounds
- Easily distracted

- Activity level that is unusually high or unusually low
- Physical clumsiness or apparent carelessness
- Impulsive, lacking in self-control
- Difficulty making transitions from one situation to another
- Inability to unwind or calm self

If you suspect that your child may have a sensory processing disorder, an evaluation can be conducted by a qualified pediatric occupational therapist. Evaluations usually consist of both standardized testing and structured observations of responses to sensory stimulation, posture, balance, coordination, and eye movements. The therapist then analyzes test results and other assessment data along with information from other professionals and parents, and makes recommendations regarding appropriate treatment. If therapy is recommended, your child will be guided through activities that challenge her ability to make a successful, organized response to sensory input.

Is the Problem Too Much or Too Little Information?

Looking at the sensory systems in a simplistic way, there are two ways that the processing can go awry. The system is not providing enough information to the brain or, alternatively, it is providing too much information. In the first instance, the child may underreact, or be **underresponsive**. A child who is underresponsive may not respond to the sensory input, such as temperature extremes, or pain. A child who is underreactive to touch may crave it, seeking it in any way he can get the input. These children may be constantly touching friends, fiddling with their clothes, or playing in their food. Conversely, the child who is **overresponsive** to touch reacts negatively to touch and messy tactile input. This child may cry violently or lash out when she is touched unexpectedly. She may be extremely cautious around groups of children and tentative with new textures or tastes. She may limit exploration of new toys or sensory play, such as finger paint and sand. The same phenomenon (over- or underreacting) can be seen in all sensory systems. It is possible to have underresponsivity in one sensory system and overresponsivity in another system. It is also possible to have both over- and underreactions in the same system. A child who experiences significant challenges in processing sensory information will have significant difficulties functioning in environments such as a classroom, playground, or birthday party. This child may miss out on many wonderful sensory-motor play experiences, which are the hallmark of early childhood.

The Sensory Systems

Touch, movement, body awareness, hearing, sight, taste, and smell are the systems that guide us throughout our day as we interact with the world and others. When something goes wrong with these systems, we experience everything from discomfort to panic.

Tactile System

The tactile system refers to our sense of touch. It is through this system that we first gather information from the world around us. When a baby is comforted by his mother's touch, that touch is processed effectively; it allows the baby to feel safe with the parent. Effective processing of touch is essential for early learning, social, and emotional development. Countless studies prove that babies who have not been picked up, held, or cuddled as infants have problems with attachment and bonding later in life. There is an innate drive to seek touch input during infancy and young childhood.

There are two parts to the tactile system, the discriminative and protective systems. The discriminative system tells us where we are being touched and by what. The protective system tells us whether we are in contact with something that might be dangerous and causes a fight-or-flight response. When a young child feels threatened, she may whine, cry, or cling to her mother. If the child continues to be bothered, the natural reaction would be to lash out against the stimuli or flee. This may look aggressive or disruptive to others, but may simply be her way of coping with the offending input.

Problems with Processing Tactile Information

Children who are not getting correct tactile feedback from the muscles in their mouths may have trouble articulating sounds for speech. These children may also be picky eaters because they can only tolerate certain textures in their mouths, and so they avoid the textures they perceive as offensive.

Children who avoid touch limit their fine motor development. If they only play with toys that are smooth or have similar textures, such as cars and trains, they may have difficulty developing the hand skills necessary for higher-level fine motor function. Children need to have a variety of experiences with different textures and materials to facilitate hand development.

Young children are driven to explore their environment through touch. When a child is unable to explore in this way, it affects his ability to participate in play. This tactile aversion may affect how he uses childhood tools such as crayons and scissors, as well as his ability to perform self-care skills.

Danielle does not appear to process tactile input accurately. She can only tolerate certain textures and avoids any skin contact that is unfamiliar. Small bumps in her socks feel like needles and pins. When familiar toys are not available, she melts down because she has little ability to play with other objects. Her social play with other children is affected because she has trouble sharing her "safe toys" and does not like other children getting too close to her. Her life is out of control and she feels as if she is a nonstop traffic jam. The adults in her life must become her stoplights so she can better organize herself and begin to learn to cope with her sensory differences.

Whether your child has a big or a little problem with tactile processing, here are some strategies to support him.

If Your Child Craves Touch

- Have your child hold or carry something that has a textured surface or provides deep pressure, such as a "stress ball," a Koosh ball, and/or squeeze toys.

INDICATORS OF A PROBLEM WITH TACTILE PROCESSING

Underresponsive	Overresponsive
Touches people and objects excessively	Withdraws from touch
Bumps into others frequently	Dislikes standing in line
Exhibits a low reaction to pain	Strikes out at other children when they come near
May not respond to hot/cold	Overreacts to small hurts/bumps
Does not react to falls, scrapes, or bumps	Has limited food repertoire
Likes highly crunchy foods	Reacts adversely to new foods, tastes, or textures
Constantly puts nonedibles in mouth	Dislikes being cuddled/held
Chews on shirts/sleeves	Dislikes playing in messy play
May have limited articulation/ speech	Is bothered by loose shirts/tags
May demonstrate poor oral motor skills (may stuff food or bite others)	Dislikes going barefoot

- Have your child carry something heavy (this provides deep input into muscles).
- Before entering a tempting new environment where there are items that he cannot touch, provide deep pressure by rubbing his shoulders or back, or the palms of his hands.
- If there are rules for touching, explain to your child what he *is* allowed to touch and not just what he is *not* allowed touch! Show him!
- Practice rules for touching: Practice gentle touch and hard touch; play games so you know your child understands the difference.
- If your child chews on clothing or toys and is past three years old: Avoid all "sippy" cups and have your child drink from a water bottle with a sturdy straw, and allow him to chew on latex-free tubing. Also provide crunchy snacks, such as crunchy hard

pretzels, chewy bagels, fruit rollups, gummy worms (chilled to harden), and, when he can handle it, teach him to chew gum. ("Chewelry" is a commercially produced necklace for children to chew. See appendix H).

Fun Activities for the Child Who Craves Touch

- Get large plastic containers and fill them with dry rice, dry beans, sand, or cornmeal, and provide your child with a variety of kitchen utensils. Hide shapes, letters, and small toys in the mixtures and have your youngster try to find the objects without looking. Use containers with lids so they can be stored easily and taken out when you need to change the activity.
- Encourage playing with Play-Doh, clay, Gak, and Silly Putty.
- Play with shaving cream or soap-based finger paints on the wall of the bathtub.
- Give baths and shampoos to dolls or plastic toy animals. Use sponges, cut into fourths, to wash dolls.
- Fill buckets with water, and have your youngster "paint" your house, using a sponge for a brush.
- Have a car or bike wash. Use spray bottles of water.
- Do finger painting. Children love to finger paint. To cut down on the mess, use an easel or a tray placed on a table. Do it with your child. Take the easel outside or tape paper to the side of your house. Painting on a vertical surface is terrific for hand development and is a great prewriting activity. Add rice, sand, or flour to the paints to give them more texture.

Don't Touch Me! . . . The Child Who Avoids Touch

Children who avoid tactile input and become distressed at unexpected touch or who actively avoid touch can be a challenge to parents and teachers. These children are constantly in a fight-or-flight mode and may need lots of assistance. However, parents, caregivers, and teachers can do much to help tactually defensive children. Keep in mind that these youngsters are more apt to tolerate new or uncomfortable input if they feel in control.

If Your Child Avoids Touch

- When possible, respect your child's desire for certain textures in clothing.
- Remove irritating clothing tags.
- Rub lotion on your child. If she will not tolerate you rubbing it on her, have her apply the lotion. Apply the lotion to her legs, arms, hands, and face.
- Massage your child with a vigorous towel rub, to increase tolerance to certain textures and provide deep pressure to her body. She may better tolerate touch if it is provided firmly.
- Remember, when touching your child, to use deep-pressure touch and try not to touch her lightly or unexpectedly. Children who display tactile defensiveness tend to enjoy big bear hugs when they initiate the contact. Let family members and teachers know that they should alert her when she is about to be touched.
- When entering a large group environment, ask your child if she would like her hand held or ask a younger child if she needs to be picked up. This will help avoid unexpected touch in crowds. Make sure there is adequate spacing of children during circle-time activities in preschool and in large group activities.
- If your child can't stand seams in socks, turn the socks inside out so the seam is on the outside or try buying tube socks, which are seamless.
- If your child dislikes having her face washed or hair washed, allow her to wash her own hair. There are commercial visor shields that will prevent water from splashing on her face.
- If your child dislikes toothbrushing, consider using a smaller toothbrush with soft bristles or a battery-powered toothbrush. Let your child control the toothbrush. Simply monitor the process. Use a sand timer to help her know how long to brush. Allow your child to choose the flavor of the toothpaste; dip the damp toothbrush into the toothpaste instead of squeezing a blob on it.

- If your child refuses to go barefoot or walk on sand, try rubbing her feet with a cloth or towel first. Use lotion on her feet; during play, have your child walk on different textures such as Bubble Wrap and textured carpets. If none of these things work or for a quick fix, compensate by having her wear "aqua socks."

When tactile issues interfere with your child's enjoyment or his ability to function with family and friends, it may be time to consult with a licensed occupational therapist trained to provide sensory integration treatment.

Vestibular System

The vestibular system is responsible for your sense of movement and gravity. It is through this system that you get your sense of the relationship between your body and the Earth. The vestibular sensors are located in the inner ear and register at the subcortical (lower) level of the brain. The vestibular system gives information on how gravity affects you when you are stationary or moving, because it registers direction and velocity of movement. This system gives you your sense of balance, posture, and muscle tone. The vestibular system also sends your brain the information about whether you are right side up or upside down. It is how you sense how your body is acting with or against gravity. Babies have an innate drive to challenge their body against gravity. They progressively test their ability to compensate for gravity as they bring up their head to look at their mother and gain head control; soon they are rolling over, sitting up, and then the ultimate challenge is rising to stand and learn how to walk.

Just as the tactile system gives you a sense of safety, the vestibular system gives you a sense of safety that comes from knowing your feet are firmly planted on the ground. It also provides the visual reference you need to keep your balance in relation to the environment.

When There Is a Problem in the Vestibular System

Children with inadequate processing of the vestibular system may be either under- or overresponsive. The child whose vestibular system is overresponsive may easily feel motion sick on a car ride or on a simple playground swing. He may not be able to tolerate amusement park rides, going down sliding boards, or rocking on a rocking horse. Conversely, the child who is underresponsive may seek out movement constantly. He may whirl and twirl and never get dizzy and often the only way to get him to sleep is to rock him or take a ride in the car. Some toddlers start in fast speed and run randomly just for the sheer need for the movement. But when this level of activity persists after the toddler stage, children may appear to be hyperactive when in fact they may have an inadequately processing vestibular system.

Muscle Tone and Muscle Strength

The vestibular system is one of the regulators of muscle tone that is important for posture and sensory feedback. **Muscle tone** is the **set point** of your muscles and is not a reflection of the strength of the muscle. When muscle tone is not adequate, it does not support good postural control or correct feedback to your muscles and joints. A child with inadequate muscle tone may have trouble sitting cross-legged at circle time or may lean on his friend for support. These children expend an enormous amount of energy simply trying to support themselves against gravity. They tend to continue to stay close to the ground, rarely exploring playground equipment. Often, these children are content to watch TV or play computer games and are reluctant to engage in physical play. A child with inadequate muscle tone usually uses lots of energy performing tasks that come automatically to other children. Keeping his head up while writing or coloring may be challenging for this child. He may have low tone in his face, resulting in a flat expression, and may appear to be a little sad or tired. This lack of facial expression can result in ineffective social feedback and can be perceived by others as disinterest or lack of enthusiasm.

Vestibular System and Bilateral Coordination

Another important aspect of the vestibular system is its relation to **bilateral coordination**, or the ability to use both sides of the body efficiently. To do such activities as clap hands, climb a ladder, skip, use scissors, and write, one must have the ability to coordinate both sides of the body. A child who does not process vestibular information adequately may have difficulty establishing hand dominance and/or the ability to use the other hand as a helper hand.

The Fear Factor: Fearfulness Associated with Inadequate Vestibular Processing

As if all of these problems with the vestibular system are not enough, the child with inadequate vestibular processing may have inappropriate emotional responses. The child who is overresponsive to vestibular input may demonstrate gravitational insecurity. **Gravitational insecurity** is an "emotional or fear reaction that is out of proportion to the actual threat or danger of the vestibular-proprioceptive stimuli or the position of the body in space (especially those body positions when the feet are no longer in contact with the floor)" (Fisher, Murray, Bundy.) A child with gravitational insecurity may be extremely fearful and may not move with confidence and ease. He rarely explores environments that have different terrains, and tends to stay planted to the ground during playground play. This fear may hinder social interactions and learning opportunities.

Children who are fearful of movement need a great deal of gentle encouragement. They have a fear of falling and are hesitant to use playground equipment or participate in games where they lose contact with the ground.

If Your Child Avoids Climbing, Sliding, or Swinging

- Initially allow the child to direct the movement. If she will only walk out to the playground and then sit, encourage her to walk with you on the outskirts. Hold your child's hand as you walk on the railroad ties that surround the playground or jump off the curb. Find a piece of equipment that she views as safe and play together on it. Make the experience pleasurable so she will want to come again.
- Hold your child in your lap firmly and swing on a swing.

- Climb up climbers and playground equipment *with* your child. She will be motivated to attempt equipment that is "scary" if you are there encouraging and participating.
- Break down skills into smaller parts. If your child finally climbed up the ladder of a slide but is fearful of sliding down, give positive reinforcement. Next time, you will both go down the slide together.
- Remember that little accomplishments will build on future success.

The child with an underresponsive vestibular system needs and often craves movement and is constantly on the go. He may have trouble sitting still enough to adequately take in the information from his environment. For this child, the drive for movement is greater than the drive to sit and pay attention to a story, or read the social cues from a peer or an adult. These children try to seek new and more intense movements to satisfy their craving for vestibular input and may be oblivious to safety issues. This craving for movement is often first noted as a concern by the preschool teacher and seen as a behavioral problem.

"He just won't sit still at circle; he is always bothering the other children . . . he runs and runs at playground time . . ."

If Your Child Seeks Movement Constantly

- Children with an underaroused vestibular system need opportunities for movement prior to times when they are expected to sit for long periods of time.
- Provide frequent opportunities for motor play. This may include walking, bike riding, and active playground play. Add some structure to this play (e.g., take turns running after the ball rather than random running).
- It would be beneficial to have physical play interspersed with more sedentary activities.
- Encourage moving in different ways: Encourage playground play prior to going into school.

- Combine movement activities with reciting nursery rhymes that you read. Have your child act out "Humpty Dumpty" by sitting on a pile of pillows and "falling off" at the appropriate time. Use climbers and slides to play "Jack and Jill." Climb up the ladder and slide down the hill.
- Swing on swings or hammocks.
- Do wheelbarrow-walking.
- Jump on a mini trampoline or bounce on hippity-hop balls.
- Rock in a rocking chair or on a rocking horse (rocking horses on springs are great!).
- Roll down hills. Rolling in grass appears to be a lost art! Don't be afraid of a little dirt!
- Encourage relay races: crawling, jumping, hopping, skipping, and marching.
- Introduce your child to rhythmic posture games such as "Simon Says" or "Going on a Bear Hunt."

Proprioceptive System

The proprioceptive system is the sensory system that gives information about body awareness. It tells you where a certain body part is and how it is moving. The receptors are located in muscles, joints, and tendons and are activated by muscle contractions and movement. It is this system that lets you know how to sit down in a chair without looking, or find your mouth without looking in a mirror. It gives you the information you need to adjust and control the pressure; for example, the ability to know "gentle touch" when you are touching a baby vs. "hard touch" when you are trying to push a car. The proprioceptive system is linked to the vestibular system and tactile systems. A child learns quickly that if she handles a balloon roughly it will explode, or if she pushes too hard on the juice box that juice will spurt out all over her. On the other hand, if the child doesn't exert enough pressure when grasping, she will have trouble feeding herself, drawing, or completing fine motor tasks.

Problems in the Proprioceptive System

"Why does he act like such a bully? He is really a sweet kid!"

A child who has trouble with his proprioceptive system may push too hard, walk over toys, or handle toys too roughly. These children are often characterized as a "bull in the china shop" or the cartoon character Marmaduke. This child can get so excited when he sees a group of children building a block building that he runs over, pushes it down, and destroys the building, not realizing the consequences of his behavior. It is possible that he didn't have the ability to stop and control his movements and it felt good to give that tall wooden block building a push, which provides input to his proprioceptive system. He was happy—it fulfilled his need. He never meant to destroy the building; he couldn't control his movements or his desire to get the deep pressure input. The result, however, is upsetting and unacceptable to the other children.

Some children with proprioceptive problems attempt to give their body the input they are craving. For example, a youngster may crash into walls, hug too tightly, walk over toys, or push their friends when he only means to say "hello." While this can be mistaken for aggressive behavior, it is *not* aggressive. The child is simply seeking deep pressure or proprioceptive input. Someone who leans on others when trying to sit upright at circle time could also have inadequate processing of his proprioceptive system. He does not have the postural control to maintain an upright sitting position, so leaning on a friend gives the needed support.

The feedback you get from your proprioceptive system allows you to refine your fine motor skills. When you repeat a task, you get feedback about how it feels and you adjust until the movement is just right. For example, when a child is learning to write his name for the first time, the positioning of the pencil is awkward, and each stroke is a major effort. Hopefully, if the proprioceptive, tactile, and visual systems are all working together, the child grips the pencil with the correct pressure and eventually a motor memory results. Thus writing your name becomes automatic. You remember what it feels like when you write it correctly due to your motor memory. When the child's proprioceptive system does not give the correct feedback, he must work very hard to perform the correct motor action and may not be able to remember it automatically and has to relearn it constantly. This results in frustration and difficulty learning functional skills.

Children who have **underreactive** proprioceptive systems seek out deep pressure in lots of ways. It is up to the adults in their lives to help them obtain what their body seems to be craving.

If Your Child Squeezes, Pushes, and Hugs Too Hard

- Provide activities that provide "heavy work" to muscles and joints, such as crab walks, and wall push-ups.
- Ask your child to help in the garden by wheeling a wheelbarrow or pulling a wagon full of dirt. Rake the leaves and dig dirt to help plant flowers.
- Have your child carry heavy items, such as laundry baskets, milk containers, and waste baskets. Fill plastic liter bottles with water and play "delivery man."
- Suggest that your child push shopping carts and doll carriages: Weight them so they require more exertion.
- Build obstacle courses where the child crawls in, out, and through furniture, tunnels, or objects in your home.
- Play jumping games on trampoline.
- Initiate marching games when taking walks.
- Encourage playground play, including climbing and hanging on monkey bars.
- Engage in active play with Play-Doh, clay, Silly Putty, therapy putty, and dough.
- Pinch large and small clothespins—set up a wash line for doll clothes.
- Use stretchy resistive bands like the ones adults use in exercise classes, to play with your child. Sing: "Row, Row, Your Boat" while each of you is holding an end of the band and moving back and forth. Try different songs and movements together with the bands.

Auditory System

The auditory system provides information about the sounds in our environment. Just as some children have trouble tolerating tactile or vestibular input, some have difficulty with noises and sounds. When such youngsters experience difficulty processing auditory information they may respond negatively to unexpected noises, or may not respond consistently when their name is called. A child may scream when the blender is running or hide when the vacuum is turned on. Conversely, a child may not respond to his name being called, or his attention seems fleeting during large group activity time. He may hum and sing to screen out unwanted noises. A child may not notice sounds in his environment, have trouble processing the sounds, or have trouble knowing which sound to attend to. This may commonly be seen in a busy, stimulating classroom when children are talking and background music is playing. It may be hard for a child to attend to the teacher's voice. A child who is experiencing difficulty with hearing needs to be examined by a physician and receive a complete audiological examination. Once medical or hearing problems have been ruled out, it is then time to consider an evaluation by a speech and language pathologist. Often, children who are experiencing other sensory processing problems also have difficulty processing auditory information. Determining whether this is a big problem or a little one depends on how noises and sounds interfere with a child's functioning in his natural environments.

Managing Noise or Sound Sensitivities

Helping a Child Cope with a Particularly Upsetting Noise or Sound

- Expose the child to the irritating noise in small steps and gradually increase the duration as your child's tolerance improves.
- Warn your child that the appliance is going to be turned on so he won't be taken by surprise. If appropriate, have your child participate in using the appliance.
- Lessen the unpleasant effect of the noise by combining it with alternative sound such as music, or pair the noise or sound with a preferred activity.

Helping a Child Who Notices Every Little Sound in the Environment

- Keep auditory distractions to a minimum.
- Set up quiet places for the child.
- Provide headphones or earplugs for your child to wear during exposure in noisy environments, such as on airplanes.

Helping a Child Who Hums or Sings Constantly

- If the child is humming to concentrate, use other techniques such as chewing gum or chewing on a tube necklace.
- Allow your child to use and play with vibration by using such items as a battery-operated toothbrush or a kazoo.
- A child may be humming to block out overstimulating noises in the classroom or the environment. If the noise or activity level is a concern, move the child away form the source of the noise.

Helping a Child Who Is Easily Distracted by and Fearful of Loud Noise

- Approach the child with singing or talking in a soft voice.
- Use soft classical background music for calming.
- In situations or places where a child may experience a lot of loud noises, use headphones or earphones to buffer the noise.
- Whenever possible alert the child that there may be a loud noise before it occurs.
- Avoid using appliances when your child needs to attend and focus.

Increasing Sound Awareness and Response to Name

- Plan activities that will help teach the child to attend to various sounds.
- Play listening games such as "Mother May I?" or "Red Light/ Green Light."
- Play "Marco Polo" in the swimming pool. Children have to call each other and go to the source of the sound.

- Have your child call a name out before throwing a ball to a specific friend. This also provides social interaction with young children.
- Use a visual cue to gain the child's attention.
- Teach the child to attend to his name by using games that involve saying his name and then praising him for responding.
- Vary your intonation or add a melody using a singsong manner.
- Pair a novel auditory cue with his name such as clapping hands or clicking fingers.

Visual System

The visual system is responsible for sight and coordinates the eyes to interpret visual images. Activities that encourage moving the eyes through their full range, visually locating objects, fixing (holding) the eyes on a target, or alternating focusing between near and far are all good for eye motor development.

- Play any kind of throw-and-catch game with a beach ball. Beach balls are easy to throw and catch because they move slowly, allowing a young child time to be more successful.
- Play flashlight tag. (Have an adult shine and move a light beam, while the child tries to "tag" it with her own light beam.) Teach two children to play and enjoy this game outside on a summer evening.
- Remember to catch lightning bugs. A child must follow and catch the source of light. (Of course, release the bug after it is caught!)
- Draw a chalkline maze on the sidewalk and have your youngster follow a specific path until the end. Change directions and overlap lines.
- Bounce a balloon on a badminton racket and keep it going. (Supervise balloon use carefully.)
- Throw beanbags at a target or a box. Vary the distance and the angle.
- Reduce glare; glare is the visual equivalent of sound reverberation and a major source of visual overload.

- Decrease clutter in your child's bedroom and play rooms: Designate certain places for toys; keep toys in bins or baskets.

The Taste (Gustatory) and Smell (Olfactory) Systems

The gustatory and olfactory systems work together to provide information about what you put in your mouth. Information from smell is often associated with taste. Taste accompanies smell and, if one's smell is lost so may one's taste be lost so that all that is left of food is texture and temperature. There are four basic tastes: sweet, sour, salty, and bitter. The tongue is covered with millions of sense organs that process the different tastes. Tactile sensitivity is intertwined with the taste sense and may limit exploration of textures and tastes.

Enjoy wonderful smells and tastes with your child! Point out fresh honeysuckle and ripening tomatoes on a vine. Pay attention to the ordinary smells of cooking and baking, and have your child identify ingredi-

INDICATORS OF A PROBLEM WITH THE GUSTATORY AND OLFACTORY SENSES: TASTE AND SMELL

Taste	Smell
Chooses very limited repertoire of foods (may be due to tactile defensiveness)	Complains of things smelling bad
Chews constantly on nonfood items—wants to taste everything	Notices how people smell
Strong reactions to certain foods	Reacts violently to smells
Refuses to try new textures or tastes	Smells objects constantly
Has unusual cravings for certain foods—may like very spicy foods	Ignores unpleasant odors
Likes highly textured or crunchy food, avoids mushy food, or *only* likes soft, bland food	Seems uninterested in eating
May be indifferent to food	

ents by smell and taste when appropriate. The more experiences your child has with new smells and tastes, the more likely he is to try new foods. A youngster who helps prepare food is also more likely to eat it. If your child is a picky eater, you may have her put the food to her lips for a brief taste to increase her familiarity with it. Encourage her to look at it, smell it, touch it, and, eventually, take a tiny taste.

Working with Taste and Smell Sensitivities

- Use the foods that a child enjoys and put them in a different form: If he loves apple juice, make frozen juice pops or make a slushy.
- Fill small containers with different scents and play a guessing game of smells.
- Use scratch-and-sniff stickers.
- Cook with your child, using herbs, spices, and flavors like chocolate and vanilla.
- Read books about different foods and try them.

If your child won't eat certain foods (beyond being just a picky eater), the textures of the foods may be unpleasant or the child may be sensitive to the temperature or oversensitive to certain tastes. Introduce new foods by expanding one sensory characteristic at a time. For example, if your child only eats yogurt, place a raisin or a cornflake or oat square on the side of his bowl. Work gradually. First, just have your child tolerate the new food next to his yogurt, then ask him to touch the new food, next bring the new food to his lips, and last, actually taste the new food. If he can tolerate the new taste, put the new food in his favorite yogurt.

These are just a few of the strategies that you may find helpful when working with a child who may have a sensory processing difference. All of these activities can be implemented with children that are typically developing and just need a little tune-up or practice from time to time. Remember, when a child's sensory system is suspected of interfering with his ability to function in his home, preschool, or social interactions with adults and peers, it is not necessarily a little problem, and may be a bigger problem in need of professional intervention.

Praxis, or Motor Planning

One important outcome of normal sensory processing is the ability to motor-plan movements in a refined or efficient way. This ability is known as **praxis**. Praxis is the ability to integrate your sensory and motor systems to be able to organize and make graded, controlled movements or new movements. Praxis is necessary for learning both gross motor movements such as walking, running, and climbing; skilled movements; and fine motor movements such as those required for speech production, writing, or using the computer.

When There Is a Problem with Motor Planning

Joe is a four-year-old who is having a "terrible, horrible, very hard time," in his movement class at preschool where the children imitate movements to a new song. He tried to participate briefly but this is way too hard an activity for him and he is feeling confused and frustrated. He takes a truck off a shelf and runs it repeatedly up and down the floor until he is stopped and admonished by a teacher.

Joe is not being "bad"; the movement class is just too darn difficult for him. Children with difficulties with praxis do not tend to show muscle weakness; rather, they tend to be limited in how they use their body or mouth movements and do the same highly familiar movements over and over. They are often clumsy, due to difficulty sequencing, grading, and/or controlling movement sequences. They may play repeatedly in the same way with toys and may have trouble varying their routine. They may be able to perform some tasks spontaneously, but not on demand. Joe is having trouble following the sequence of motor movements. Because of these difficulties, children with **dyspraxia** may demonstrate real difficulty playing with peers. They may appear obstinate or only agree to play in one way. This behavior often appears oppositional but may simply reflect the child's extreme difficulty changing gears or coming up with a new plan. It is very challenging for dyspraxic children to create new play patterns.

A key piece of motor planning is the ability to initiate an action. This is critical for the play and activities in preschool and early elementary school. Some children can't get started with a task and seem unable to get their *engines* going or get their bodies in gear to begin a particular task. When a child does not attempt the task because he is overwhelmed, he gets stuck in a **closed loop.** A closed loop is when a child plays repetitively over and over performing a task in the same way, thus not learning higher-level skills.

Everyone has trouble learning new skills from time to time; and most people learn to compensate or avoid things they cannot do well. When a child is in preschool or early elementary school, he is learning basic foundational skills. If he continues to avoid attempting tasks because they are too difficult, he will have difficulty moving on to higher-level motor and language skills. To achieve success, he needs the adults in his life to break down the task into smaller, manageable steps. Joe's parents realized that Joe was clumsy and having trouble in many aspects of his life and took him to an occupational therapist to evaluate his sensory-motor system. The therapist came up with a treatment plan to help him be more successful in home and classroom.

His therapist coached his parents and teachers on how to break down motor tasks into smaller, more manageable steps. For example, they played "Simon Says" games and presented the directions at a slower rate. At group movement times, a teacher now stayed close to Joe to help him break down the movements and be a more active participant. Structured obstacle courses were introduced at home and school for Joe and his friends to practice moving their bodies.

Outside, Joe eventually learned to play catch with a beach ball, which was slower and easier to catch than other types of balls. He and his buddies also liked playing "beach ball soccer."

Joe's occupational therapist worked closely with his parents and they began to join him in his play as well. With practice, Joe began to be more flexible and develop new ways to play. At home, his parents discovered that he enjoyed reading a story and acting it out if they provided simple props from the story to help him organize his play.

BREAKING DOWN TASKS

Any child can benefit from learning how to break down a big task or project into smaller, more manageable steps:

1. When you are working with glue and paper, first show the child how to tear paper. Use hand-over-hand prompting initially, so he experiences what it feels like.
2. Next, show him how to crumple the paper in his hand. Help him feel the crumpling and then have him do it himself (color tissue paper works best).
3. Last, show him how to put glue on the paper and then how to put the crumpled paper on the glue.
4. Have a visual or picture of each step available if he needs a reminder.
5. Stay with the child until he feels he has learned the task and then gradually introduce other activities that incorporate similar skills. The child will be more likely to try this kind of activity next time and be able to initiate or begin the task independently.

Modulation: Arousal Levels and Alertness

Young children are active; they learn by moving and doing. It is parents' greatest joy to see their baby crawl and then eventually stand and toddle away to explore. Babies are into everything and it is fantastic to watch them explore and look at the world from many different angles and points of view. Young children have a fairly short attention span, and are not wired to sit for long periods of time engaged in particular tasks. However, when something is wrong with a child's **arousal level,** which is a part of his sensory processing system, he may exhibit an exaggerated reaction or limited reactions that may need to be examined. For a child to behave appropriately in different situations, he must be able to take in, process, and organize information from his sensory system without becoming overloaded or shutting down. Everybody has been in situations, such as a circus, where one feels one's sensory system assaulted. When you are so overstimulated, it is hard to concentrate and you have trouble figuring out what to look at first and where to focus your attention. Most people have also experienced going into a dim, warm room after lunch where they have been expected to pay attention to a dry, monotone-voiced speaker. The content may have been interesting but it was impossible to concentrate and stay alert.

Your state of alertness fluctuates during the day and allows you to attend and learn. If your state of alertness drops or becomes overstimulated, you instinctively try to regulate it, to get to the state that is "just right" for optimal functioning. A normal state of arousal develops as a result of your ability to modulate sensory input. Children with problems in sensory processing may have more trouble obtaining and maintaining appropriate state of arousal. For instance, when small youngsters are running outside at playtime, the child with a sensory processing problem may need extra time and particular strategies to calm down before going back into the classroom to engage in academics or indoor activities. Simple strategies for calming are to dim the lights when the children return, and to have them drink from a water bottle with a straw.

When a child's arousal level is too low; he may look like he is tired or bored. Preschool teachers often comment that the child looks as though he did not get enough sleep or that all he likes to do is sit in the corner. Such children usually are reluctant to participate in activities that require physical action. They tend to want to spend more time in front of TV or computer, and less time engaged in productive play.

Eeyore . . . Slow and Low

"Josh is very bright and I think he has almost taught himself to read. He loves to play computer games at home and, when he has a neighborhood friend over to the house, they usually play with action figures on the floor. I am really concerned that he doesn't seem that interested in playing with the children in the classroom. Each day when I bring him to school, he heads straight to the book corner and takes out books and reads to himself or whomever comes over. The teacher has to practically drag him away from his books to get him to do any art activities. He tells me he likes his friends but the teacher tells me that

*he spends most of his playground time sitting next to teachers
on the bench, with complaints of being tired. I took him to the
pediatrician and she said he was perfectly healthy."*

THE PROBLEM:

*"We are not the most physical of people but Josh is such
a couch potato at such a young age. Is this a problem or will
he grow out of it?"*

Detective Work:

- Does Josh eat a good breakfast before coming to school?
- What is his bedtime? Is he getting enough sleep?
- What are Josh's motor skills?
- Has he always been more sedentary and quiet than other children?
- Does he have trouble keeping up with family members when on walks?
- Is he still asking to be carried, and do his parents carry Josh instead of having him walk?

Analysis of the Problem:

If medical issues have been investigated and dismissed, some intervention may be needed at this early age to prevent further delay in Josh's motor exploration, his social connections, and play.

Plan of Action:

Start by encouraging Josh to participate in more active forms of play. Get him to engage in physical movement through routine activities, such as carrying the trash can, setting the table, or pushing the shopping cart. Add music to a task, providing a starting and stopping point. Take him to playgrounds and play with him on the equipment. Each morning, before school, Josh should ride a bike, jump on a mini trampoline, or bounce on a hippity-hop ball to increase his arousal level. The teacher may want to change her routine and have the children go outside to the playground the first thing in the morning. Alternative indoor activities could be marching to music, kiddie aerobics, or pretending to move like different animals. Josh could be encouraged to play "Follow the Leader" on the equipment and ride a bike before free choice of activities.

Tigger . . . TIGGER!!!

When a child's state of arousal is too high, it often interferes with the ability to complete tasks. It seems like these children are in constant motion and lack purposeful play. They are easily upset and often lack impulse control. These are the children, sweet as they may be, that really upset the teacher because the teacher is constantly asking that child to "sit still" or "stop fidgeting" or "pay attention."

Such children have great trouble organizing the sensory input and maintaining an optimal state of arousal. They have difficulty filtering out stimuli. They may go through a room like a tornado or run randomly on the playground. These children are quick to have a tantrum and then have great difficulty calming themselves after they get upset. It takes them a long time to get back into control after a meltdown. Their lives seem to be out of control and chaotic, and they experience little downtime during the day. They also may have trouble falling asleep. They may appear to have attention deficient disorder with hyperactivity (ADHD) and it could be, but it also may be a sensory processing disorder or both. It may take a while to sort out the differences but, in the meantime, this child needs help to find effective strategies for self-calming and appropriate activities to help obtain that "just right" state of arousal that is so essential for learning.

A Sensory Diet

Just like a diet designed for a person's nutrition, a **sensory diet** consists of specific elements designed to meet the child's sensory integration needs. The sensory diet is based on the idea that specific intermittent sensory input can reduce the child's inappropriate responses to his environment.

Calming a Child Down

- Intersperse the child's days with active movement and deep proprioceptive input.
- Provide deep pressure and firm input to the child: With both hands press on his shoulders or head using firm pressure. Be careful, not too hard, but exert enough steady pressure that the child feels that input.
- Play-Doh or clay play is very calming: Provide cookie cutters and objects that require pushing.
- Give big bear hugs, but make sure you approach your child from the front so he knows what you are going to do. You may also first ask him if he needs a hug.
- Try neutral warmth—wrap the child in a blanket and provide slow rocking.
- Create a neutral quiet area. Have a small quiet place with a large floor pillow, which he can go into for escape. It may be a small indoor play tent or a table with a tablecloth over it. Have a box of sensory toys near the tent so he can choose something to hold, push, and pull. This arrangement is very calming and helps your child learn how to regulate his body.
- Let the child carry something heavy while transitioning from one activity to another. Have him hold the door for the class when in the hallway. Teachers may plan their lessons so children can get active movement breaks.
- Give him dry tactile experiences: Play with beans, dry rice, or sand.
- Let him spend time in a comfortable rocking chair.
- Engage in "heavy work," such as wheelbarrow-walking or push-ups against wall.
- Try yoga.
- Use low lights.
- Create orderly surroundings.
- Give him sweet, bland foods, such as yogurt drinks with a straw.

BIG PROBLEM OR Little PROBLEM
OR AN INDIVIDUAL DIFFERENCE?

It is important to note that *not* all children who have trouble following directions or acting out in shopping malls and restaurants have sensory processing difficulties. As children grow and learn, they function in the world and are exposed to more and more experiences. They are bound to have moments when their sensory systems become overloaded or overreactive. For instance, the first time a child experiences a crowded carnival, the assault to his senses of the lights, colors, sounds, smells, and crowds, may leave him feeling overwhelmed. This is a fairly natural response for both the child and the parent until they process all of the stimuli and feel comfortable. Even adults may experience such reactions in the crowded shopping mall during busy holiday seasons. As adults, we develop many habits that help us when we feel overwhelmed by our environment such as avoiding malls during the busiest times and shopping online. Children need time to learn to make those coping strategies and also may need the adults in their lives to provide help and guidance. However, if a child frequently reacts in either a shut-down mode or becomes hyperresponsive in his preschool classroom or other familiar surroundings, he may be having trouble with sensory processing, a problem warranting further investigation.

Coping with Sensory Differences

As an adult, you have learned how to cope with sensory problems. If the tag on your T-shirt bothers you, you have learned to cut it out or buy tagless T-shirts. Another way that some adults cope with their own fragile sensory system is by having a cup of coffee in order to get going in the morning, but in the evening they might have a cup of hot decaffeinated tea or hot chocolate to calm down after a hectic day. Everyone develops certain sensory preferences that help them cope with the external environment. Exercise such as jogging or aerobic class makes you alert and helps you to get your body and mind ready to think. Settling down in a big comfy chair, with the lights low and a good book, might relax and calm your sensory system.

Children also need time or strategies to settle down after an exciting outing. For instance, after a stimulating experience to the park or a birthday party, a child may need some downtime with quiet activities, such as putting together a puzzle or looking at books, or even a video or educational TV. It is important to give children such downtime as well as time to transition from exciting activities to more sedentary play. It is imperative for children, as well as adults, to begin to learn what is calming and organizing for them.

Part Three

. . .

WHERE CHILDREN STRUGGLE

Seven

Life at Home

Getting Kids to Sleep, Eat, and Dress Without Pulling Your Hair Out!

Mealtimes, bedtimes, and getting out of the house in the morning are a few of the daily events that can give parents gray hair and premature wrinkles. In the face of constant whining, disagreeing, negotiating, or tantrums, even the strongest parents can lose their composure and find themselves yelling, threatening, pleading, or bribing.

These essential daily routines are extremely stressful in some families. The good news is that parents can change the tone of these daily routines and get the kind of behavior they are looking for from their child.

Here are strategies for everyday routines.

Morning

Morning is often rushed and stressful because there is so much to do and so little time. It may sound obvious, but children who have difficulty waking up may need to go to bed earlier. Most young children need ten hours of sleep. For the slow riser, try a fun alarm clock and set the alarm at night with your child so he is part of the process. Teach the good habit of hopping right out of bed to turn off the alarm or to respond to a parent's wake-up call.

Morning Routine

A morning routine (followed by memory or picture schedule) should include a trip to the bathroom for toileting and toothbrush ing, then getting dressed. Clothes should be chosen and laid out the night before (make your child a part of this process). A young child is going to need help or supervision getting dressed. When helping, it is always a good idea for the adult to begin the process and let the child complete the final step. For example, help get a foot into a sock and then let the child pull it up. If the child is a dawdler, it may be helpful to use a timer and play a little game of "Beat the Clock." Hair care should be the final step to dressing. Keep in mind that an easy-to-care-for hairstyle can save time and tears.

Keep breakfast simple. Because children like to make choices, a picture or check-off menu could be completed before bedtime, eliminating last-minute indecision or tears over "I wanted waffles, not cereal!"

"Catch Me if You Can" David

"He runs away whenever it's time to do something, like it's a game, until I get really mad."

THE PROBLEM:

David's parents were at their wit's end with their four-and-a-half-year-old because he never responded to requests or directions the first time. He'd giggle and run away. After several requests and/or attempts to tie in consequences ("If you don't come eat your dinner, you can't have dessert" or "If we don't get to school on time, you won't have very much free play"), they'd turn their attention to their other two sons who were more cooperative. Once those children were settled, they'd go back to the first child and typically have to physically carry him or lead him to the next activity. By this point, he was usually giggling and acting like a wet noodle, falling to the floor while his parents became increasingly angry and frustrated. They were nagging and negotiating with David instead of following through immediately on their directions. At school, his teachers expressed concern about his explosive tantrums and occasional aggression, and his difficulty with peers.

Detective Work:

- Which transitions are the hardest?
- Are these consistently difficult for David?
- Are some transitions consistently smooth for him?
- What factors might be contributing to his difficulty, such as time of day, the specific activity he is beginning or ending, or other people being present?
- What is the typical consequence to his behavior? Is he left alone? Sent to his room? Given undivided negative attention from parents?

Analysis of the Problem:

Whether this is a big problem or a little one depends on the parents' perception and how much of this behavior they can cope with. At first, it may seem like a little problem, but after months of difficult transitions it may become a bigger issue. Because most of the changes that need to be made to help with morning routines are on the part of the parents, they need to be sufficiently concerned and committed to changing their patterns at home if they hope to see meaningful changes in David's behavior. The teachers' concerns are another red flag, because typically teachers are experts at managing run-of-the-mill behavior problems at school. If they express concerns about David's development and behavior, his parents may want to seek outside professional help with evaluating the nature and cause of his problems.

Plan of Action:

In general, David's family had very few routines and was perpetually running late. When the family realized that David functioned much better when he knew what was expected of him and had ample warning before transitions, they attempted to tweak their lifestyle and begin building in routines where none had existed before. They gave themselves more time in which to complete major transitions during the day, and worked on one period of the day at a time so that they could all get used to the changes. Their goal was to be consistent about doing things more or less the same way each time.

They also made picture books showing David at each step in a sequence of an activity, such as getting ready for bed, leaving for school, and other spots in the day that had been challenging. He read these books to himself or with a parent throughout the day (children love books about themselves!) but especially right before the transition would occur, so that he was primed to handle it successfully.

His parents also realized that by asking him to do things multiple times and nagging him, they were lessening the importance of their own words and inadvertently letting him know that there were no real consequences when he ignored what they said. They began to aim for quality over quantity, only giving him an instruction when they had his full attention, and were prepared to follow through to ensure right then that he followed directions.

As they changed their behavior at home, they also had their son evaluated and subsequently treated for moderate sensory integration disorder. This explained why he could not cope as well as his brothers could with the family's lifestyle. The occupational therapist made further recommendations that the family incorporated in their home life, and the teachers also incorporated into school.

For More Information, See:

Although David's difficulties at home were compounded by sensory processing differences, his parents were able to shape his behavior significantly through changes to their own family's routine. They were able to markedly improve their home life despite his underlying problems with underlying sensory issues.

Family Chores

Young children love to be helpful and feel needed. Having a special job that contributes to the family will help teach a child responsibility and will make him feel very needed and important. Suggestions for jobs include: setting the table, folding towels, walking the dog, or bringing in the mail.

When giving a child a job, keep in mind the following: be sure he can handle the task, because you are aiming for success, not failure. Help your child learn to do the job better, but never let him see you redo what he just did. Let him know how much you appreciate what he did. Set yourself up for success by asking him to help you when he's not playing his favorite game or watching his favorite show. A power struggle is to be avoided at all costs here because, truthfully, you could probably do the chore in a fraction of the time that it will take your child to complete it. Giving your child chores isn't for the purpose of getting the work done, but for teaching him to contribute to the family.

Scott, the "Button Pusher"

"His teachers say he's fine at school, so why do we have so much trouble at home?"

THE PROBLEM:

Three-and-a-half-year-old Scott constantly challenged his parents. If they said, "Let's go this way," he'd say, "No, I want to go that way." They tried reasoning with him, and to talk him out of tantrums when he was really upset. Scott and his parents disagreed and argued over everything. He was the master of the third option—if they gave him two choices, he'd come up with a third. He tried to negotiate everything. They tried to compromise and respect his desires, but then he'd completely change his mind. They were exhausted by him and couldn't understand how his teachers could insist that he was a perfectly delightful, cooperative, caring, and helpful child at preschool.

Detective Work:

- Are there consistent routines at home as there are at preschool?
- Are there clear rules and behavioral expectations at home as there are at school?
- What is the typical outcome in these "negotiations"? Does he get yelled at or punished in some way? Does everyone involved become frustrated?

Analysis of the Problem:

Although this seems like a big problem to the family, Scott's parents are in a position to dramatically shape their child's behavior by changing their own. Because the teachers have ruled out any learning differences and can attest to his cooperative nature at school as well as willingness to follow rules and get along with peers and staff, this appears to be a little problem.

Plan of Action:

There was nothing wrong with Scott—the problem was in the way his family interacted with him. Young children constantly test and push their limits to experience where those limits are. They don't really want to be able to negotiate with parents or change parents' minds—that would give them a scary amount of power that they aren't really comfortable with.

In an effort to respect youngsters' wants or preferences, parents often misguidedly treat their young children as peers, and then are surprised and confused when their children do not respond as an adult would. Scott's parents were talking way above him and attributing a degree of reasoning and cognition that a three-year-old simply does not have yet. They were talking to him as they would talk to an adult.

This problem was exacerbated when Scott was upset. When in the throes of a tantrum, most of a child's systems shut down and he cannot completely process what is being said to him, nor can he generate a cogent thought or response of his own. A child having a tantrum is not functioning as he normally would. Language, if any, needs to be dramatically simplified.

They began to ask Scott to help with dinner preparation. First, he was allowed to make choices (within parameters) about what the family would eat for dinner. For example, his mom would say, "Pick something green. We have frozen broccoli, green beans, and peas. Which would you like?" Once he realized that he'd have some control over the meal, he became more interested in helping to make it. He dumped the frozen peas into a pan or pulled out the pot holders for his mom to use when the food was ready. He helped stir in seasonings and test the food to judge if it tasted good.

Once he was engaged in the kitchen, it was easy for his mother to hand him the silverware or napkins to set the table. However, had she just said, "Scott, come set the table," while he was watching TV, she would have met much more resistance. She used a more desirable task to get him started and then worked in the less desirable but more helpful tasks. Incidentally, when Scott helped with the meal prep, he was much more inclined to eat the food as well, so battles at the dinner table also diminished.

For More Information, See:

Chapter 3: *Social Emotional Development and Managing Behavior*

Dressing for Success

How Can Sean Get Started?

"My four-year-old son Sean has been identified as having developmental delays. He needs so much more help with dressing than does his younger brother. It seems as if he has trouble even figuring out where to begin. He just can't seem to coordinate his body movements to get his clothes on and off. Even when he gets started, he is slow and awkward. In order to save Sean frustration and to save time, we are doing almost all of the dressing for him. This has been a real time saver, and his nanny loves being able to help him in this way. Now he is dressed and ready to go just as quickly as his brother. Is this okay? If not, how do we help?"

THE PROBLEM:

With several children to get dressed, it sometimes simply seems easier to do the dressing, especially when a child is having such a hard time getting started. Sean needs opportunities to practice dressing skills for him to achieve success. However, getting started is daunting for this family because dressing independently feels like an insurmountable task for him right now.

Detective Work:

- Does Sean have the motor skills for dressing?
- Is it typical for Sean to have difficulty knowing how to start a task?
- Is Sean generally cooperative with the tasks that he is able to do?
- Are his clothes large enough and easy to get on and off?
- Do the family and nanny do things for Sean for convenience, at the expense of teaching him the skills?

Analysis of the Problem:

The family needs to do some thinking about what factors are getting in the way of Sean's dressing himself in the morning. Does his "attitude" or complacency interfere with achieving this goal? Do they have a particularly rushed morning routine that makes it difficult to allow Sean the time he needs to work on dressing? Are the nanny and parents so willing to help that they don't give him time to problem solve and make mistakes needed to figure out how to put his clothes on more successfully?

There is often a fine line between assisting a child to develop a skill and creating a situation of learned helplessness. In response to his slow progress and need for help, this family and nanny (out of kindness and caring) have deprived Sean of opportunities for practicing the skill development he needs for the early stages of independence.

Plan of Action:

The first step is making sure that Sean has pajamas and clothes that are large enough and easy to take on and off. Then take this daunting task and break it into small, measurable pieces. (See below for specific strategies.) The first goal, for example, may be to put on his pants. The second goal would be to show him how to put on his pants and then his shirt with minimal adult help. The next goal would be for him to put on his shirt independently. Now that the stage has been set and goals clarified, it is important for everyone working with and caring for Sean to be consistent with the amount and kind of assistance they give to him. As he gains skills, reduce assistance and increase the expectations.

Dressing Independently

- Start at bedtime; undressing is easier than dressing and pajamas are the easiest clothes to put on.
- Structure for success: Buy clothes that are on the large size and that are easy to put on (e.g., elastic waists; knit shirts, pullovers, or

tops with three buttons at neck; tube socks; and Velcro-closed or slip-on shoes).

- Let your child help choose the clothes the night before and lay them out so there won't be any hassle about what to wear in the morning.
- Use visual aids, such as picture sequences. This works well if your child has difficulty getting started, trouble organizing movements, or a hard time remembering the order for undressing or dressing.

Techniques for Teaching Dressing

You may need to experiment to see what techniques are the most successful with your child.

- **Give "hand-over-hand" assistance.** Place your hand over child's hand and guide him through the process, reducing the amount of assistance as he is able to do more.
- **Chaining is one method of teaching a new skill. Backward chaining** is when the adult does all but the last step of a process and then lets the child do the final steps. When the youngster is successful at that, he will do the two last steps and so on until he has learned the entire process. To put on a T-shirt, the adult helps get the arms in and the shirt lined up at the head. The child completes the final task of pulling it over his head and into place on his body. **Forward chaining** is the reverse process, whereby the child does the first step and the adult completes the process. As the youngster learns a new step, he connects it to the previously learned steps until he has the entire sequence. A good example of forward chaining is shoe tying. The child does the initial step of crossing the laces, and the adult completes the process until the child has learned each successive step.
- **Provide only enough assistance to help your child successfully achieve the desired outcome.** Reduce assistance as the youngster gains skills. Reinforce independence.

- **Remember that it is easier to teach these self-help skills when the child is motivated to learn.** Encourage these skills during the window of opportunity when the child is striving for independence and declaring, "I do it myself!" If you wait too long, he may become complacent and remain content to let adults do things for him rather than be bothered with learning how to do them himself. This is called "learned helplessness."

Expectations for Dressing Skills

Less than two years of age: Almost totally dependent on adult for dressing; however, they would like more independence. The child may help with the final step of pulling off a shirt or will assist by pushing her arms and legs through openings.

2 to 3 years: Will begin to take off or assist more in the undressing process.

3 years: Will start to dress self; need assistance with turning clothes right side out, with fastenings, and with belts and tying shoes.

4 years: Most four-year-olds can completely dress themselves. However, they still need guidance and help with difficult fasteners, boots, and heavy outdoor wear.

Toilet Training

Toilet training can be a real challenge for many families. The key factors for success are timing and consistency. To maximize the possibility of success, the child needs to be physiologically ready, which usually occurs around the age of three. To set the stage for successful toilet training, children over the age of one should ideally have their diapers changed in the bathroom rather than in other places in the home. This helps to establish the idea that the bathroom is where all toileting should occur. This also makes for easier cleanup and begins to teach modesty. If your bathroom is not large enough to accommodate a changing table, find another area that offers privacy and consistency.

Signs that your child may be ready to be toilet trained are: staying dry for longer periods of time, and being aware of when diapers are wet or soiled. There are many different approaches to the plan of action but, whatever plan you use, it is critical to be consistent and maintain the plan throughout the day. It is very confusing to a child when he is expected to use the potty sometimes but, at other times when it is not convenient for the parent or caregiver, it is okay to wear a diaper and wet himself. Choosing a specific toilet training plan or just doing what comes naturally is a personal choice parents need to make, depending on their lifestyle and the needs of their child.

When children do not take the initiative to begin using the toilet, typically it is because they are not motivated to do so, or because they are not expected to do so. There is a fine line between gently encouraging and matter-of-factly expecting, and each child seems to need a unique blend of the two. Some children put so much pressure on themselves when it comes to almost anything, that parents need to do very little other than to reassure them that mistakes (or accidents) happen and it is no big deal.

Other children need more prodding because they'll never wake up one day and say, "I want to wear undies!" For these children, parents may have to initiate the changeover, and be prepared for several soggy days. The parent may say, "Okay, you're a big kid so starting today, you're wearing undies." Hide the diapers and hunker down for a few days of laundry. This is a good three-day-weekend undertaking, so that the day-care providers or teachers don't have to deal with the first (and presumably worst) days. Being firm but neutral (not angry) and insisting that the child help with the cleanup and clothes-changing are essential components for this approach.

Make sure children feel that this is *their* work and not yours. Adults cannot do this for them. They have to be motivated and interested to be successful. In this scenario, let them pull their own pants down and up, flush the toilet, and so forth. Try to avoid getting in the habit of reminding them a thousand times a day. You don't want them dependent on your reminders; you want them to depend on their body's signals. Typically, after children are trained during the day, they will continue to need to wear a diaper or pull-up at night until they are no longer wet in the morning.

Don't make a big deal out of accidents. Shame doesn't help the process and only reinforces children's feelings of uncertainty about their ability to stay dry.

Scott, "the Pampers King"

"He knows exactly what it is all about and he knows when he is going, so why won't he just use the toilet?"

THE PROBLEM:

For Scott, toilet training provided the perfect opportunity for a battle of wills with his parents. No matter what they did or said, this was one area over which he had total control. They could not make him use the toilet. He'd sit on the toilet but nothing would happen. As soon as he had the diaper back on, he'd go.

Detective Work:

- What have they tried so far?
- How quickly do they give up on one strategy in favor of another?
- What has their attitude been?
- Is Scott routinely around other children who are already using the toilet?
- How is toilet training handled at school?

Analysis of the Problem:

Given what we already know about Scott, it seems that he is ready and able to wear underwear. His parents have tried numerous strategies but all have been fairly short lived. He'll aim a few times at floating targets in the toilet, like Cheerios, then stop. He'll earn stickers a few times, then stop. He loves sitting on the toilet if his

Mom will read books to him, but he doesn't go. When the novelty of the above strategies wore off, he just went back to the old, reliable diapers. As long as they are still an option and still available, he'd rather use them because they are easier. However, the fact that he is able to control his bladder and be successful *when motivated*, shows that he is clearly ready to be in underwear.

Plan of Action:

It is time to pitch the diapers and go cold turkey. Simply raise the bar—no more Cheerios or token reinforcements, just declare the expectation. Scott's parents told him that he was a big boy now and they knew he could do this. They waited for a long weekend and kept their calendar fairly free, so that one of them could be home at all times (if necessary) with Scott. They didn't want to give themselves any excuse to whip out the diapers, like having to be in the car for an extended time, or being out at a store. As it turned out, after he did use the toilet, they were able to take him to the park and play outside for a bit, which was good for all of them. They also gave him lots of fluids so he had lots of opportunities to go. They insisted he help with the cleanup of accidents, and gave him specific praise when he was successful at avoiding them. "You got to the potty in time! You felt like you needed to go and you remembered to stop playing and run to the bathroom! Super, honey!"

For More Information, See:
Chapter 3: *Social Emotional Development and Managing Behavior*
Appendix F: *How to Make and Use Behavior Plans and Star Charts*

Will Jake Wear Pull-ups for Forever?

THE PROBLEM:

At three and a half, Jake showed no indication that he was interested in or ready for toilet training. In his preschool class of eighteen three-year-olds, most of the other children were either trained or in the process. Jake had some successes at home with urinating while seated on the toilet; however, he was far from dependable and always had his bowel movements in his pants. He wore pull-ups to school, where children were taken to the bathroom every two hours. Jake consistently sat on the toilet for a few minutes without success, and then, almost like clockwork, had a bowel movement within the next thirty minutes. These were always very soft and messy. He seemed oblivious to the evidence, the mess, and smell, and he was uncooperative when he was taken to the bathroom for cleanup.

Jake's teachers were at their wit's end and his parents were stressed. They had read many books on toilet training and tried everything with very little success. They were beginning to wonder if his lack of toilet training was going to endanger his school placement.

Detective Work:

- What methods have been tried so far?
- What is Jake's diet?
- Is it possible that he does not feel the urge to go?
- Have his parents conferred with their pediatrician?

Analysis of the Problem:

It is entirely possible that Jake is not aware when he needs to use the toilet. He may have a high threshold for sensory awareness. Additionally, he does not have a regular schedule for bedtime, eating, and using the bathroom. His lack of awareness that his pants are messed may also be an indicator of inefficient sensory registration. Regardless of the problem, he and his parents need a strategy that will help them get Jake potty trained.

Plan of Action:

After consulting with their pediatrician and a behavioral specialist, Jake's parents decided to make an all out effort to train their son. Jake's diet was changed to include more fiber. His bedtime was moved to eight o'clock and he was woken up at seven thirty each morning to allow sufficient time for breakfast and toileting before he left for preschool. Approximately fifteen minutes after breakfast, Jake was taken to the bathroom. He was seated on the toilet until he had a bowel movement or until ten minutes had passed. His mom stayed nearby to immediately reinforce any success. Jake was allowed to "read" books while he sat on the toilet. Any success was immediately reinforced with a star chart. If he had not been successful after ten minutes, he was allowed to leave, but had to try again before leaving for school. After three days of this new routine, Jake began to have a bowel movement every morning before leaving for school. At around the same time, he began to urinate in the toilet at home and also later at school. He continued to wear pull-ups for the next two weeks and then advanced to regular underwear during the day. He continues to wear pull-ups at bedtime and wakes up wet most mornings but, happily the dry mornings are more frequent.

. . .

Yes, there is life after toilet training!

Remember that children need close supervision in the bathroom while you teach them the beginning skills necessary for independence in self-care. Although a child is toilet trained, assistance will continue to be necessary with regard to wiping, flushing, and arranging clothing. Reduce this assistance as the youngster shows the skills to be independent. Teach even the youngest child to wash and dry his hands every time he uses the toilet.

Play and Cleanup Time

Play helps youngsters to understand their world. Playing with a variety of materials assists them in learning how to problem solve, manipulate materials, and develop creativity, and also facilitates interactions with peers. It is important for parents and teachers to expose youngsters to a variety of types of toys.

Children often begin playing by using items for real functions. For example, many two-year-olds enjoy pushing a pretend lawn mower or vacuum or talking on a pretend phone. Two- to six-year-olds like using materials to build structures. For preschoolers and young school-age children, this may involve building with cardboard or wooden blocks or using manipulatives such as Legos and Bristle Blocks. During these early years, children also engage in pretend play. They may make elaborate meals in a pretend kitchen or develop complex play scenarios using dress-up clothes and props.

After she's been playing with toys, getting your child to clean up is no easy feat. The best approach is a two- or five-minute warning before commencing cleanup, give her time to finish her work. This time might be spent figuring out how the two of you will reconcile your need to clean up with her need to preserve something she's worked hard to create. You can, have her draw a picture of her building-block fortress or snap a photo before dismantling it or set aside unfinished artwork, in a safe place so that work can be resumed later.

Cleaning Up Toys Together

- **Build in time for cleaning up.** If children have ample time to do the cleanup themselves, parents will be less likely to become stressed out. Teachers build in anywhere from five to fifteen minutes for cleanup after virtually every activity. It takes children longer than it would take an adult, but the point is that they are learning to do it themselves.

- **Be present.** Children need guidance, specific directions, and a model, especially at first. Eventually, they will be able to clean up the whole room independently but first an adult needs to be with them, showing them what to do and helping them to stay on task. You don't want to do it all for them but you do want to support them and teach them how to clean up.

- **Build clean up into the transition to the next activity.** Young children are especially prone to challenging behavior during transitions because they are acutely aware of what is ending (playtime) and don't quite have a vision of what is coming next.

You can help by putting the emphasis on what is happening next. "We'll have a snack as soon as we've got this room clean. What do you think we should have—crackers or grapes?" If what comes next is not particularly appealing, still try to shift their focus to what lies ahead. "Your favorite jammies are in the basket of clean laundry upstairs, let's go find them." Or add in a desired activity such as: "As soon as you clean up, Daddy will read a story. How about one of your new library books?"

- **Give very specific instructions, paired with gestures**. Specific tasks are more manageable for children and give them a focus. Instead of saying, "Clean up the playroom," try "Put all the play food in your kitchen." Or, "You put all the red blocks in this bucket and I'll do the blue ones." Young children are still learning to process verbal instructions. Pointing to what you are talking about or counting out on our fingers ("First, pick up blocks and second, stack the puzzles") gives them a visual cue, which will help them understand. To make sure they've understood a request, ask, "Now what are you going to put away first?"

- **Sing a song to help with the transition to cleaning up.** Young children respond well to music. They associate certain songs with certain activities (think bedtime lullabies). If you don't know a cleanup song off the top of your head, ask your child's teacher. Then start the cleanup process with the same song each time. This repetition is another reminder of the expectation. A child thinks, "When we sing this song, I'm supposed to put my toys away," or "Oh, we're still singing this song, so I guess I'm still supposed to be looking for things to clean up."

- **Make it a game or a race.** Assign each sibling a task and see who finishes first, or set them up assembly line style so they can pitch items to each other. Set a timer and see if they can clean up the room in five minutes. Their time will be the time to beat during the next cleanup. Do anything to make it fun and challenging. Avoid nagging, remember to praise their actions or speed, and tell them how much you appreciate their help.

- **Take preventative measures: Encourage children to put away one toy before taking another one out.** Try calling a time-out in the middle of their play and ask everyone to put away two things before resuming their play.
- **Keep the room manageable by rotating toys.** Paring down what's out at any one time not only limits the scope of how messy the room can get, but also reduces boredom. Kids can be so enthusiastic about a bunch of old toys that have been boxed up and "out of the rotation" for a month. A couple weeks later when those have lost their luster, swap again for whatever is currently boxed in the closet.
- **Create organized storage systems for toys so that the children can both clean up and find things easily.** Open-topped or clear bins on shelves are great. The bins can be labeled with words or cutout pictures for ease in finding and putting away. Children should be able to handle the bins and be able to comfortably fit contents into them. Nothing drives a toddler nuts like a container that is too full for the lid to stay on, or a box that isn't quite big enough to hold a particular toy. They derive great satisfaction from knowing that everything is in its place and that they put it there, all by themselves.

"Play It Again, Sean"

THE PROBLEM:

When Sean was two and a half, he was frequently content to play with his toy garage for long periods of time. He would often lie down on his side, rolling his car back and forth, and rolling it down the ramp. Sean enjoyed looking at his picture books by himself and would name familiar pictures when looking at them with his parents. Occasionally, his mother would introduce books that had a simple story. Sean would yell in protest or push the book away.

Cleanup time was challenging, as Sean often seemed oblivious when asked to pick up his toys. His parents had more success when they showed him what to clean up or provided him with physical assistance, taking his hand in theirs and putting toys away together or holding an empty container next to him that he could fill.

Many times during the day, Sean would wander around his playroom. He appeared to have difficulty finding a toy that would interest him. Sometimes he would dump toys off his shelves and seemed a bit perplexed about the chaos he had created.

Detective work:

- Has he had many colds and/or ear infections?
- Has he ever had a complete hearing test?
- What kind of toys does he enjoy?
- Are there other toys that Sean will play with, when given adult support?
- How does he communicate?
- What types of commands does Sean appear to understand?
- What are Sean's motor skills like?

Analysis of the Problem:

Sean acquired some early skills, but there appear to be some gaps in his development. He is able to identify pictures but has difficulty attending to even simple stories. Sean's play skills are limited; he appears to have some difficulty organizing and sequencing his play. Dumping toys off the shelves may be due to his difficulty in engaging in purposeful play or an attempt to do some cause-and-effect play. Younger children engage in this sort of play. Sean may be overwhelmed with too many choices, which results in sensory overload. A professional evaluation was helpful in determining how to best help Sean.

Plan of Action:

When a parent sees several areas of development lagging behind, the first step may be a **complete developmental evaluation**. A **developmental pediatrician** or a **developmental team** may do this. After the assessment, the team will come up with a plan. They may recommend speech and/or occupational therapy or an early intervention class to help Sean bridge the gaps in his development. (See appendix G.)

Sean's parents can begin to work with him on their own. They can:

- **Increase interaction and turn taking:** Get down on the floor and play with Sean. Initially these sessions can work most optimally if done for short intervals, several times during the day. Use short phrases and sentences as you talk about the play. Take turns pointing to pictures in a book or rolling a car back and forth.

- **Expand types of play:** Encourage Sean to play with a variety of toys. Present them one at a time to encourage exploration. Introduce modeling dough, such as Play-Doh, and encourage him to squeeze, pull, and roll it. Bring out large crayons and encourage Sean to make marks on the paper. Present musical instruments and blocks. Keep initial playtimes short, and present the toys another day if he loses interest.

- **Add a "novel twist" to the play:** Show him how to play with his toys in a different way. Take a toy he likes and add another element to the play. This will encourage Sean to build on his play skills. For example, cut a clean sponge into two pieces. Show Sean how to use the sponges and a squirt bottle to wash his garage and cars. Another way to add a novel twist to the vehicle play is to draw a road on a large piece of paper and show Sean how he can drive his cars along it.

- **Increase eye contact:** Playtime provides a great opportunity to work on increasing eye contact with others. Use bubbles! Hold the bubble wand up to your mouth and talk about the bubbles, using short phrases. Wait for Sean to look at your mouth before you blow the bubbles. A pregnant pause is another way to give a child time to look at you. For example, play "Ring Around the Rosy" and stop before you say the last word and sit down.

- **Develop motor skills:** Encourage him to use riding toys. Set up an obstacle course. Help Sean to follow you climbing over pillows and crawling under a table. Provide opportunities for him to push a shopping cart or his own stroller with a doll seated in it, and let him help push/pull a wagon. Pushing gives a lot of input to his muscles and joints and helps to strengthen them.

- **Limit the number of toys available at one time:** Some toys can be put in plastic boxes and taken out to play with when needed. Label the shelves with large pictures of his toys. Help Sean take out a toy and play with it and then, when he is done, put it back on the shelf where it belongs.

For More Information, See:
Chapter 2: *Play*
Chapter 4: *Speech and Language Development*
Chapter 5: *Motor Development*
Appendix G: *Working with Other Professionals*

"Mommy's Busy" Time

Every day, at some point, children have to entertain themselves. Perhaps you're on the phone, feeding a younger sibling, cooking dinner, or trying to work in the home office. Children have an uncanny ability to "cross the line" at the exact moment you throw something into a hot frying pan and can't leave the stove, are trying to move a barely sleeping baby from point A to point B, or are talking about an important deal with a client.

You can try to plan for these moments, because they will surely occur. If you think two steps ahead of the children, with any luck you'll manage to stay half a step ahead of them! It's best to anticipate when they'll be tired or hungry or bored, and to make a plan to keep them busy and happy.

An activity can be set up or a book pulled out for reading together when it is time to nurse the younger sibling. A video can be turned on as dinner prep commences. Save the most desired activities for the most critical times of day. Let the kids have their TV time at the end of the day when they are running out of energy, which will give Mom or Dad some fairly uninterrupted time to get dinner on the table or to finish an assignment for work. Resorting to take-out dinners on a regular basis can help with particularly stressful periods, such as when there is a new baby or increased work demands on one parent.

Despite the best-laid plans, there will always be periods of chaos. In such cases, use a "triage approach." Deal first with the most dangerous, safety-related issues, such as a child's real or imagined injury, and then move on. Sending one child to his room to "cool down" is a great option— not as a punishment but just as a time to chill out and collect himself before rejoining the rest of the family. Then, move on to the next most essential task, such as removing those damp sheets from a child's naptime "accident." Anything that can wait until after the children are in bed for the night, should, especially if they are having a particularly rough evening. And if you are a "morning person," for heaven's sake, go to bed yourself when you're exhausted and deal with the mess in the morning, or pawn it off on your spouse if she or he tends to be a night-owl!

Scott, the "WWE Heavyweight"

"Scott does pretty well at entertaining himself or playing nicely with his brother, but the moment I get on to the computer, they become wound up and start wrestling, and someone is in tears within minutes."

THE PROBLEM:

Whenever Scott's mother tried to work from home, he and his brother would become especially demanding and break all the household rules about playing calmly inside, taking turns with toys, and so on. She'd warn them that she needed to do work and remind them of the rules, but to no avail. Inevitably, she'd become angry, they'd be in tears, and very little work would be accomplished before they were in bed for the night.

Detective Work:

- How often does Mom try to work from home? Is this part of the daily or weekly routine or less frequent?

- How long does Mom try to work?
- Does she typically try to work at the same time of day or does it vary? What time is it?
- What is Scott typically doing when she begins working? Playing? Watching TV? Napping? What about his brother?
- How does she respond to Scott's attention-seeking behavior?

Analysis of the Problem:

Scott's mom does not routinely work from home while simultaneously trying to care for him. Most of the time, she can complete her work while he is in preschool or while her part-time nanny is with the boys. Because it is not a routine event, Scott is not accustomed to having his mom unavailable. Therefore, he pulls out all the stops when she tries to put her foot down, and to test her limits. He intentionally does things that he knows will get her attention, such as wrestle on the couch with his brother, even though it is negative attention. Furthermore, since it is not a routine event, Scott's mom has not devised a consistent plan for managing the situation. Each time she tries a little different tactic. But each time, she ends up abandoning her strategy (and her work) and gives the boys her undivided, furious, attention.

Plan of Action:

Scott's mom understands the motive for her son's behavior: He wants her attention. Regretfully, thus far her response reinforces his behavior. It always eventually gets him her full attention, which is exactly what he wants.

She needs to make a plan that addresses her need for uninterrupted time, and his need for attention. Next time, she should first separate the boys before attempting to work. Because the toddler still takes afternoon naps, that could be a good time for her to work, but she will first have to find something really rewarding or fun for Scott that doesn't require her attention. A video is a great option, especially if it is one he hasn't seen recently or a new rental from the library or video store. Alternatively, she could set him up with a special snack and a new coloring book. Because working from home is not a routine occurrence, Scott's mom could try to make it special for him, too, with a new video, coloring book, can of Play-Doh, toy car, or special snack. Making this time special for Scott will motivate him to leave her alone. If he bothers her, she will immediately take away the special toy/video and then ignore his protests. She wants to avoid giving him any attention, even negative attention, because that would reinforce the behavior that she's trying to eliminate (bothering her while she's working). This consequence should motivate him to follow her instructions.

She should also set a timer near Scott. This will let him hear time passing (on an egg timer), or see it passing (on a digital clock, like on the microwave or a watch). When the timer goes off, Scott's mom will be done with work *and* she gives him some undivided *positive* attention. The catch for Mom is that she can't work indefinitely. Scott is only three, after all, and she needs to have realistic, age-appropriate expectations of what he can handle, even when he's highly motivated. A half hour or so is probably reasonable, but it depends on the child. She knows how long he is able to play independently when she is nearby, so that may give her a rough idea of his attention span. She'll likely be burning the midnight oil later that night to finish her work, but at least she'll have made some headway, midday, without interruption. Further, this is an important accomplishment in its own right: Scott responds to his mother's directions, and his mother is able to set down a limit and stick to it.

For More Information, See:
Chapter 3: *Social Emotional Development and Managing Behavior*
Appendix F: *How to Make and Use Behavior Plans and Star Charts*

Mealtimes—Eat, Drink and Be Independent

Having a relatively consistent mealtime is best for children. Meals should be simple, enjoyable, and healthy. Whenever possible make dinner a family affair. Include your child in the preparation and cleanup of dinner as often as you can. In fact, when children help make the food or plan the menu, they are more likely to eat their meal. Preschoolers are quite capable of clearing their own dishes and helping to set the table.

Make your dining table as "kid friendly" as possible. This is not a time for tablecloths that can be pulled off the table, or breakable dishes. A vinyl placemat works well with unbreakable dishes and sturdy tableware. Most children like having their own assigned spot at the table. If a child is seated in a chair that is at an appropriate height to the table and has a footrest so his feet are not dangling, he is more apt to pay attention and less likely to fall off his chair or leave the table.

Teach your children they need to remain seated at mealtimes, as this provides you with an excellent time to include them in the conversation. Reinforce the rule that if a child leaves the table, his meal is finished.

Maintain consistent expectations at meals. Give choices within parameters (e.g., "You need to eat something green. Would you like broccoli or peas?"). Do not allow grazing. Plan a well-balanced meal for the family, including at least two items you know will appeal to your young child. Remember to keep reintroducing foods. Encourage your child to try a bite of something new, without pressuring her to eat all of the new food. A preschooler may not like string beans one week, but after watching the family enjoy them, may be willing to try again next month.

A healthy dessert is often part of an evening meal. Vary desserts so a child is not expecting cake and ice cream every night. Jell-O, pudding, yogurt, fruit, sherbet, or ice cream can be good choices. Often children will be more willing to eat a healthy dessert such as fruit if you include a novel element, for example, yogurt for dipping, kids' chopsticks to pick up cut-up pieces of fruit, or yogurt served in an ice-cream cone. Have small dessert bowls that you regularly use, for portion control. Dessert can be offered if a good effort has been made eating and drinking during mealtime. It is not a good idea to use a clean plate as a criterion for receiving a dessert. Some children will eat more then they need just to earn the treat, and this can have other implications in this age of increasing childhood obesity.

"Hurricane Danielle"

"She won't sit at the table and eat—she's up and down and just picks at her food."

THE PROBLEM:

Mealtime was a priority for Danielle's mother, both from a nutritional as well as behavioral standpoint. Danielle grazed at meals—running by the table for a bite or two and running off again to play with her Disney toys. Her mother could not get her to sit at the table. When Danielle did come, she'd squirm around in her chair until she slid off or fell off. Her mother could not get her to eat a balanced diet because her daughter had very narrow food preferences. Throughout the day, Danielle snacked frequently and drank substantial amounts of apple juice in a "sippy" cup and was always on the go. Whenever she did not get what she wanted in terms of food, she threw a tantrum.

Detective Work:

- How frequently is she snacking?
- What is she eating?
- Does she show preferences for dry and crunchy vs. soft or wet foods?
- Is she a messy eater or does she become upset if she gets food on her hands or face?
- Does she always have difficulty sitting in chairs or is the dining room chair particularly difficult for her?
- Are there clear expectations at mealtime, such as "Try one bite"?
- Is her speech and language adequate to express her needs or preferences, and to understand what is said to her?

Analysis of the Problem:

Mealtime behavior may be a big problem or a little one depending on the child's age and eating habits. Toddlers are notoriously picky eaters, but older preschoolers should have outgrown this stage.

All of us have likes and dislikes for certain tastes and textures. However, a strong preference for certain textures or an aversion to others could also indicate that her sensory system is interfering with her normal daily functioning (i.e., her ability to eat a balanced diet), which might indicate a bigger problem. Her posture at the table and in other seated activities could be contributing to difficulty at mealtime—if she is too busy trying to get comfortable or stable in the chair, she is not focusing on her food. Discomfort in the chair could contribute to her eating on the go.

Behaviorally, if her mother is inconsistent in her expectations, Danielle will be less likely to do what she asks because she knows that those "rules" are subject to change.

Plan of Action:

Since she was filling up on snacks and especially juice, Danielle had no motivation or desire to sit at the table and eat what was in front of her—she simply wasn't hungry. Her mother first tackled the snacking. She watered down Danielle's juice gradually and then switched to water altogether. She eliminated all snacks in the afternoon (choosing to tackle dinner issues rather than lunch or breakfast first). Without the snacks, Danielle's hunger at dinnertime became a motivator that her mother could really work with.

She was more willing to sit at the table because she was hungry. Her mother also gave her a more supportive chair at the dinner table to help her stay in one place.

Her mother then instituted a simple "one bite" rule, whereby she just needed to try what was on her plate to get dessert later. As Danielle became accustomed to this, Mom upped the ante and gradually moved to two bites of everything, then three.

Additionally, her mother worked with a pediatric occupational therapist to analyze Danielle's sensory system by using both a questionnaire and evaluation to determine whether outside intervention was needed.

For More Information, See:
Chapter 3: *Social Emotional Development and Managing Behavior*
Chapter 6: *Sensory Processing*
Appendix F: *How to Make and Use Behavior Plans and Star Charts*
Appendix G: *Working with Other Professionals*

Instilling Good Eating Habits

- **Try to have fairly consistent mealtimes.**
- **Carefully plan for snacks.** *Nothing takes away the motivation for eating more than not feeling hungry.*
- **If your child doesn't want to eat, don't make a big deal out of it.** She will then have the natural consequence of feeling hungry and will need to wait until the next meal or planned snack. (Children will not starve by missing a meal or two, but may learn a lesson about eating when food is available.) If your child is frequently missing or refusing meals, discuss this with your pediatrician.
- **Teach mealtime skills and manners.** Use modeling and incorporating gentle prompts. Remember to keep these lessons positive. These may include: encouraging the use of silverware when applicable, taking small bites, chewing each bite and swallowing before the next, and using the napkin to clean the face.

Ages and Stages for Eating: What to Expect from Your Child

Age 1–2: This is the age range for giving up the bottle and beginning to drink from a cup, and shifting to getting most of their nutrition by eating a variety of foods. Children will finger-feed and begin to experiment with a child-size spoon and/or fork. Up until the age of two, a child needs close adult supervision and some assistance with eating. Until this age, he will do best seated in a high chair or in a chair where he is well supported.

Age 2–3: Children over the age of two should be learning to drink from an open, lidless cup. Discourage "sippy" or spouted cups, because they encourage an immature drinking pattern. If you need a cup that is less apt to spill, get a covered cup that has a cutout area for the liquid (like a travel coffee cup) or a cup with a lid and a hole that can be used with a straw. A cup should be not only unbreakable but easily held by your child.

Children at this age eat a lot of finger food; however, they are also beginning to eat more competently with utensils. Expect some spills and messes. Adult supervision is still necessary. Watch for choking hazards such as grapes, sliced hotdogs, or other pieces of food that are not cut into child-size pieces. (Always cut grapes in half and cut hotdog pieces lengthwise as well as into bite-size pieces; when in doubt always make the piece smaller.)

Age 3–4: At this age, children can independently feed themselves and most are able to pour milk or juice into their own cup from a small pitcher. They often continue to need help opening food packets and milk/juice boxes. Some children are able to spread peanut butter or cream cheese. They can successfully use a napkin, but sometimes need a reminder.

Age 5: Most five-year-olds are independent and can be expected to use reasonable manners. They still need help cutting foods and opening some difficult containers. Many five-year-olds are already experimenting with chopsticks, eating more complex foods, and even preparing some simple snacks.

Bedtime

Bedtime is extremely difficult for so many children and consequently their families. A regular bedtime and a consistent routine can go a long way toward making this a positive experience. Always allow enough time so the routine can be carried out with quality time rather than having to rush or be inconsistent. Many children have difficulty slowing down enough to accept the slower, calm pace needed prior to bedtime. Pre-bedtime is not a good time for roughhouse play, scary stories, or other overstimulating activities.

Depending on the child, a bath is often a good way to start the bedtime routine (note, however, that for some children bathtime can be overstimulating). During bathtime, children need close supervision for safety and to ensure success. Teach an organized approach to bathing to ensure getting clean all over, safely exiting the tub, and drying their body. Parents often wonder how frequently children needs to be bathed. Until a child is toilet trained, a daily bath is a good idea. After that, two or three times a week will suffice except for those days of messy play. In the winter months, too-frequent bathing can contribute to dry skin.

Toothbrushing is the next step in the bedtime routine. Regular and careful toothbrushing is critical to good hygiene and essential for maintaining healthy teeth and gums. Parents should begin to brush a child's teeth as soon as they come in. By two to three years of age, toothbrushing should have two phases: kids brush first and then the parent does a quick and thorough brushing to ensure that all teeth have been cleaned adequately. Many families prefer to use children's electric or battery-operated toothbrushes, and there are "kid friendly" flavored toothpastes that delight even the fussiest of children.

As a final step in the bedtime routine, be sure that the child has used the bathroom and had a drink of water, if necessary. Then go with her to her room for pajamas (if not changed at bathroom), a story and goodnight hugs and kisses, before turning out the light.

Whether to use a night-light or leave a door partially open is a personal choice, and can be very reassuring for some children. For children who have difficulty falling asleep, it is sometimes helpful to turn on music or books on tape. For children who are repeatedly getting out of bed for a variety of reasons, it may be helpful to use a star chart or other system that rewards them for staying in bed. (See appendix F).

Danielle, the "Energizer Battery"—She Just Keeps Going and Going . . .

"Danielle is so tired she is falling on her face, but she won't give up, calm down, and just go to bed . . . I have to go back to her dozens of times and even when she finally falls asleep in tears, her sleep is fretful, and she wakes many times during the night . . . I have given up and have just let her come into bed with me . . . I am just too tired to deal with it."

THE PROBLEM:

This five-year-old has unpredictable, explosive behavior throughout the day at both preschool and at home. Her mother loves seeing her daughter at the end of her day and Danielle rushes into her mom's arms when she picks her up from preschool. Danielle loves touching and squeezing her mom even to the point that her mother has black and blue marks from the child's hugs. They hurry home and Danielle tries to tell her mom about her day. Her mother does not always understand the stories because they are somewhat disorganized, but she tries her best to connect the dots and figure out what Danielle is trying to tell her.

Once the dinner battles are through, Danielle's mom wants to relax and have some quality time with her daughter. However, as her parent attempts to have a cup of tea and watch the evening news, Danielle just wants to play physically, jumping on the sofa, running randomly in the living room. Danielle's mother just wants a moment to catch her breath and doesn't understand why her daughter just can't quietly play with toys for thirty minutes.

Danielle has great difficulty calming herself. She resists going to

bed and fights sleep. Her body always seems to be in "overdrive" ...
she is in constant motion and goes from 0 to 60 mph in a fraction of
a second. One moment, Danielle could be happy, and the next she
is yelling or crying. It is difficult to predict her emotions; she is constantly on edge and blows up frequently.

Danielle loves her bath but screams hysterically when her hair is
washed, or if her face is wet. She will only wear one pair of pajamas
and if they are not available she will refuse to get dressed for bed. She
cries and screams until they are taken out of the laundry bin so she
can wear them. Needless to say, this makes for a difficult bedtime.

Eventually, her mother gives up on watching the news, becomes
upset with Danielle, and says she has had enough, and they head for
the bedroom. Danielle starts screaming that she is not ready for
bed. She is promised that if she gets ready for bed, her mother will
read two stories. Danielle bargains for more stories and a song. This
"negotiation" goes on until her mom gives in. After reading four
books and singing several songs, her mother gets frustrated and
tells Danielle, "Just go to bed!" and rapidly leaves the room. This
typical nightly exchange leaves the mother feeling guilty and overwhelmed with doubts about her ability to parent.

Detective Work:

- How much sleep does Danielle need?
- What time is she getting up in the morning?
- How long is she napping each day?
- How much time is Mom spending with her in "play" without any
  agenda?
- Does Danielle know the routine and understand time con-
  cepts?
- Is bath time calming for Danielle or arousing?
- When Danielle was a baby and toddler, how did her mom get her
  to sleep?
- Does Danielle fall asleep when there is soft music in the
  background or when listening to a quiet story with lights off?
- Does Danielle fall asleep in cars?

Analysis of the Problem:

This bedtime behavior may be a big or a little problem depending on the child's age and sleeping patterns. Infants and babies may have trouble establishing sleeping patterns, until they are six months old. After that age, most infants can and do sleep through the night. By the time a child is in preschool, her sleeping patterns should be well established, with the child being able to self-soothe and sleep all night.

The most common sleep problems during the first years of life are night waking and bedtime struggles. Night waking is generally due to an inability to soothe oneself back to sleep after normal brief awaking following REM (deep) sleep. Most commonly, bedtime struggles are due to the child's resistance to separation from a parent and her stopping enjoyable nighttime activities.

Behaviorally, if Danielle's mom is inconsistent in her expectations, Danielle is less likely to follow the rules about getting and staying in her bed. She knows she will be able to sleep in her mother's bed if she just ups the ante.

Plan of Action:

Appropriate bedtime routines help a child get to sleep and or go back to sleep after waking. These routines include bathing, reading a book, singing a song, bedtime snack, toothbrushing, and playing a quiet game.

In Danielle's case, her mom tackled her need for attention. When they got home from school, Danielle's mother put down the mail and they sat down at the kitchen table and planned out the schedule of the evening. First, they discussed the choices for dinner. Next, Danielle's mom gave her the choice of helping her prepare the dinner or going to watch a quiet video. A kitchen timer was set, with Danielle's help, to organize the time frame in which dinner would be prepared and TV be watched.

Danielle's mother prepared dinner, interacting both verbally and nonverbally with her daughter. This allowed Danielle to have downtime but also reassured her that Mom was home and involved. When the timer went off, dinner was on the table, the TV was off, and all phone calls were diverted to voice mail. Danielle had undivided attention from her mom. Following dinner, a picture schedule illustrating each step of bedtime routine was taken out with the plan for the evening. Picture schedules are reassuring for a child because they show them what is expected. Danielle's mom reviewed the schedule to help Danielle get through her nighttime routine. Realizing that Danielle required her undivided attention after a long day at child care, her mom set the VCR to record the evening news, and she instead played a variety of calming games with Danielle. The amount and time were predetermined with the use of a timer and a choice board. (See appendix E.) Once the timer went off, playtime was finished and it was time for bath, books, toothbrushing, and so on. The picture schedule was then "read." The schedule told Danielle what would be happening next, and helped support Mom with following through on the plan. She could refer to it as they wound down toward bedtime (e.g., "The schedule tells us it is time for bathtime"). Schedules can reduce power struggles: It's not Mom saying it's bedtime, it's what the schedule says!

Bathtime was then used as a calming activity. Danielle played in the bath and her mom interacted with her, playing imaginatively while drinking that necessary cup of tea. Danielle's mother recognized that hair washing has been a problem, so she has eliminated shampoos until the weekends when there would be more time to deal with Danielle's sensory difficulties, and bought a face shield to assist in the process. A large bath sheet was warmed for calming effect and after the bath her mom wrapped it tightly around Danielle, just like when she swaddled her as a baby. Providing the youngster with this deep pressure was calming and got her prepared and quieted for bed.

Instead of getting into bed with her daughter to read books, Danielle's mom sat in a large rocking chair in the child's room and read her the agreed-upon stories. Danielle chose the books and they rocked together in the chair. Following the stories and a predecided song, Danielle willingly got into her bed. Her mom has realized that her child sleeps best when she is swaddled or cradled with cushions. Danielle crawled into a child's sleeping bag with her favorite "lovey" and stuffed animals. Her mother played a tape recording consisting of a book read by Mom, followed by a few quiet songs. She turned on the night-light and left the room. Danielle was instructed how to rewind the tape if she needed to listen to it again.

A simple behavior plan was set up with a visual chart. Every time Danielle managed to stay in her bed and fall asleep by herself there was a star waiting for her the next morning. When she had five stars at the end of one week, she got a favorite reward or special activity with Mom. As Danielle became more accustomed to the routines and the calming strategies, her sleep patterns improved, as did Mom's quality time with her daughter. Additionally, Danielle's Mom worked with an occupational therapist to assess Danielle's sensory processing to determine if therapy was indicated.

For More Information, See:
Chapter 3: *Social Emotional Development and Managing Behavior*
Chapter 6: *Sensory Processing*
Appendix E: *Using Visuals to Support Children and Enhance Learning*
Appendix F: *How to Make and Use Behavior Plans and Star Charts*
Appendix G: *Working with Other Professionals*

Life with kids is never easy, but by putting some of these daily routines and strategies in place you can get your kids to sleep, eat, and dress without pulling your hair out!

Eight

Life away from Home

*Ensuring Successful Experiences
at Childcare Centers,
Preschool, School, and After-
school Programs*

Today, young children may spend as much awake time at child-care or preschool as they do at home. Childcare centers have become a "home away from home" for many children. Elementary schools often have built-in early care and after-school care programs as well.

Teachers and other caregivers often encounter behavior problems among the children, just as parents do. They may have concerns about how a child interacts with his friends, how he communicates, or how he plays. A child may have difficulty in one part of the day or in many. Like parents, teachers can feel incredibly frustrated when they are unable to give a child what he needs (or figure out what he needs in the first place!).

Teachers and parents need to work together and listen to each other. Just as parents may turn to teachers for support or advice about managing a child's behavior at home, teachers may be eager to have increased communication with a family when a child is having trouble at school. Although frustration levels may be high among all involved, it is important to maintain a positive attitude and open mind when collaborating with teachers to change a child's behavior at school. While the focus of conversation may be the negative aspects of a child's day, it is important to be cognizant of his strengths at school. Those strengths may be drawn upon to address his weaknesses. This chapter highlights parts of a typical preschool day so that you have an idea of what is expected of children, where problems might occur and why, and what you can do to support children and their teachers when faced with a challenge at school.

Arrival

Saying good-bye to Mom or Dad is the first big transition faced by children at school or day care. Leaving one grown-up and going to another is a big deal for children: Aside from attachment issues, they are leaving one person's set of expectations, ways of doing things and communicating things, for another person's. In many homes, the morning is rushed, harried, and not particularly pleasant. Children may be especially resistant to saying good-bye if they feel that things are not "right"

"I need 2 hugs, 3 kisses, and 1 story before you go."

with their parent—if there are residual or unresolved bad feelings from a bad morning at home. Once in the classroom, some children may have an elaborate ritual of hugs, kisses, and "Have a good day," whereas other children prefer a quick split without lingering on the good-byes and prolonging the agony. For them, it may be all they can do to keep their emotions in check until their parents leave the room!

Saying good-bye is only half the challenge: Immersing oneself into the classroom is the other half. Having routines associated with arrival can be helpful, such as a check-in board where a child moves his picture from a "home" sign to a "school" one. Older children may practice signing in at a writing table or on a white board. Children who ride the bus may have the duration of the bus ride to shift their thinking away from home and to their school day (much like we may use our commute time to mentally shift gears between home and work). Going through the same arrival routine every morning can be very comforting to children. They know what to expect, they do it every day, and the familiarity brings comfort. Where parents fit into this routine, if at all, depends on the individual school.

Dropping Off at Preschool or Child Care

- Make the morning as smooth as possible at home so that you start your day on a positive note with your child. Prepare as much as possible the night before, such as lunches. Be close by to ensure the morning doesn't derail. For example, if your child tends to wander half-dressed toward a television, make sure you are nearby to "put the morning train back on the track."
- Encourage your child to eat a healthy breakfast. This helps to ensure a good start to the day.
- Try to give yourself an extra five minutes so that you can spend time in the classroom with your child if that is what he needs, without being stressed about what time it is.
- Don't tell him how *sad* you'll be all day without him and how much you'll miss him, or otherwise dwell on the negative— he'll start to worry about you! Focus on the positive and what he can do when he's thinking about you, such as draw you a picture, call you on the toy phone, or write you a letter.
- Make sure a very young child has a "lovey" from home, such as a favorite pillow, doll, or even a photograph of the family to look at when he is missing you. Talk to the teacher about what the school suggests along this line.

- Arrive on time! Teachers plan their days very carefully and your child is more likely to have a smooth separation if he arrives when the teacher is expecting him.
- If your child has trouble with separating, leave him in the teacher's capable hands as you leave. Give the teacher space to do her "work" of comforting and reassuring your child. This will enable the teacher to form her own positive relationship as your child learns that his teacher is an adult whom he can trust and turn to for support in stressful moments.

Scott, a.k.a. Dr. Jekyll and Mr. Hyde

"He loves school, so why is he so difficult in the mornings now that we've started early-bird drop-off? We thought he'd be thrilled to have the extra playtime at school."

THE PROBLEM:

As a way to squeeze in a bit more work time, Scott's mother signed him up for an early-morning drop-off option at nursery school. The extra hour seemed like it wouldn't be an issue for Scott because he enjoys school. However, the compressed time at home before school became more stressful and chaotic for everyone. Scott lost his playtime at home before school and felt pressure to get out of bed quicker, eat quicker, and get dressed quicker. He had less positive attention from his mother because she was trying to do the same. He responded by becoming silly and stubborn in the morning: refusing to get in and out of the car, leaving his lunchbox in the car, insisting on walking up the longer path to the school's door, and every other delaying tactic in the book. In response, his mom became more brusque and irritated with him. They typically parted on a sour note.

Detective Work:

- Does Scott now have to wake up earlier than before?
- Have his parents made adjustments to the morning routine to make things smoother now that there is less time at home, such as packing lunches or laying out his clothes the night before?
- Before starting early-birds, was the transition to school smooth for Scott?
- Does he have friends at early-birds or is he with children from other classes?
- Does he arrive in his own classroom with his own teacher or do the early-birds start in a different room or with different staff?

Analysis of the Problem:

There were several issues here. First, at home: Scott's mom is trying to cram the morning routine into an hour-less time slot. Something has to give and unfortunately it has been the relaxed atmosphere, breakfast conversation, and unhurried pace. Rather than letting Scott dress himself, she hustles him into his clothes. Some days, she gives him a juice box and toaster waffle to eat in the car on the way to school. These have been dramatic changes for Scott.

Second, the atmosphere at school is very different. Scott's teacher is not in charge of early-birds, so there's a new staffer for him to get to know. The early-birds meet in a different room, with children from several classes. Scott's favorite pals are not among them. Just at the time when he needs extra support and comfort from his mother to handle this new transition, she is less available because she is more harried than ever.

Plan of Action:

Scott's parents not only began more preparations the night before (lunches packed, clothes laid out, coffeepot ready to start, cereal and fruit on the kitchen table), but they set their alarm to go off forty-five minutes earlier. After a few weeks, they also started going to bed earlier! They didn't wake up Scott any earlier but they were able to get themselves ready sooner so that they were more available to Scott and his brother in the morning. They effectively *eliminated some of the causes* of stress in the morning routine by taking preventative measures the night before.

Additionally, Scott's mom resigned herself to the fact that dropping him off an hour earlier didn't mean she'd get an hour's more work done because, as an early-bird, he needed her to stick around for a little longer. His silly, stubborn behavior decreased somewhat as a result of less stress at home in the morning; however, because he didn't much like being an early-bird, he still used various delay tactics once they arrived at school. As with most aspects of parenting, "two steps forward, one step back" seemed to describe the net result of this shift in the family's schedule.

For More Information, See:

Chapter 3: *Social Emotional Development and Managing Behavior*

Appendix F: *How to Make and Use Behavior Plans and Star Charts*

Free Play/Free Choice Time

The bulk of the day at most early childhood programs consists of free play. We know from developmental experts that young children learn by doing: active, hands-on exploration of materials, toys, and so on. We also know that children's play is most meaningful, that is, they learn the most from it, when it is self-directed (as opposed to teacher-directed). To that end, children have long periods of time where they may choose and move among a variety of activities. Free play is long because children typically need a long period of time in which to become fully engaged or absorbed in their play. As any child will tell you, there is nothing worse than being told to clean up right after you've begun to play! The self-directed nature of this time allows children to find a comfort level both with the activities and their degree of interaction with others.

School is work for children, even when they are "just playing." They are sizing up the options, making choices about where to go, whom to be with, how long to continue with an activity, and what to do next. Free play can be overwhelming for some children for this very reason: There aren't the clear expectations as during other parts of the day such as circle time, nor are there tight time frames—free play typically goes on for quite a while. Managing this lack of structure requires higher-level skills found in the executive functioning part of the brain. Children who have trouble focusing, maintaining attention to one thing, and sequencing their actions, for example, can find free play challenging. Refer to chapter 2 for strategies to support children who are experiencing difficulty in different aspects of their play, including those described here.

"The Flitter"

Some children flit from activity to activity without deeply engaging in anything. Their response to all the choices is to try to do everything all at once, in a disorganized fashion. From child development experts, we know that real learning only occurs when children are fully engrossed in what they are doing. If they only superficially stop by an activity without really participating, they aren't learning anything.

"The Destroyer"

In lieu of saying, "Hi, can I play with you?" some children choose to knock down or scribble on a friend's work. This is some children's way of joining in play. Obviously, this doesn't gain them any friends! However, we see children destroying each other's work all the time, in an effort to get another child's attention or maybe the teacher's attention. The Destroyer can't quite come up with the right words but he knows that this is a sure-fire way to get a response! At two years of age, this is annoying but typical. Toddlers are very new language users, and their emotions and desire to play often overwhelm their budding language skills. However, such destructive behavior at age four or five is cause for concern, since these older children should be much more adept at entering play, getting along with peers, and using language to sort things out.

The Destroyer

"Hi! Can I play, too?"

"The Cling-on"

Some children are more comfortable with adults than with other children, to the extent that they rarely interact with their peers because they are attached to the hip of their favorite teacher. Yes, adults make better communication partners than do children (because they have years more of experience!), but children learn so much from interacting with each other, figuring out how to explain things to each other, negotiate with each other, and so on. A child who doesn't do this is missing out on a key piece of her social skills development as well as related language and cognitive development. (However, very young children, such as two-year-olds, may be "cling-ons" simply because they are still grappling with separation issues. The fact that they've formed a strong attachment to a teacher is actually a healthy, positive development. As they grow though, they should begin to venture away from the teacher and interact with peers a bit more.)

"The Train Lover"

There are kids who love trains and other toy vehicles, and then there are kids who *love* them. Typical kids who love trains may set up the tracks in different ways, crawl around to set things up just so, enjoy hooking the trains together in different combinations, and most important, interact with other train lovers all the while. With such toy vehicles, they are experimenting with weight, gravity, and magnetization (how many cars can one engine pull up a ramp?). With their peers, they are negotiating track design and train distribution among themselves, the "engineers." These are not the children we are concerned about.

The one-track behavior we're concerned about is a solitary player who sticks with one thing, to the exclusion of all else and everyone else. He typically keeps his body in one position, usually lying on his side on the floor. He moves one train or other toy along the same path, back and forth. There is no trial and error, no experimentation. His is a closed loop—the same exact motion over and over. Most likely this child has raised other red flags. His intense play, *combined with other concerns*, may warrant further evaluation by professionals.

Sean Goes to Nursery School

"By the time our son was two and a half years old, we knew that Sean was delayed in several areas of development. A complete developmental evaluation revealed delays in motor, speech, and social language development. Sean began to attend a therapeutic nursery school program. When our son turned four, we enrolled him in a regular nursery school class, three afternoons a week, to supplement the therapeutic program he attended every weekday morning."

THE PROBLEM:

Initially the typical nursery school program was a considerable challenge for Sean, in spite of the progress he made in his therapeutic class. During free play, Sean often wandered around the room without engaging in a specific activity. He appeared lost and overwhelmed. At his parents' request, Sean's teachers and therapists from both programs met to discuss strategies, review goals, and brainstorm ways they could work together to help this youngster be successful in both programs.

Detective Work:

- What kind of free play was Sean most successful at in this therapeutic program?
- What kinds of support did his therapists and teachers provide to facilitate success in the therapeutic class?
- What type of aid was available in his typical nursery school class? How could the therapeutic program provide support for Sean in the additional nursery school program? What kinds of support would assist the teachers to help him?
- How would the professionals communicate on a regular basis with each other and with Sean's parents?

Analysis of the Problem:

Sean needs support to play successfully in a busy nursery school environment. He experienced some success in his highly structured therapeutic program, but he, like many children with difficulties in several developmental areas, needs support to generalize his skills to other environments.

When a child is enrolled in both a typical and therapeutic nursery school program, careful planning is a key factor as to whether he will have a successful year. It is imperative for the parents to co-ordinate or facilitate communication between the two programs so they can share goals and effective teaching strategies. The therapeutic program may also share resources to support the teachers in the typical program. Sometimes this communication can be the make-or-break factor about whether a child with significant needs can be successful in a program designed for typically developing children.

Plan of Action:

The professionals and parents set up regular ways to communicate. They exchanged e-mail addresses and began using a notebook in which teachers from both programs could write a brief note to highlight Sean's successes as well as difficulties. At his parents' urging, teachers from both programs visited Sean in his other class, which gave them a better understanding of the rest of his day.

Sean's teachers worked together to structure some play activities so he could organize and sequence his play more readily. For example, the teacher in his typical program began to set up play scenarios by introducing the theme in a circle time. The class began to read simple books on restaurants with key props such as a tablecloth, apron, and menu being added to the kitchen area, to encourage the play. Sean's parents also practiced the play scenario with him. Within the scenario were opportunities to sweep the floor, wipe the table, take the orders, or be a customer. These organized play scenarios also provided an opportunity to play and interact with classmates. Sean needed a great deal of teacher support initially, but as his play became more familiar, his teacher provided less guidance.

The teachers from Sean's therapeutic nursery school also demonstrated how to use visuals (picture boards) to help him make a choice from two acceptable choices. They demonstrated techniques to assist Sean in completing an activity rather than wander the room. They gave him simple instructions, such as "Put two puzzle pieces in" or "Clean up three blocks. Now you're done." Sean began to smile more in his typical nursery school class as he experienced more success.

For More Information, See:
Chapter 2: *Play*
Appendix G: *Working with Other Professionals*

Circle Time

Large group, structured activities also known as circle time, sharing time, or class meeting allow teachers to present new information to the whole group at once, and give children the opportunity to begin developing skills to learn and function in a large group, as they'll be required to do for the majority of their school years ahead. In general, the children are expected to sit still on a carpet, be quiet, and listen to the teacher or whoever is speaking, though they may have opportunities to get up and move, sing, and answer questions. Their attention should be focused on the teacher.

For some children, the demands of circle time are too much to handle. Maybe it is sitting still, maybe it is attending for a prolonged period of time to the teacher, maybe it is the distraction of having so many children close by. Occasionally we see squirmy children who may do things to bring the attention back to themselves, such as bother the child next to them, do or say something silly to get a reaction from peers. Children may do something intentional to get themselves kicked out of circle if it isn't enjoyable to them.

Circle time is a challenging yet important part of most programs. It provides a unique opportunity to develop as a group and build a sense of community. It brings together children who might not otherwise interact. Finally, it prepares children for large-group learning down the road.

Outside Play, a.k.a. Recess

Elements of recess at school are unique within the larger sphere of outdoor play. Specifically, children tend to be supervised less closely during recess. Also, although teachers may be outside, they are rarely up on the climbing structures with the children or out in the field playing ball with them.

Ironically, recess is the time when children frequently have their most spectacular falls or biggest fights. In other words, it is the time when children need close supervision more than ever. They ride tricycles too fast or too close to one another. They jump off equipment from unsafe heights, or play a bit too rough with friends. The huge space facilitates running and jumping and high-energy activity, which children need. Yet, they also need to be reminded of limits and rules which will help them to stay safe. As with Free Play, some children find the demands of recess to be overwhelming. Some children flit from area to area, while others may stay near the building without engaging at all.

Communication Is Vital!

Parents are the first and most important teachers and advocates for their children. However, teachers have expertise in how to teach young children and support youngsters' development in ways that surpass what parents alone can offer their children. Children clearly benefit from a collaborative, cooperative relationship between parents and teachers. While parents may be the "experts" on their children, teachers are the experts on how to teach those children. By pooling their respective areas of knowledge, parents and professionals can create an enhanced learning environment. Because children often act differently at home vs. school, it is essential for parents to listen to their child's teacher and collaborate with the teacher to ensure that the child is having the best experience possible.

For some children, it is truly a challenge to get through the hours that they are in day care or school. Many youngsters feel unsuccessful, and this may be expressed by demonstrating behavioral outbursts, shying away from peers, or avoiding activities. If a child is having difficulty at school, parents need to be proactive: Find out what is happening and work together with the school staff to formulate a plan of action to help the child be more successful. Always follow through to see if little problems resolve. If little problems continue or get bigger, consider seeking additional advice from an educational consultant, your pediatrician, or a developmental clinic. Advocate to secure any needed special service or therapy for your child. Never underestimate how important a good beginning is: A little intervention at an early age can ensure future success for a child.

Working with Teachers When a Child Is Having Trouble

- **Communicate daily.** Pick-up and drop-off are not the best times, however, because they are hectic, not private, and both your and other children are present. Use a notebook that goes back and forth between home and school, or have a regular time to check in via e-mail or phone. Let the staff know you care and are concerned.

- **Listen with an open mind.** Consider teachers' opinions carefully and remember that they know your child in a different environment, where he may behave much differently than he does at home.
- **Ask what she needs.** Look for ways to support the teacher and to let her know that you appreciate her efforts. She may be frustrated and feeling down because the child's behavior is challenging her.
- **Consider all possibilities.** Attending for shorter hours or fewer days, having an earlier dismissal, or hiring a "shadow" to stay close to your child (if safety is an issue) are all options that may help a child experience more success at school.
- **Remember that this is a fluid situation and be flexible.** A child may need extra supervision for a month or two, but then staff and parents may decide to phase it out. A child who has trouble at recess at the end of the day may be picked up early for a few weeks before slowly working back up to a full day. A promising plan may not work out so well for unforeseen reasons, so generate a "plan B" together.
- **Stay positive and work as a team.**

Nine

Siblings and Playmates

Can't We All Just Get Along?

For most parents there is no greater satisfaction than observing two offspring building a tower, coloring in a giant coloring book together or simply talking to each other nicely. However, what does a parent do with a child who really has difficulty sharing or lashes out at siblings or peers? This certainly feels like a big problem!

"Why is it so hard for my kids to get along?" is a common lament heard from mothers' coffee klatches to the water coolers at work. As usual, this problem calls for a little detective work. Over the course of several days, take some time to observe and to clarify specifically where and when the problems arise between your children.

Is there a specific time of day in which the altercations take place? Do the squabbles break out when the play is unstructured or going on for long periods of time, or during the "bewitching" hour before dinner?

Many a desperate parent has sought assistance to help brothers and sisters live together in perfect harmony or at least with occasional peace! This is a goal that can be more successfully approached if it is broken into smaller pieces.

Cohabiting Peacefully with Siblings

- **Set up the environment to promote peace and harmony.** For example, if your toddler is constantly knocking down your older child's structures and causing the younger one to scream in frustration, you may consider dividing a room with baby gates so that older children can sometimes play without this aggravation. (One of the authors used this technique for years in her own home and still uses it at home when her youngster wants to play with dolls, without interference from the dog!). Encourage older children to do puzzles, play with Legos, or do artwork at the table or kitchen counter where their work is out of reach from curious toddlers.

- **"Does anybody really know what time it is?"** There are certain times of the day when everyone's reserves for handling stress are very low, which sets up increased possibilities for conflict. Many parents find this to be when they are making dinner or coming in the house after work. In this situation, a little planning goes a long way.

  You can try bringing out the giant coloring books, new boxes of crayons, or special markers. Ideally each child can have a box of his own markers and coloring book so there won't be a fight over who has the red marker. This is not a time to work on sharing, because parents are tied up with cooking, going through mail, and so on. The children can sit at the kitchen table (in visual range) while you work on dinner preparations. You could add a novel twist to coloring time by covering your kitchen table with brown paper for them to make an illustrated tablecloth for dinner. (It certainly works in a lot of kid-friendly restaurants!) Or get a page of multicolored dot stickers and have the children decorate paper cups for the dinner beverages.

- **Calm down!** Put on soothing classical music. Provide calming activities. Show your child how to cut Play-Doh "snakes" or straws with child scissors, or how to pick up the imprint of the Sunday comics with Silly Putty. Even rolling out bread dough (you can use store-bought, refrigerated dough) can be calming and relaxing. Set out water bottles with straws for your children, because drinking from straws can be calming to the sensory system.

- **Regulation, regulation, regulation . . .** Getting along with siblings is a bigger problem if the children are tired or hungry. Some parents find that children handle the ups and downs of life with a sibling when they provide a snack of cut-up vegetables for the kids to nibble on before dinner. This gets a less favorite food group out of the way and gives nourishment, but doesn't fill them up.

- **Proximity control (or, "My eyes are watching you!"):** An effective tool for helping children get along is simply to be in close physical proximity. Having you close by and in visual range will often decrease the possibility of conflict. This is a principle that most adults understand. Certainly most drivers are more cognizant of using turn signals and driving the speed limit when a police officer is in sight. Proximity control can also help siblings follow the household rules. Being in visual range sounds reasonable, but what if making dinner pulls you out of range? Initially, it may mean that you will be more successful if you simplify dinner menus (e.g., make pasta or macaroni and cheese the night before, or cut up vegetables and fruits in advance). The goal is to first increase positive interaction by providing maximum assistance and then to gradually reduce assistance.

  You can also provide proximity control by having the children "get in on the act," when it comes to fixing dinner. You might work one-on-one with each by giving them different meal preparation tasks. Have one child spin the lettuce in a salad spinner or help you wash vegetables while his sibling assists by washing the kitchen table with a wet sponge. Make sure everyone has a little time with you as that can certainly calm those end-of-the-day nerves. While dinner preparation may seem like a chore to us, young children are often happy to help with "real" jobs around the house.

Another solution may be finding a "parent helper": a responsible eleven- or twelve-year-old in the neighborhood who would be thrilled to play with your children for a nominal fee while you make dinner and attend to other household matters.

- **Pair a less favorable activity with a more desirable activity.** Pair a less-liked activity with a more motivating activity, such as cleanup time with playground play, by stating, "Once we clean up these toys we can go to the playground." Specify what you are looking for (e.g., pick up five toys, put these cars in the box). At other times, you could try setting a timer and then reward successful completion (being done by the time the timer goes off) with playground time, an extra book at bedtime, or other favorite activities.

- **Catch your children being good.** Praise your children when you see them getting along. Regularly and specifically praise this behavior (e.g., "You used nice words," "You shared a toy with your brother"). When your child is having difficulty with a sibling, also give specifics about what they should do rather than what they shouldn't do (e.g., "Keep your hands to yourself," rather than "Don't hit").

- **Structure the environment for unstructured play.** As one member of our team so aptly explains, "Five minutes of planning gives you twenty." Set up the environment to pique your children's interest. For example, take out all of the zoo Beanie Babies and nursery blocks so that your children can create a zoo. Take down a cash register, a couple pairs of your kids' shoes, and several empty shoe boxes and you have helped them create a shoe store. Cover the kitchen table with a tablecloth and give your kids flashlights—they have a fort. Help them put the kitchen chairs in a row and they have an instant train. The possibilities, with just a little environmental tweaking, are endless! Adding a little novelty into the day can sometimes bring out the best in siblings. They'll have more fun with the new items or new setup and forget about some of their squabbles.

- **Where you lead, I will follow . . . sometimes.** Help your children take turns being the leader as well as the follower in play with a sibling. This activity takes adult support and facilitation. Support each child with both roles and this will truly improve their play together.

- **Teach "old fashioned" table and board games!** Structured games provide an organized way for siblings and families to interact. Begin with "Memory" or board games. One excellent teacher we know teaches her youngsters that there are two games going on at the same time. One game is the game of being a good friend, the other is the game that is actually being played. As the kids get older, introduce card games. Cards are easy to throw in a purse for restaurant entertainment. Set up game nights for all family members to interact. Not only do these activities foster good family social skills, but they also provide an opportunity to practice skills that can be used to have a successful playdate.

Playdates

Why Have a Playdate?

Interaction and play with peers is essential for social and emotional development in the preschool years. Learning to communicate, play, and develop friendships is an important life skill. Some children learn to socialize with other children easily, whereas others need more support and systematic practice to learn to make friends. Parents play an integral role in supporting a child's development of social skills with peers. One of the best ways to facilitate social skill development is to invite another child over for a playdate.

Today's children are exposed much earlier to group learning experiences than previous generations. Many children go to child care or nursery school before the age of three. Although these environments can provide valuable social experiences, preschoolers also benefit from one-to-one play with a peer.

Preschool is a sensory-rich environment, and some children are easily overwhelmed by the noise and tumult of a classroom. A child who is experiencing some social difficulties may more fully enjoy his nursery school experience once she has had some playdates with classmates.

Also, consider that children have a mix of strengths and challenges. A child may be a whiz on the playground equipment but need support to share toys or to communicate with peers. Inviting another child over can help both children continue to develop motor, communication, and play skills. For example, a youngster may more readily attempt to try a new slide if a peer ventures down it first. Tasting a new food, playing a novel game, or exploring a sandbox may all be accomplished more easily if a peer leads the way. (See chapter 2.)

Two Is Company, Three Is a Potential Disaster

Invite one friend over to play at a time. This allows children to get to know each other and interact more easily. Adding an extra child to the mix often leads to someone's feeling left out. A child may find playmates in school or the neighborhood. If she goes to preschool, ask the teacher to suggest a youngster from the class to invite to a playdate.

Consider inviting a child to your home who shares similar interests with your youngster. At other times, you may extend an invitation to a child who has different strengths than your own child. For example, with some adult support, you may help your child who loves dramatic play to join forces with a child who has amazing playground skills. Each may come away from the encounter with new abilities. Sometimes a peer can open up new horizons in a way no adult can.

Keep Them Wanting More

Keep first playdates short, with initial visits lasting no more than one and a half hours. It is better for the children to end their playtime wanting more. Strive to end the visit on a positive note. Some children, particularly three-year-olds, may initially need a parent or special adult to accompany them on first playdates so they will feel comfortable in new surroundings. Some preschoolers may be able to have an after-school play session, while others may need to plan these excursions on un-scheduled days, weekends, or after a nap. If you individualize the plan to accommodate a child's particular needs, you are halfway down the road to success!

Stay Within Earshot

Stay in close proximity to the children during a playdate, because some children need adult facilitation and support to play with peers, particularly if they are new friends. As the play evolves the adult will facilitate less and can stay in the background, ready to provide assistance if needed.

Reinforce the children's behavior as they are playing nicely together. Give specific praise, such as "Nice job taking turns" or "Good job sharing the bike." Nonverbal praise works well, too, such as using a "thumbs-up" sign to let your preschooler know you saw her share her toys.

It Takes a Plan

A planned playdate is a successful playdate. Talk to your child about what will happen when his friend arrives. Discuss sharing toys and putting away items that are too hard to share. Talk with your youngster about taking turns with a friend to pick the next activity.

Plan several different types of activities. Present a sensory-based experience, such as playing with Play-Doh or Silly Putty, or washing dolls in a sink of warm sudsy water. Encourage the children to create a picture using rubber stamps or a collage out of a variety of materials. Take the children outside to gather up leaves and jump into them.

You may incorporate some motor activities into your play by using your own equipment such as hula hoops, bikes, or wagons. Stop by a nearby park to allow the children to let off steam on your way home. Perhaps you and the children can collect some snacks and go for a walk.

Have an alternate plan when children need to slow down and shift gears. If the activity gets too rambunctious inside your home you may move to outdoor play. If children have trouble calming down for indoor play, turn the lights off, put a blanket over your kitchen table, and read them a story in the "tent." If interest in pretend play has waned, take out large rolls of brown paper and help the children draw each other's portraits.

Pull out new or different toys and let the children come up with a plan to use them. For example, strategically leave out a suitcase and the preschoolers may decide to go on a trip. Leave several kitchen chairs set up in two rows and they may go for a car ride. A toy doctor's bag, bandages, and stuffed animals can provide a great deal of entertainment!

Let Them Eat Cake (or Crackers, or Fruit . . .)

Snack time offers a superb opportunity to facilitate interaction between children, both verbally and nonverbally. Check first with your guest's parents about food allergies, then let the children work together to prepare a special snack.

Young chefs may enjoy taking turns shaking a covered container to make instant pudding. They might want to try making a "trail mix" by combining interesting goodies such as cereal, bite-size crackers, and raisins and stirring them together. Or they may delight in making sandwiches and then using cookie cutters to cut them into interesting shapes.

Motivating the Reluctant Player

Some children have a difficult time playing with peers and may require some specific intervention strategies. For example, encourage nonverbal as well as verbal interaction. You might bring out some edible bubbles (available at many specialty toy stores) and have one child blow them and the other try to catch them in her mouth! Take them on a wagon ride and have them face each other to encourage conversation. The youngsters can also take turns pulling each other.

Try an art project that two children can create together such as ball painting. Put practice golf balls in a box with paper and paint, and have the children hold the box and move it around to create a picture.

Encourage four-year-olds to play games together. You may try old favorites such as "Memory," "Don't Break the Ice" or "Topple." These types of games organize the child and provide a structure, allowing some children to more successfully play with a peer.

Picture This!!!

Take photos during the playdate! Make copies for your child as well as for your guest. The pictures will help your child talk about the special activities the youngsters shared and help her relate the events to other family members. Other special projects, such as the artwork they created, will also remind the children about the playdate.

"My younger child gets so jealous when my older child has a playdate. I understand that it is a good idea for my child to have playdates. But whenever he brings a friend over, his younger sister wants to play, he gets upset, and soon everyone is yelling (or crying). How do I make playdates work with younger siblings?"

Many a parent laments over this issue. Some families with two children find that it actually works best if each have a friend over at the same time. Others use the time to provide some quality one-to-one time with the other youngster. Many a younger sibling has happily left an older child and his playdate to sit down and play dolls (or a board game or blocks) with a parent. Some families may invite a playdate over while the other sibling goes to a friend's house. Another way to solve this can be to give the younger sibling a "piece of the playdate." For example, help the younger child make invitations for the older children to come to the grand opening of your new pretend family restaurant at a specific time. Set up the restaurant and prepare a snack. Give the younger sibling an apron or a chef's hat and make cookies, fruit kabobs, or fruit smoothies for the restaurant that all the children can enjoy together.

To quote the divine Bette Midler, "You've gotta have friends . . ." However, acquiring them can be a daunting task for a young child. With your support and some well-organized playdates, the good times will roll.

Ten

Parks and Playgrounds

*For Some Kids, This Type
of Outing Is Not a
"Walk in the Park"*

Taking children to the park is a great way to burn off their excess energy, give a spouse a break on the weekend, or socialize with friends both big and little. Most children love the opportunity to practice new skills, move in new ways, and role-play various scenarios with gusto. The thrill of trying the "big slide" for the first time or successfully crossing the monkey bars can be the high point of the day for a child and an exciting moment for a parent.

However, trying to get a child off the park bench to "go play" can be as exasperating as constantly needing to apologize for the youngster who runs roughshod through the playground, inadvertently knocking down or troubling other children. Some parents stop going to the park altogether because a child always whines he's "too tired," or is so full of energy as to be a problem for others. While some children refuse to climb or run, others can't seem to slow down their bodies, despite reminders, threats, or incentives.

Whether your child is a "wallflower" or a "wild thing," most little problems resolve over time with a little maturation and regular opportunities to play at the park or playground. Big problems tend to be those where there are issues in other contexts or environments in addition to the park or playground. Lagging coordination or motor skills, excessive fearfulness or clinginess, frequent bumps and bruises, and limited or repetitive play at the park are all indicators that a child may have a problem. A child who is left out or feared by other children on the playground also may be experiencing a developmental glitch.

A Tale of Two Children: The Wallflower and the Wild Thing

All children need physical activity and most love to spend time in the park or playground. Playgrounds are an important arena for practicing motor skills and for social interaction. Learning to play is the work of children. Learning to play on the playground requires using cognitive, motor, social, and communication skills in an unstructured environment where there are many competing stimuli. The playground is where all of a child's developing skills are put to the test. Some children thrive and shine but others resist and retreat, possibly due to some underlying differences in their development.

As young children develop, motor skills are interwoven with cognitive, language and sensory abilities. Toddlers and preschoolers are able to quickly acquire new skills because growth in one area leads to new connections in other areas of development. Conversely, if a child is having difficulty in one area, it may negatively impact other areas of his development and he may have difficulty participating successfully with peers in playground play.

A child with a speech and language delay may have difficulty calling a playmate by name, commenting, or even protesting to friends. He may not be able to engage in the volley of conversation that occurs on the playground to assign roles or negotiate turn-taking for a desired swing.

The Wallflower

"Help! My three-and-half-year-old whines and throws a fit every time we want to take her to the community playground. The teachers at preschool tell me she sits and chats with them throughout recess. Is this normal and what should we do?"

When a child is having difficulty participating in playground play, parents and teachers need to carefully observe her behavior and examine what is really happening. Consider her skills in other contexts besides the playground or park: her ability to express herself, follow directions, negotiate with peers, imitate other kinds of movement, and play in a variety of ways as both leader and follower. Are there other sources of anxiety for the child, such as large groups, loud noise, other sorts of movement, or changes to routines? Difficulty in any of these areas could contribute to her reticence to play at the playground. Honing in on the underlying contributors will put parents and teachers in a much better position to effectively support her while at the playground or park.

A child may shy away from the playground for a number of reasons. First, consider the impact of other children. Is she more inclined to try new things on an empty playground? If so, the mere presence of other youngsters may be the biggest impediment to her play because peers are unpredictable. Trying something risky, like climbing on a structure, is even riskier when a child is unsure about the possible reaction or actions of other children already up on the structure. Jostling for a spot in line in the classroom can be uncomfortable but jostling for a spot in line to go down a slide six feet up in the air can be downright scary for some children. Similarly, if a child has trouble understanding peers or expressing herself with them, she may shy away from playing too closely with them on playground equipment because she's afraid of a misunderstanding or inadvertent altercation.

A child who refuses to climb or play at the park *regardless* of the presence of other children may be experiencing a developmental glitch. Different kinds of movement or being off the ground may feel threatening to her. However, without experience, she won't learn to tolerate new sensations any better; and without actively moving her body, she won't improve her coordination or strength. This child clearly needs extra encouragement and close-proximity adult support to explore the various structures at the park. A special snack for the walk home can provide added incentive for going to the park in the first place.

Other children (like some adults) simply don't like to get dirty, overheated, or cold. These children may need extra reassurances that their clothes can be washed, their sneakers are perfect for climbing, and their layering of clothing will ensure that they feel neither too hot nor too cold. Bring an old, small towel to wipe off any wet slides or swings, and a pack of wipes or dry soap to clean off dirty hands.

Power struggles with parents, or refusing to go to the park just for the sake of being argumentative, may also come into play. Usually, though, once the decision has been made and the transition from home to park has been completed, children will forget their gripes and run off happily to play. If this is the case, don't worry about a child's motor skills but do continue to work on planning transitions, following routines, setting limits, and all that other good behavioral information that can be found in chapter 3.

Helping Wallflowers at the Park

- **Play with her.** Throw on sneakers and be prepared to do a bit of climbing. Join a child in her play on the playground equipment by going down a slide or climbing a ladder and then encouraging her to do the same. Don't be afraid to climb up on a piece of equipment with your child! Your child will love you for it. Staying in close proximity is reassuring for the reluctant climber. When she sees a parent climbing up to the top of the jungle gym, she will be more likely to try it herself. When trying to entice a child to dig in a sandbox, describe to her how it feels, how easy or hard it is to dig, and offer several tools or "jobs" that would be helpful for her to do as you build a castle together. When making an impromptu structure out of sticks and leaves, be sure to keep it simple so that the child doesn't feel incompetent next to her adult play partner or simply request that the adult do all the building.

- **Don't draw attention to her timidity.** If being around other children is a factor, encourage her to play near others on lower, less intimidating equipment or on the swings. When aiming for more physically challenging play, do so when fewer peers are around so she can focus on the activity without being distracted by or concerned about their presence.

- **Go to the park with a playmate.** She will have a trusted peer to interact with. Consider walking to the park together so that they warm up to each other before facing the challenges of the park.

The Wild Thing

"David is a five-year-old who exuberantly runs the entire length of the fenced-in play area. At times, he is moving so quickly that he is a danger to himself and others. He doesn't mean to run into others but, given his constant whirlwind speed, it is inevitable."

David enjoys moving and does not modulate his movements. He may need adult assistance to vary his play and to develop a broader play repertoire. A closer look at his language, sensory, and problem solving abilities would be appropriate as well. Children who constantly move in one gear—*fast*—with little regard for safety or for others around them, may have underlying issues that contribute to their behavior. For example, a child who doesn't get accurate feedback from his sensory system about where his body is in space may need to move extra-fast, jump extra-high, or use his muscles in extra-exhausting ways to feel comfortable, and to sense where his body ends and the ground begins. (See chapter 6.)

For other children who have difficulty with planned, coordinated movement, running at full speed may be the most familiar and therefore comfortable method of "play." For these children, motor planning problems significantly interfere with their ability to play in a wide range of ways, so they tend to do the same thing over and over on the playground. (See chapter 6.)

The first goal for David is to help him slow down so that he's available for more purposeful and varied play. Adding structure and even a bit of organization to his adventures at the playground will help.

Helping Wild Things at the Park

- **Teach him to check his movement by playing simple games.** If he is going down the slide, have him stop at the top and wait for the adult to tell him, "1-2-3 go!" "Red Light, Green Light" is another simple game that requires children to modulate their speed or movement. While he's moving or running, call out "Red Light!" which means he should "freeze," and then say "Green Light!" to indicate that he can start moving again.

- **Play "Follow the Leader."** This game encourages him to slow down to the leader's pace and to copy the leader rather than just moving in his preferred ways. This will help him organize and sequence his movements. Sequencing play actions is an essential part of higher-level play skill development. Lead him under and over climbing structures and through tunnels, which will further encourage him to be more aware of where his body is and of what he needs to do to successfully get through the "obstacle course" that the adult is spontaneously creating. Then, of course, let him be the leader!

- **Provide supportive reminders.** When he becomes frenetic or seems to be stuck in high gear, pair verbal reminders with physical and visual cues. For example, rather than calling out to him to slow down, put yourself in his path, and tell him to stop as you put your hands on his shoulders and wait for his eye contact and attention before giving him a reminder about how he needs to behave at the park. Ask him to say it back to you, so you're sure he was listening and understanding. Before letting him go, ask him where he's going to play next or suggest a calming activity to help bring down his energy level.

- **Plan ahead.** Anticipate that he will need help settling down and plan accordingly. Bring a juice box or sport bottle: Drinking through a straw is a calming activity. Think about where you two can go or what you can do if he needs to settle down. Is there a walking trail into the woods? A 7-Eleven nearby that sells Slurpees? Or think of five items that might be found nearby, and challenge him to a short scavenger hunt. Try to use these strategies preventatively, before he's so out of control that he's hard to communicate with and likely to throw a tantrum.

- **Assuming he *loves* the park, be sure to have a good "hook" to get him out when it is time to leave.** A snack on the way home or the possibility of a favorite activity upon reaching home may ease the transition out of the park.

Violent Television Play on the Playground

"Scott and a small group of boys are huddled together. They are acting out antics and scripts from a television show. Although their intent is dramatic play, the boys do not know how to act out the complicated plot depicted in the show. Their play quickly deteriorates into karate kicks."

Children who are acting out scenarios they watched on television need closer adult supervision. They require the adult to stay close by, provide support, and help them organize their play and shift gears as needed. This type of dramatic play is complex and children are often not clear about the scenario they are acting out. Consequently, their play often deteriorates into kicks and pushes. This is quite a common phenomenon on playgrounds everywhere. It is a problem when it cannot be redirected to more purposeful play. If a child hurts others repeatedly in the play or repeatedly throws the sand, then we need to look at underlying behaviors that might be causing this play. However, the majority of children will shift their Ninja fighting, karate kicking, and other purposeless yet dangerous play for more appropriate play with a little bit of assistance from an adult friend.

Help the children shift into another similar, appropriate, and more familiar role by encouraging them to pretend to be community helpers such as firefighters and police. Initially support them to develop scenarios that they can act out, such as rescuing a cat that is stuck in a tree, or helping you fix a flat tire. Bring out plastic fire hats to help develop this play scenario. Talk about how strong a community helper, such as a firefighter, needs to be. Develop an obstacle course that includes running, going down a fire pole, and hanging from a bar to develop their muscles. As the children develop their own ideas, the adult takes on a lesser role in the play.

Add novel items such as chalk courses on a blacktop, stop signs, and vehicles. Encourage the youngsters to be explorers and to go on a scavenger hunt. Use stories at other times during your day to give children ideas on how to develop their dramatic play.

. . .

There is no more challenging or rewarding job for a parent or teacher than helping a child enjoy the freedom and exhilaration of playground play. In today's "wired" world of portable electronic devices, getting kids to go outside and "just play" is more challenging than ever. The foundational skills and memories that parents and teachers help create can last a lifetime. Shaping, nurturing, and supporting both skill development and simply the habit of spending time outdoors together is invaluable to our children.

Eleven

Holidays, Celebrations, and Birthday Parties

"It's My Party, I Can Cry if I Want To!"

Are you someone who *used* to look forward to parties, holidays, and family celebrations? Now that you are a parent, these very same events may evoke a sense of dread or fear because they are so hard for your child! You look forward to your family reunion next summer, but you know your child will be traumatized by the entire event.

Some youngsters thrive on the excitement and novelty of these events, whereas others with a more sensitive sensory system or a quiet temperament do not fare as well. Your child may be overwhelmed, pained, or troubled by the bombardment of sensory overload, social expectation, and unpredictability. Whether this is a big problem or a little one can usually be answered by asking a few questions. How pervasive is the problem; does it always happen in these settings? Is his reaction or behavior so strong that it is disruptive? If it is disrupting the function and you have made necessary preparations and accommodations, but the behavior still has not eased, this may be an indicator of a more significant problem. In most cases with preparation, accommodations, and a few strategies to deal with these uncomfortable social situations, a child will fare better. Structure for success: One successful

"It's my party, I can cry if I want to!!!"

event helps a child build skills and confidence that he'll draw on at the next event.

Parents experience many thoughts and emotions when their child seems different from other youngsters of their age in group situations. Anger, embarrassment, or empathy for their child are all normal feelings at these times. Parents often struggle with the dilemma of helping their child escape the situation and/or save face vs. pushing the child in the hope that he will rise to the occasion. Parents know their children best, and most adults intuitively know when to protect and when to prod *regardless* of their own expectations and desires. Children need their parents to understand and help them at these troubling times.

Holidays and Celebrations

Holidays and celebrations usually mean lots of people, noise, and heightened social expectations. Everybody knows adults who would rather spend the holidays at home, avoiding large social gatherings so as to avoid what seems to them like chaos instead of delightful fanfare. Some children feel the same way, but if they can't express their reluctance or disinterest and instead go along and try to participate, they ultimately fall apart or act out.

Why Do Children Act This Way?

- They don't know what to expect! What are they going to do? What will they eat? Where are the bathrooms? Who will be there?
- They receive unwanted attention—too much attention focused on the child, the child is put on the spot—or they may find themselves ignored in a crowd of adults.
- They are bombarded with a sensory barrage: a touch, kiss, hug, pat on the head, or unwanted vestibular input (thrown in the air or twirled around). Everyone wants a piece of the child, but the overly sensitive child just wants his space or to be left alone. Many well-meaning adults may come on too strong, with loud voices, act too touchy-feely, or are simply inept at interacting with children. They tease, embarrass, poke fun at the child, or just joke in a sarcastic manner (which children don't under-stand). Most adults are doing this in a good-natured way; how-ever that may not be how your child perceives the interaction.

Each child is unique and some children thrive on the atmosphere of the excitement and unpredictability; others have much more difficulty and most have a few moments of apprehension, but usually rise to the occasion and enjoy themselves. What is a party for an adult may not feel at all like a party to a child, who may end up confused, scared, or overwhelmed.

Surviving Family Gatherings and Holidays

What can a parent do to help increase comfort level and hopefully prepare their child for success or at least a bearable time?

- **Prepare your child.** Anticipate and plan for the glitches. Let her know who will be there and what is going to happen. For ex-ample: "Uncle Jon and Aunt Peg and their children Sally and

Bob will be at Grandma's house. You remember how much fun you had playing with Cousin Sally last time. First there will be time for kids to have a snack and watch a special video that Grandma got for you. I told Grandma not to turn out the lights because I know that scares you. Then Grandma and Grandpa will need your help before dinner. Bob can help Grandpa bring in firewood and you and Sally can help Grandma put special decorations on the table." This advance conversation has set the stage about who and what to expect. For many children just knowing what will happen and what is expected of them will put them at ease. By putting in the piece about not turning the lights out, you will let your child know that you are looking out for her and have removed this roadblock.

Children often have anxiety or strong food preferences that make eating at someone else's home or celebration difficult. Your contribution to the family feast or celebration could be a favorite comfort food of your child. Consider feeding your child beforehand if you know that he will be hungry but is a very picky eater.

- **Use visuals.** A picture is worth a thousand words. Before an extended family event, get out some photographs and talk about the key people who will be there. A picture of your child with that relative is terrific, and pictures taken at the last family event would be ideal. Create a small book of photographs for your child. Looking at a picture of Uncle Nick reading her a story would bring back happy memories and a picture of Aunt Kay and her little dog would be an entrée into talking and wondering if Rex the "Wonder Dog" would be there again and reviewing the rules about playing with dogs.

For young children who need structure and need to know what to expect, a visual schedule can be very useful. This simple schedule could use photographs, or words for the child who can read (e.g., a car to depict the travel, knocking at the door for arrival, playing with children, dinner, the playground, eating dessert, waving good-bye, then the car for the trip home). When your child starts to ask when you are going home, you can refer him to his schedule. Kids love to cross off each activity as it is completed. (See appendix E.)

- **Develop entry and exit strategies.** Even the youngest child can benefit from having a plan or prop to enter a social situation. Bringing a small gift of food or flowers to the hostess can make a child feel special and, more important, give him a role or a job to ease those first uncomfortable moments of arriving.

Practice a scripted greeting. "Hi Grandma, I'm so glad to be here. I always have so much fun at your house!" or a simple, "Happy Thanksgiving!"

If your child has tactile sensitivities or is uncomfortable with hugs and kisses, teach him to offer his hand for a firm handshake. (Cue friends and relatives in advance when possible.) Being set off at the start by a well-meaning adult who ruffles his hair, can be the beginning of a downward spiral in a child with sensory sensitivities. (See chapter 6.)

Having a way to leave or avoid an uncomfortable situation will enable your child to save face and as result be more comfortable in a variety of settings. For example, let your hostess know that you will be leaving early for Zach's soccer game. Advance warning will eliminate questions at the time you leave and help the hostess pace the event. It will also have the added advantage of giving the people an opportunity to talk with your son about his passion, soccer. Another exit strategy is to watch your child closely and intervene before a situation falls apart. For example, if the kids are starting to squabble and you see her putting her hands over her ears, give her a break by having Daddy take her to the car to get her books or special doll or have a special activity in your bag or purse, and bring it out to reenergize and/or restructure the social dynamics. If you know your child tends to get hysterical when the lights are turned out while blowing out the candles, have the hostess let you know when that will happen, and that can be the time you take your child to the bathroom or to run an errand in another room. By telling your child this plan ahead of time, you will help to relieve her anxiety. These strategies will help you and your child save face; however, it is important to remember to reduce these assists as soon as your child gains more comfort and control in social situations or is able to act as her own advocate.

Learn to read your child's face and comfort level. Just as you would rescue your spouse from a boring conversation at a cocktail party, you need to be prepared to rescue your child. *Remember that there is a fine line between rescue and overprotection* and only you as parents know your child well enough determine when a rescue is necessary. Some examples might be: Too much roughhouse play with cousins is about to end in tears, or one too many "coin in the ear" tricks by a favorite uncle is about to cause your child to run and hide, or an adult is relentless in ordering her to taste an undesired vegetable dish and you can see signs of a total meltdown, or the kids have pushed her onto the dreaded merry-go-round. These are all times that you could and *should* tactfully rescue your child.

- Teach and expect children to be pleasant and polite. However, do not force social interaction, insist on your child's eating new foods against her will, or ask a reluctant child to perform. She may be just "holding on" by a thread, and one more expectation or demand may lead to a total meltdown.

These assists can make the difference between a miserable time or a successful experience that will build confidence and help your child develop skills for future success.

Parties

For many young children, their own birthday is the most exciting day of the year. As soon as one birthday passes, they begin to plan and talk about the next one. Unfortunately, this long-awaited special day sometimes goes awry. It seems that in our society, the birthday party circuit starts young (often before age two), with many children invited to several birthday parties each month. For most children, this is just a piece of cake, literally and figuratively, but for some it is an event that can cause anxiety, sensory overload, and social and behavioral challenges. Some children simply lack the constitution or maturity to handle parties.

For some children their own party is the most difficult, whereas others are in their glory on their special day but have difficulty at others' parties. Some children have difficulty at all parties. The good news is that the majority of children are naturals at parties and social events.

"My child does not want to go to parties! Is this a big problem or a little problem?"

Temperament, sensory system functioning, and past experiences are factors to consider when determining whether there is a problem here. A two-year-old that cannot handle a party may simply be too young to successfully integrate into a group, and he'll need more time. Missing the party circuit at age two is not a big deal!

Some three- and four-year-olds may have difficulty at parties because of the sensory overload that comes from the noise and commotion of a larger group, and may need more adult help to negotiate this social setting. A child who has difficulties with separation, transitions, and different routines, may find a party difficult. These reasons are no need to assume a big problem with a three- or four-year-old. With a little support these children will soon look forward to the next party. When a five-year-old is excruciatingly uncomfortable at birthday parties, it may be time to look closer and see if this is an isolated or global problem.

Being Guests at a Birthday Party

Prepare

- **Let your child know what to expect.** Read stories about parties. Include your child in wrapping the present and making a card.
- **Be creative.** Help your child to wrap the gift in the comics section of the paper, or decorate plain brown or white wrapping paper with stickers, stamps, or markers.

- **Talk about the party.** Tell your child who else may be at the party. Let him know where the party will be—at Sally's house, at a park, or at a pizza restaurant. This can help your child prepare mentally. Let him know if you will stay at the party, bring him in and stay for a few minutes, and then return to pick him up; or that Johnny's mom will pick him up and drive him home afterward. These details may be trivial for you, but are *huge* to your child. *You know your child best and should carefully choose options for maximizing the possibility of success.*

BE SURE HE IS "HOOKED" BEFORE LEAVING!

Many children have difficulty separating from their parent or caregiver. In fact this is perfectly normal in twos and threes. At this age, parents usually stay at the party and fade a bit into the background, often helping the host family. Your child can participate in the party with you nearby, but not needing your one-on-one support so you can wait until he is comfortable and engaged before you move away. By age four and five, many parties are planned for children to be dropped off, with their parents picking them up at a designated time. If you have a child who is tentative about parties and leaving you, you will want to be sure that he is comfortable and is engaged or with a friend before you say good-bye. Be sure to arrive for pickup on time or even a bit early. The tentative youngster may become very anxious if you are not there when other parents arrive to pick up their children. Carpooling is great, but until your child is very comfortable with the party scene, it will be better if a parent takes him and picks him up.

"What if my five-year-old will not stay at a party unless I am there?"

If this is the case, call the party hostess and find out if you could be an adult helper at the party. Being there may give you some valuable insight into how your child interacts at the party. It will be important for you to shift your role as parent to that of a party helper. Maybe at the next party, you can help for a part of the event and then leave. Always work toward lessening supports so your child will gain confidence and become more self-reliant.

TEACH YOUR CHILD TO BE A GOOD GUEST

Teach children to be polite. Practicing greetings and saying thank-you before leaving will help your child be more comfortable in social settings. You can role-play with your child; practice makes perfect. Children learn by watching others and especially their parents, so it is important to model good manners and gracious party behavior.

It is important for children to realize that different families do things differently. Some parties are extravagant, some simple. Some are theme parties, others have games and entertainment. Some parties are held at the birthday child's home and others at community or commercial sites. Some parties have a meal and others just cake and ice cream. At some parties children bring gifts, at others children may bring a theme item for charity, or some may be "no gift" parties. At some parties the gifts are opened, at others they are saved until the guests have left. In this day of over-the-top parties, the simple goodie bag has taken on a new meaning, and at some parties there is no goodie bag. None of these practices are right or wrong, but simply reflect personal preferences or traditions. Your child should know that whatever the situation is, this is how *this* family does birthdays. A good guest will accept that and not question or complain, but rather go with the flow. Help your child appreciate the variety and how lucky he is to have so many friends who share their families and traditions with him.

Planning a Birthday Party

Know your audience and plan accordingly! A group of mostly boys will not do well at a tea party, but a group of all girls aged four and five will be in their glory, wearing their dress-up clothes and sharing tea with their friends and favorite dolls.

HELP YOUR CHILD BE A GRACIOUS GUEST OF HONOR

Some children find it harder to be the guest of honor than to be a guest because, although some children like to be in the spotlight, others need to withdraw or even misbehave when too much attention is directed toward them. Another problem with being the Birthday Girl is that you have to have the maturity to share parents' attention and home turf.

MAXIMIZE THE POTENTIAL FOR SUCCESS

Include your child in the decision to have a party and with the planning. Be sure that the party is something that he wants to do! Just because most children have birthday parties, a parent shouldn't assume that their child will enjoy his party or even want a party. Some children would be much more comfortable with a quiet family celebration, or celebrating his birthday at preschool with a special snack or treat. If you plan to have a party, practice party behavior by having a make-believe party with stuffed animals. Pretend to greet guests, accept gifts, and talk about what to do if you don't like the cake, and so on.

HOW MANY GUESTS?

An old rule of thumb is that there should be as many guests as the child's age. In theory this sounds good; however, it is seldom practical because of the large social circle of most young children. Remember that more is not always better. Some preschool programs make a policy to invite the entire class or no one from the class. If you are in this situation, it will affect your party options. A shy and/or tentative child may be much more successful with a few good friends rather than his whole preschool class. The type of party that you plan will also influence how many guests that you will invite.

WHAT KIND OF A PARTY SHOULD YOU HAVE?

Many families prefer to have the party at a venue that provides a "total party," such as gymnastics party, or an amusement center with pizza, or a movie theater. Other families prefer to have the party at their home and either hire some entertainment or do all the planning themselves. Most parties focus on a theme that is of interest to the child; having a theme often makes planning the food, games, crafts, and treats much easier. Remember that every birthday does not need to be celebrated with a big birthday party for multiple children. Some years can be a family-only party or a special outing with one or two special friends. Let your child be a part in deciding how he wants to celebrate his birthday.

Making a Birthday Party Run Smoothly:
"Hostess with the Mostest"

- Having a party theme makes planning much easier.
- Overplan the activities. You may not need them all, but it is better to be prepared.
- Enlist enough adult volunteers so you are available to the children.
- Help your child take time to make each guest feel special and welcome.
- Use a "magic name jar" to eliminate the arguments over "It's my turn to be first!" or "I want to pass out the buckets!" or "Can I turn out the light when we sing 'Happy Birthday'?" When each child arrives, write his name on a slip of paper and have him put it in a large plastic jar. Draw names for turns and other activities. When a name is drawn, it is taken out and put aside. Just be sure there are enough turns that everyone's name is drawn.
- If a guest is having a difficult time, try to enlist his help so he will feel needed. For example, give him a job passing out the picture lists for the scavenger hunt.
- Remember to keep a close eye on your own child and see that he is having a good time. Remember, it is his party. If your child is anxious or easily upset by too much stimulation, remember to read his cues and help him regroup if necessary.
- Keep the food simple and kid friendly.
- Consider a project to make and take home rather than goodie bags, or use a party favor during the party and let the child take it home. Small chalkboards can be used as place markers and the chalkboard, with a bag of colored chalk, can go home with each child as a party favor. A plastic pail with the child's name printed on it with puffy paint or a permanent marker can be used to gather up the candy and prizes from a piñata. A small magnifying glass for each child can be used at a science party and then taken home as a favor.
- There are countless ideas that may fit into a party theme and be more creative and used in place of a "goodie bag."

- Consider not opening gifts at the party or having a "no gift" policy.
- Make it short and sweet! A *successful* party ends on a good note when everyone is still enjoying himself. A common mistake is to have the party last too long, when children become restless, tired, and cranky.
- If there are enough adult helpers, have someone take a picture of each child, to use in a thank-you card. If gifts will be unwrapped later, it would be great to get a picture of the child unwrapping each gift. Then include that photo in the thank-you card.
- Pickup is not a time to have a lengthy conversation with parents. The child wants and needs his parent's undivided attention at that time. A sincere good-bye and thank-you are enough. Every child loves a compliment, so give her one in front of her parent, e.g., "Sally was such a good helper when we decorated cookies" or "It is always nice to have Max here; he is so thoughtful."

Real-Life Party Tales

"My three-year-old does not do well at parties. She doesn't want to go, cries when we get there, and clings to me."

Most likely it is a little problem, and the solution would be to take a break from parties for a while. Keep the door open, but don't continually test the waters. Her refusal to attend parties should not be an everyday conversation, but can be revisited when a new party invitation arrives. Let your child know she has been invited to a party and help her make the decision about attending. A little bit of encouragement goes a long way, and if you help to structure the experience, she has the best chance of feeling good about attending her next party.

On the other hand, her negative reaction to attending parties may be just the tip of the iceberg for a child who is having difficulty in other areas. If your child is refusing to leave the house, having multiple meltdowns at school, or in general being very fearful and tentative about all novel social situations, you may want to seek a professional opinion.

"At five, Andy loves going to parties; he is said to be the 'life of the party,' but it is a totally different situation when it is his birthday party. He becomes a tyrannical dictator, bossing his guests around, refusing to share toys, and needing to win every game. What can I do to prevent a rerun of this party-to-forget next year?"

This situation may pass by his next birthday, simply through maturity. If evidence seems to point to a rerun, plan a different kind of party, outside of his home where he feels he needs to be in control. An activity-based party at a location that offers a structured plan, such as a gymnastics party or a movie party, is a good idea and may be just the ticket so he can relax and just be one of the kids.

The "Party Spoiler"

"At almost every party we host or go to, there is one child who is 'the spoiler.' He is in overdrive when he arrives. Even

Spinning out of Control

before all the guests are there, he has taken out all the toys and is running nonstop through the house. His boisterous behavior and loud voice are frightening for some children, and magnets to others. What can be done to harness this child and get the party back on track?"

Some children have difficulty with self-regulation and easily become overstimulated. A party is a perfect scenario for this behavior: a novel setting, without his parents, excitement and anticipation. If this sounds like your child, you can do him a big favor by being sure that he is well fed and rested before the party. Plan the day so that he has sufficient time to "chill out" before the big event.

Managing a "Wild Child" at a Birthday Party

If you are the hostess, here are a few tips that should help get things back on track:

- Give the "spoiler" a job. Heavy work tends to calm children. Have him carry the big box of gifts to the area where they will be opened, or put him to work in the kitchen.
- A cognitive, or "thinking," job can also reverse the "overdrive" gear. Have him count the guests or pass out nametags.
- Be prepared to be flexible with your plans. A "wild child" will only become more wound up with a loosely organized game of chase. If things are spinning out of control, switch to "story-time" or some other more sedentary activity.
- If all else fails, engage all the other children and withdraw attention from the offender. Usually this will work; if not, you may have to have one adult tend to that child and go on with the party for the others.
- Remember that although it may not seem possible, the "wild child" would prefer to be in control and one of the group.

Most children thrive in social situations but they do not develop on a clear upward continuum: What is difficult one day may be easy another day. As a parent, there is no greater reward than watching your reluctant party-goer or wallflower turning into the "belle of the ball" or "life of the party"! But just knowing that a child can have fun in these social settings and can fend for himself is reward enough. Concerns are for the child who shows a pattern of difficulty in these situations. If your child continues to avoid and struggle with the social situations around holidays, celebrations, and parties, it may be time for a closer look. Talk to your pediatrician for advice, recommendations, and referrals.

Twelve

Out and About

*Unforgettable Scenes from a
Shopping Mall (or Restaurant,
or Vacation)*

No parents go into a nice restaurant expecting their children to be terrors. They give them a pep talk ahead of time, maybe a promise of sweets if they behave, and hope for the best. But there is more that you can do to increase the odds that your children will rise to the occasion and bring out their best in situations that are inherently challenging for them.

Learning of the challenges posed by public outings will help you to be more sympathetic to your children and aware of what they are coping with. If you understand the stressors and recognize which act as potential triggers of challenging behavior, you can make specific preparations and contingency plans to mitigate these triggers before you've even left the house.

Crowds and Noise

Public places tend to be noisy and crowded. From busy parking lots to busy food courts, the stimulation is unbelievable. Kids' attention is drawn in a million directions at once and they have a hard time filtering out the extraneous and concentrating on the important (like keeping up with you as you hustle through a store). Parents' attention is obviously split between keeping track of kids and actually finding what they, the adults, are looking for. Kids want our undivided attention, so this split is difficult for them. There is a lot of waiting—waiting in line, waiting for a parking place, waiting to ask someone for help. Kids don't wait well, so this, too, is challenging. Getting basic needs met in public can also be tough. Industrial-size toilets with motion-activated flushing devices in loud, echoing public restrooms can create anxiety and resistance in the most competent of young bathroom-users.

The Novelty Factor

Unless you're on a routine errand or heading to a usual destination, you're dealing with the novelty factor as well. Children may want to check out an interesting-looking object, touch a plant to see if it is real, watch a fascinating interaction between some other child and his parent, or ride the elevator just because it is see-through. These are generally things we'd say no to: "Don't touch," "Don't stare," or "We don't have time." Yet from a child's perspective, these are of high interest but parents are ignoring them. Disappointment can easily lead to whining, protesting, and other challenging behaviors.

Considering a child's perspective, review a few guidelines and key points before leaving the house for errands or a restaurant. Think about **timing**, such as when did he (and you) last eat and sleep. Hunger and fatigue do not meld well with being out and about, for him or you. Traffic and crowds are another factor: *Never do on a Saturday afternoon what could be done on a Tuesday morning!*

Prioritize

Is this outing really necessary? Why are you doing this? Are your expectations of your children realistic, given their ages and the demands of the outing? Excursions into public with kids fall into two categories: those that are unavoidable and must be endured, such as trips to the shoe store, grocery store, and "nice" dinners with the in-laws; and those that are optional and often occur because we think they will be fun or worthwhile in some way. While it is good to stretch and challenge kids, do so when they are at their best. Going to the zoo may seem like a fun idea, but if a child has missed his nap or is coming off a cold, it could be a disaster!

Simplicity Is the Key

When planning a "fun" outing (a.k.a. getting the kids out of the house for a while), *keep it simple*. Walking to the library or park, or taking a bus or subway ride just for the sake of taking the ride, can be more than enough entertainment. Going to a museum will be sufficient adventure— don't feel compelled to buy tickets to the nausea-inducing IMAX movie just because it is there. Running around a new park or going out to lunch at a familiar, casual eatery is plenty. *"More" usually equals "too much" when it comes to outings with young kids. Keep it simple!* A large zoo may be too much for one day, so pick out two animals ahead of time that the children want to see, to provide some focus in an otherwise overwhelming setting. Try to end the adventure on a positive note, before kids become too tired or cranky, even if it means leaving a bit earlier than planned.

Realistic Expectations

Once you've determined that this outing is happening, the next step is to figure out how to set up a child for success. Realistic expectations for both adults and children are important. Conceding beforehand that yes, the outing will be much more work than it would be without children along, and no, you won't have as much stimulating conversation as you might otherwise, can prevent frustration among the adults as much as among the children! They will need your frequent if not constant attention and support to handle the demands of the occasion, and you need to arrive prepared and try to stay one step ahead of them at all times if you are to avoid a nuclear meltdown. Be prepared to leave abruptly should that meltdown begin.

Please Remember This!

As hard as it is to believe, no one loves or appreciates your children as much as you do. Those around you will be grateful when you bite the bullet and haul away a disruptive, out-of-control child. Doing this too soon is nearly impossible—by the time a child's behavior crosses a line in a parent's eyes, chances are he's long ago become an unwelcome distraction to others around him.

Be Prepared

By telling the child exactly what you are doing, you are preparing him for what to expect. Using your fingers to add a visual cue as you review the plan ("First we're going here, second there, and third to the park. What's first?") To make sure he understands, ask him to remind you where you need to go. Consider giving him a list, in picture and print form, so that he can keep track and cross off items as they are completed. Planning in a kid-friendly stop for a snack or playtime in the park can also serve to prevent challenging behavior, because the child sees that there is something in this trip just for him and can count down the stops until his special time. Plan to actively involve him in the errands by having him look for items, cross stops off a list, draw a picture of what you're looking for, or match coupons to items. By giving him specific jobs, you are creating opportunities to give him praise for a job well done. If he feels like he's really helping, chances are he'll be more cooperative and willing to participate in the task at hand.

Prevent Boredom

The second key to preparation is having multiple ways to combat boredom. Think Mary Poppins. A bag full of surprises can derail many budding tantrums and prevent boredom from setting in. Reliable distractors include snacks, small toys, pen and notepad, interesting grown-up things like lotion, keys, or cell phone (turned off). Keep in mind games like "Twenty Questions" and "I Spy," and be ready to launch them, ideally before the whining starts. *It's best if you can give attention for good behavior, not undesirable behavior.*

Be Supportive

Provide support throughout the trip or meal by giving your child lots of positive reinforcement and lots of praise. Look for opportunities to tell him what a big help he is, when he helps you with lists and such. Visual props such as a list also help him keep track of how much more he has to endure: Knowing where he stands often reduces whinings of "How much longer, Mom? This is taking foreeeeever!" Finger-cue progress as well: "First we did this, then this, and now we just have to do this and we'll be done!" Giving him specific jobs, as described above, also helps him stay focused and be less available for tempting diversions for which you have no time or interest.

Motivation Helps

Will he get a balloon from the checkout clerk, or dessert if he eats all his dinner at a restaurant? Maybe change for a ride on one of the automated toys outside the toy store or a stop at the video store for a new rental? These can provide needed incentive for a child's being asked to endure a boring or stressful or even excruciating outing. (Buying a toy for someone else's birthday would certainly qualify as excruciating for some children!)

Keep It Short

Whether running errands or eating a meal, keep it short. Don't browse, linger over an extra cup of coffee, stop to chat with a friend, or try to go it alone in the self-checkout line while Junior destroys the adjacent candy display. As they say in the Special Forces community, rapid insertion and rapid extraction increase the odds of a successful mission. A child can only hold it together for so long, so don't push your luck!

Restaurants

It is so nice to let someone else do the cooking and the cleaning that you can be easily tempted to take your kids out to dinner on a regular basis. (Eating good food is an added bonus!) But parents of active, impatient (read: typical!) young kids often ask themselves afterward, "Was that even worth it?"

Two key factors in a successful and pleasant restaurant experience are the age of the child and the particulars of the restaurant. A certain bliss typically surrounds a meal out with a small infant: The waiters coo, the baby gurgles at the lights from the comfort of his infant seat, and the meal goes on more or less the way it did before he was born. But when mobility sets in, meals out will never be the same! All the strategies in the world won't make much difference for the typical six- to twelve-month-old, so for that time period, stick with take-out or babysitters and save yourself (and your child!) the frustration.

Having said that, most children can tolerate, and enjoy, eating out at certain types of restaurants under certain circumstances. After fast food, the next-easiest restaurants are typically casual places with kids' menus or fairly quick service, such as diners. Anything fancier requires a good hard look at your child's capabilities and the particulars of the restaurant and greater situation.

In general, children behave better at restaurants if they practice good behaviors at home. Have meals together as a family and expect that children will sit for the duration of their meal or snack; grazing should be prohibited! Practice good manners at home, such as using utensils and napkins appropriately and making pleasant conversation. It is unrealistic to expect children to do such things in restaurants if they don't do them at home.

Managing Children in Restaurants

- **Feed your child ahead of time to take the edge off his behavior.** If it is a new restaurant for him, chances are good that he won't like its particular version of macaroni and cheese anyway. Similarly, avoid ordering foods that your child hasn't tried before, in case he doesn't like them. Children tend to not eat much anyway when out, because there are so many distractions. Just being in a restaurant is highly stimulating. Knowing that he's had a small yet well-balanced meal before arriving may help parents feel less concerned with the fact that he's just nibbling on bread.

- **Never go somewhere that has a wait.** Waiting once seated will be hard enough! Aim for dinner or brunch on the early side, before the rush.
- **Ask for seating in a corner or back room.** There, you'll be the least disruptive to other diners. Most restaurant staff do this anyway when they see families with small kids coming, but it doesn't hurt to ask.
- **Order as soon as possible.** Before the children do anything, nail down their order so you're ready when the waiter arrives. Avoid appetizers, as they prolong the meal. Decisions about dessert can be made at the end of the meal, after sizing up everyone's mood and energy level.
- **Call in your order ahead of time.** Some restaurants will indulge frequent customers with that option, so that both table and food are ready upon a family's arrival. This can be a win-win situation for everyone: Families get the restaurant experience without the wait and the staff can turn the table quickly since there's no time wasted with reading the menu.
- **Explore diversions.** Combat boredom with runs to the bathroom and watching the action in the kitchen if it is visible. Giving children short bursts of undivided attention is helpful, too. Get them started with a game or activity and then try to turn your attention back to the conversation or menu.
- **Be creative while waiting!** In addition to "I Spy" and "Twenty Questions," use what is handy. Play "Hangman" on a napkin. Make a tic-tac-toe board out of utensils and use two colors of sugar packets for the X's and O's. Hide a sugar packet and let children guess the color. Start a pattern across the table out of sugar packets and let your preschooler complete it with the remaining packets. Form simple shapes or make pictures out of sugar packets, such as a yellow truck with a white window and pink wheels driving on a blue road. At a pizzeria, ask for a piece of pizza dough and let the children use it like Play-Doh to make snakes, cakes, and other delights. It is always a good idea to bring paper and crayons with you, or small books or a board book for a smaller child to "read."

- **If a nice meal is required, try for brunch over dinner.** Children typically have more energy at midday and therefore are better able to cope with the challenges of a fancy restaurant. Buffet lines typically have fresh fruit and muffins or other baked goods that they will reliably eat. Plus, they can see the food before making a choice, which also helps limit what is on their plates to things they'll actually eat.
- **You can take out a sit-down meal.** Never question the wisdom of asking for your food to go if your child really falls apart before the meal has arrived. Hopefully, one adult can take the child outside while the other pays and waits for the food to be boxed.
- **Always, always leave a generous tip!** Children are messy, parents can be demanding, and time is always of the essence. Try to tip generously to thank the staff for putting up with you—no doubt, other customers would have been easier to serve.

Errands and Shopping

In addition to the tips previously described (using lists, actively involving children in finding things, playing games on the go), consider token reinforcements, such as a quarter for every store in which your child behaves appropriately, an invitation to bring along allowance money and make a purchase at some point along the way, and the previously mentioned balloons or coin-fed prize machines or rides. Some children may enjoy keeping a running list of what they'd like for their birthday or holidays. When they see something in a store that they really want, remind them to add it to their list at home. That way, they leave the store with the hope that it is a possibility at least.

Navigating the Grocery Store

- Ask the older child to look for the items on the list.
- Give a younger child coupons to match to the corresponding items.

- Have him cross off items on the list, if he can read.
- Give him items to put in the cart.
- Make a guessing game out of your list. "I'm thinking of a vegetable . . ."
- Bring a pocket-size Etch A Sketch or Magna Doodle, to reduce boredom.
- Give him choices between two similar items, such as types of cereal.

Never-a-Dull-Moment David

"David and his brothers usually come along when I run errands. He's just all over the place and makes what should be a fifteen-minute quick grocery run into an hourlong ordeal. Between negotiating over what he wants to buy, bumping into things, and having to use the bathroom, it is amazing we get out of the store at all."

THE PROBLEM:

David's mom had her hands full with three children in the grocery store. They were too big to fit into the cart along with the food, yet David's impulsivity and distractibility made errands quite a challenge.

Detective Work:

- Could shopping be done so that David doesn't have to come along—late at night, early in the morning, or weekends when Dad is around? How about an online grocery delivery service?
- Is there a nearby grocery store with a child-care service or big clunky carts with seats in front for kids? The extra time it would take to get to a kid-friendly store may actually be less than the time it currently takes to chase him around the store.

- How often is David's shopping meltdown occurring? Every week, several times a week, or just once a month at a warehouse-type store?

Analysis of the Problem:

We know his family's strong suit is not preparation and planning, yet these are exactly the qualities that David relies on to function successfully. With more planning, perhaps there can be fewer runs to the store and even these may be worked in to the weekends more often. David needs clear expectations and visual prompts to stay on task.

Plan of Action:

Because spending time together as a family was very important on the weekends, David's parents wanted to make a trip to the store a fun event, maybe tied in with lunch at a fast-food restaurant with an indoor playground. They started setting aside one weekend afternoon a month for a big run to a warehouse grocery, where they'd take two carts: one for the kids and one for the shopping. The kids' cart had a list (made ahead of time by Mom or Dad with drawings next to the items) of a few items that the kids could find and make choices about, such as which kind of juice boxes to buy. After they found their items, they searched out the other parent, transferred the items, and headed to the snack bar to eat while waiting for the "shopping" parent to finish.

Alternatively, one parent might go with the other two kids, leaving David at home one-on-one with the other parent to go to the park, library, or other place where he enjoyed himself yet really needed constant supervision and support to behave appropriately.

David's mother tried to be more thoughtful about planning out meals for the week and ensuring that she had what she needed so she wouldn't have to take her son to the grocery store. If she needed something midweek, she or her husband would flip a coin to see who would run out to the 24-hour supermarket after the kids were in bed. This plan also proved to be a cost-saver because in the past she inevitably ended up making numerous impulse buys at his demand, to hold off tantrums in the store. Now, since he wasn't there to distract her, she could be more attentive to what she was buying.

These approaches required adaptation for the family but they felt it was worth it to avoid both the awful midweek trips with David and the needless purchases. Planning meals had an unintended benefit as well. David's mother began posting the week's "menu" next to his older brother's school lunch menu on the fridge. Although he might not like what was being served, he realized it was nonnegotiable because it was in black and white. This led to fewer power struggles at the dinner table. It also helped that the family had a standing pizza delivery night, which was a favorite of David's. So, even if he didn't like dinner one night, he could count on pizza in another day or two, and see it on the schedule.

For More Information, See:

Chapter 3: *Social Emotional Development and Managing Behavior*

Appendix E: *Using Visuals to Support Children and Enhance Learning*

Religious Services, Movies, and Anywhere Else Requiring Silence

"We spend two years teaching children how to walk and talk, and the next eighteen telling them to sit down and be quiet!"

This humorous description of parenting has more than a grain of truth to it when applied to such events as religious services. The strict behavioral requirements of those times can be very difficult for young children. Not only is the content often boring to them, but their instinctive ways to counteract that boredom are off-limits as well.

Despite pep talks, reminders of what will happen, and even bribes of stopping for a treat on the way home "if you're good," children still manage to squirm, make noise, and behave inappropriately at times when it is important for them to be on their best behavior. In this case, as in many, it is important to rely on consistency, routine, and repetition. As kids learn how the service goes, and they practice over and over, week after week, what is expected of them, their behavior will improve somewhat.

However, it often takes more than familiarity to get kids to remain seated and quiet. Part of the routine may be bringing a small book or quiet toy of their choosing, stepping out at an appropriate moment to use the bathroom or get a drink of water, or whispering to children about what is happening. Some churches hand out crayons and coloring sheets to keep youngsters busy, and parents may bring these items if they are not available. Describing what is going on is a helpful way to engage children in the event. Quietly asking them questions and answering theirs at appropriate moments will help them to understand and eventually appreciate what is happening during the service. It can also be helpful to keep in mind potential times to remove a child who is on the edge, in the same way we look for highway off-ramps or rest stops on a long drive. Know where you can bail out! For example, following a song may be a long sermon during which it would be rude or inappropriate to get up. Consider removing a child during the song so that he's not stuck being a disruption during the sermon.

Finally, if services are too hard too often, consider going alone for a while so you can worship in peace. Or, look for a family service which may be tailored to kids with a more sympathetic (and boisterous!) group of participants.

Quietest Distractors*

- Small picture books (the A-1, easiest way to go, and perhaps all you need)
- Crayon or pencil and a small pad
- Pipe cleaners for making shapes or designs
- Hand lotion
- Chapstick or lip balm
- Small cloth doll or puppet
- Compact mirror
- Small sheets of stickers and a small pad

*Please be considerate of nearby children without such items by using these judiciously and discreetly!

- Hard candy or cough drop, for older children
- Felt board/book with felt story pieces

Doctors and Dentists

Trips to the doctor or dentist are usually not a big deal because there are ample toys in the waiting room or exam room. They tend to be kid-friendly spaces with kid-friendly staff. However, some children may approach such visits with much more trepidation and worry than say, they do a trip to the diner. Because of this, going to the doctor or dentist can be as challenging for parents as the longest of religious services. Just getting out the door without tears over what might happen can be trying.

The best approach here is advance preparation. A few days beforehand, begin talking about what will happen or what may happen. Books can be very helpful for describing the tools used, parts of the exam, and so on. Address any worries as matter-of-factly as possible, and if you don't know the answer, say that. A question such as will there or won't there be any shots may be answered with a quick call to the pediatrician. On the other hand, whether or not the doctor sticks a long Q-tip down a child's throat (for a throat culture) may not be determined until during the actual exam. A sticker on the way out or a snack in the car afterward may be a necessary reward for getting through a stressful appointment. Listening to a Walkman or iPod may be soothing for a child getting an injection.

Coping with an Outing Gone Awry

First, remember that everyone has hauled a screaming child out of a store or restaurant before finishing their shopping or dining. It is not the end of the world!

- Breathe. Slow and deep.
- Don't say anything right away, because you'll probably regret it later.
- Once your child is buckled in his carseat, take a moment to calm down before trying to drive.

- Put on music of your choice and sing along to help calm yourself.
- Keep breathing, slow and steady, all the way home.

Must-Haves for Mom's Purse or Dad's Backpack

- Post-Its and a pencil or pen
- Deck of cards (play from "guess black or red" to more advanced games)
- Crayons and paper
- Old magazine for ripping (2s), finding objects or animals (3s), or finding letters (4–5s) or words (6+)
- Tissues
- Band-Aids for real or imagined wounds
- Stickers
- Chapstick
- Hand lotion
- Small snack, such as crackers, dry cereal, or raisins

Vacations

"I think I'll pull my hair out if I hear 'when will we be there?' one more time!"

Life with young children is difficult and unpredictable under normal conditions, but throw in a time change, long drive, different climate, weird food, and/or a new bed, and you have got a recipe for disaster. At one time or another all parents have wished they could have a vacation to recover from their vacation! Undoubtedly such trips provide memories for years to come, but when you're in the moment, things don't seem so amusing or precious. The main thing to remember about traveling with young kids is that their priority is to be with their parents. The location is not nearly as important as the time spent with family. Enjoy this while it lasts! Before you know it, they'll be whining against particular destinations, lobbying hard for others, and clamoring to strike out on their own while on vacation, ready to do everything in their power to avoid actually spending time with their parents.

Much of the stress on vacation comes from children's unexpected reactions to events, people, or seemingly trivial matters. You assume they should enjoy something (for which you undoubtedly paid good money), but they don't. You think they overreact to something that shouldn't be a big deal, or that wouldn't normally set them off. You take things personally or feel awful that you misjudged a situation, and now you're stressed and the kids are feeding off your stress, and it all goes downhill from there. Remember that it is simply the change, not the vacation itself, that is most stress-inducing to young children.

Avoiding these mishaps requires understanding the pleasures and perils of vacation from a child's perspective. Being together, 24/7, as a family really only happens on vacation, and this alone is the highlight for young children. When you can internalize that concept, and realize that *what* you do isn't nearly as important as the fact that you are doing it together, you will be able to let go of the big plans a bit more easily, become a bit more *flexible,* and just go with the flow—the kids' flow, that is!

Successful vacations with children depend on preparation and, wherever possible, establishing routines. Much of the stress children feel on vacation comes from not knowing what to expect. Every day is different in a thousand big and little ways, and the elements that bring them comfort at home are essentially gone. Although they may have a "blankie" or favorite doll, they don't have their own bed, familiar noises, smells, or dishes. Some children manage such stress more readily than do others. Some thrive on the added stimulation; others clearly do not. If a child falls into the latter category, vacations are not necessarily a "big problem," but rather a manageable challenge that will require even more forethought, planning, preparation, and flexibility than would be necessary for other, more resilient children.

Vacation Planning

Plan a vacation with the children's needs in mind, to the extent possible. Children do best with consistency and routine, so avoid bouncing from one place to another every night. Continual long days of travel are exhausting for youngsters and adults alike. Small children generally do best with a destination vacation, whether domestic or foreign.

Establish a home away from home. By having consecutive nights at one place, your child will become familiar with the setting, night noises, and the general atmosphere. This will make it easier for him to fall asleep than if he is at a different hotel, or different relative's house each night. (While this might ruffle the feathers of various factions of the family who want equal time, everyone will be better served by the child's getting good sleep. Remind yourself (and them) that one sleeping arrangement will be easiest on the child and that a well-rested child makes for better company during the day!) Continuing with the familiar at-home bedtime routine helps a child relax and prepare to sleep well. Don't forget to bring a few familiar story books or a favorite lullaby CD (and portable player!) if this is what he is accustomed to.

Similarly, plan to work in meals with familiar foods where possible. Getting a hotel room with a microwave and small fridge for a familiar breakfast can get the day off to a smooth start for everyone. Restaurant food or fast food tends to be different than what we, and especially children, typically eat, so three meals a day of it can make even the strongest of little stomachs uncomfortable. Tummy aches are not helpful on high-activity, busy vacation days!

Intersperse "hang-out" days with planned day trips so that every day doesn't involve a long car ride. After a few lazy days, everyone will be in the mood for a mini-adventure, and parents may be ready for the break that a drive can *sometimes* provide from the demands of the children.

Vacation Preparation

Prepare a child for the vacation by checking out a book from the library about the beach, for example, and discuss the things you might do while there or who you might see. Dig out the photo albums to review pictures of past trips to the same destination, or photos of extended family members who the child will see but might not remember. Talk about where you'll stay: a hotel with a room all together, a rental house, and so on. Find a Web site with pictures of the hotel or resort you'll be staying at and show it to the child. Encourage him to ask questions. Reassure him that he will have his own bed, you'll pack his night-light, and he can bring his "lovey" or pillow.

If you know ahead of time that there will be particular challenges, such as a large family dinner with relatives he doesn't really know, or perpetually long lines at an amusement park, discuss how to handle these situations ahead of time. Role-playing can be helpful (especially for handling encounters with wacky relatives). Give a child scripts to use in different situations; discuss questions relatives may ask him, and how to answer them; or brainstorm ways to pass the time in a long, hot line or at a very long dinner.

Establishing a Routine on Vacation

Once on vacation, use a commercial calendar (or a homemade version designed for this purpose by the family's budding artist) to mark off the days as the vacation progresses toward the return to home. This can be as simple as marking off the day, or it can include the day's activities so the child knows what to expect each day, or when a very anticipated event will occur. (See appendix E.)

Try to eat at regular times, nap at regular times (parents, too, it's vacation, after all!), and balance active play with more sedentary activities. Kids gravitate toward routines. Whether at the beach or an amusement park, it is not difficult to ease into a routine of early-morning inside play or a walk to pick up a newspaper or coffee, followed by outside play, lunch, and a siesta during the hottest hours, then a snack and more outside play, followed by a nice bath, dinner, maybe a game or video, and bedtime.

Transitions between activities will become easier as children learn the routine, because they will know when to expect certain things. They won't have to clamor for the beach at 6:30 A.M. because they'll learn that they always get to go to the beach after breakfast. Teaching young children to read a digital clock can be a lifesaver, both at home and on vacation. ("We'll go to the beach when the first number is a nine," for example.)

Enjoying (or Enduring) Car Trips

- MapQuest favorite stops along the way, such as restaurants, coffee shops, or bookstores with good children's departments (for a nonfood break). Many fast-food chains' Web sites allow users to figure out which franchises have playgrounds, for example. Use the Web to locate public parks with playgrounds along the travel route as well.

- The night before, put the children to bed in sweats and leave very early to avoid dealing with breakfast dishes and a new toy pile in the family room. Stopping for breakfast, either at a restaurant or a rest stop (who doesn't love those little boxes of cereal?) after getting a few miles out of the way can be a nice way to start the day.
- Play "I Spy" for road signs or license plates.
- Give a toddler Crayola's "magic" markers, which only work on "magic" paper, so there are no worries about drawing on the seats or on himself.
- Bring a felt board with felt dolls, trains, or other pieces to recreate familiar songs or familiar stories.
- Bring magnetic "paper" dolls or other magnetic toys, so the pieces don't fall under the seat as easily.
- Try Colorforms.
- Consider putting the nondriving adult in a seat that is in closer proximity to the child or children, for easier entertaining and assistance with juice boxes, snacks, or games.
- DVDs, books and music on CD, electronic portable games, and other high-tech diversions can be a big help on long drives, particularly if they are new (e.g., a new movie or a new game cartridge). Don't forget extra batteries!
- Buy each child a cheap, disposable camera for recording his version of the trip—everyone will get a kick out of seeing the drive and vacation through a child's eyes.

Traveling by Air

- Sensory overload, both in the airport and on the airplane, is a real hazard for little ones. Minimize crowd exposure by waiting in a nearby, empty gate area for as long as possible, before heading over to the designated gate for preboarding with other families.
- Have gum or lollipops for children to suck on during take-off

and landing. This helps to minimize the pressure difference in the ear and hopefully prevent the pain or discomfort associated with blocked Eustachian tubes.

- Think strategically about snacks and meals. Take advantage of the hot water and milk available on airplanes by bringing a disposable plastic lidded bowl

Bye-bye, noise . . . hello, tray table fun!

for instant oatmeal, a small box of dry cereal, or a Styrofoam cup of dehydrated soup-style noodles, for example. If liquids and gels are currently allowed on board, consider packing frozen kids' yogurt tubes (which will slowly thaw but are not likely to get warm enough to go bad), or a peanut butter sandwich—comfort food that doesn't require refrigeration.

- Dress children in layers, as the temperature on a plane can fluctuate widely.
- Reduce your child's exposure to noise. Children with significant auditory sensitivities may find great relief from the roaring jet engine sounds by wearing noise-reduction earphones which will block out the sound. These could also be helpful in the crowded airport.
- Bring favorite "loveys" (blankets or stuffed animals), which will provide comfort as well as cushioning when your child's dozing off for a nap.
- Bring favorite games or toys, and extra batteries! Remove the small screws to battery compartments and seal them with masking tape instead, so that the batteries will be easy to change if necessary.
- Many of the car tips apply to airplanes as well. Any toys with a self-adhesive component like magnets or felt will be less likely to fall between seats—a definite plus.
- Make designs, pictures, or words on tray tables, using colored

electrical or craft tape. When it is time to go, just pull it off and throw it away.

- Check airline policy and then think carefully about whether to use a child's car seat on the plane. It may be impossible to fold down a tray table for meals and play, and it may give the child easier access to kicking the seat in front of him, which won't be appreciated by anyone.
- Do not plan on renting car seats with a rental car. They are not always available, and they may not be up to the standards that you want for your child. Having his own familiar seat will be comforting for your child and a comfort for you, knowing that he is safe.
- Children over the age of three might enjoy keeping their belongings in a small backpack that they can carry on and off the plane. This small gesture gives them a comforting feeling of being in control (of something!) on a day full of overwhelming new stimuli.

Avoid Big Problems

Traveling with young children is always an adventure. Although it may not be convenient, always consider a child's unique temperament when making plans, which may mean more frequent stops on a drive, fewer sightseeing adventures, more meals "in" and fewer out at restaurants, and generally a vacation that is very different from those taken "pre-kids." Know this, accept this going in and it'll be more fun. Prevention pays off: The more accommodating done in the planning phase of a trip to eliminate potential problems and minimize stress on a child, the more likely the trip will be a success for everyone. And that, fun times and good memories, is the goal for every vacation. Bon voyage!

Epilogue

Falling Down, Reaching for the Stars, and Coping with Feelings

Sometimes, parents have a tendency in their zeal to provide a perfect environment for their children, to be overprotective and overly cautious. The downside of this is that children then don't have the opportunity to learn that yes, they can get back up if they fall, and yes, they can fail at something and be okay. Children learn their own strength, as everyone does, when they face a challenge or an obstacle or a disappointment. You may protect them from things but you also need to give them the opportunity and encouragement to move outside of their comfort zone occasionally, to try something new, or to take a risk. Some children need this encouragement more than others. Every child is unique: One sibling may always need more prodding while another may be constantly testing the limits and need frequent reminders about boundaries. As a parent, you perform a delicate balancing act between pushing your children and reining them in.

"Pushing your children" simply means encouraging them and showing them that you have confidence in their abilities. Believe in them. The first time they try something new, rather than dwelling on the possible things that could go wrong, focus on the things that they can do to be successful in the situation. Don't inadvertently plant seeds of worry that weren't previously there or dwell on your doubts with them. The first day of kindergarten is typically harder on the parent than on the child, yet it's important to also recognize (and tell him) that you're excited for him and thrilled that he's growing and developing into a big boy who can do big, independent things.

On a day-to-day basis, you show our confidence in him and his abilities by expecting that he takes care of himself and his belongings, and that he contributes to the family in a meaningful way by helping out with meal preparation and cleanup and other manageable chores around the house. Expecting that he will be a competent, contributing member of the family builds his self-esteem because he sees that he is needed and able to help out in a real way. Once he's learned to dress himself, he'll love making independent decisions about what he'll wear each day. These little moments build his confidence and remind him that, in a world where so much is too big or too hard for him, there *are* things that he can do "all by himself."

Taking care of himself and helping around the house also gives him a chance to practice such skills as sorting (laundry, toys, or clean silverware), sequencing (making his bed by pulling up the flat sheet before straightening the quilt, washing vegetables before putting them in a pot), visual discrimination (finding the can of red beans in the cupboard), fine motor control (squeezing toothpaste onto a toothbrush, brushing teeth and hair), and general coordination and balance (carrying food to the table, clearing dishes, pouring cups of water for everyone). The list goes on and on. Some things may be easy to work in on a daily basis so they become habitual, such as clearing dishes, whereas others may be used on occasion when a child needs a diversion ("Come help me with the laundry!" or "Can you pick out a can of fruit to go with our sandwiches?"). Instilling these practices and habits when children are young gives you a base on which to build as they grow older. If a child never lifts a finger around the house, it will be nearly impossible to convince him to start when he's twelve.

Finally, children need to learn how to cope constructively, with feelings such as anger, sadness, disappointment, jealousy, and fear. As a parent, you are their primary role model. How you manage your emotions sets an example for your children. When you pretend that nothing is wrong, you send a mixed message; children see right through you and know when you're upset or stressed but they hear you denying it. This may leave them with two impressions: First, that feeling stressed isn't okay to talk about and it is something to be hidden or denied; and second, that whatever you're stressed about must be their fault. (After all, young children are egocentric and think that the world revolves around them—assuming that they caused your stress is a natural supposition at this age). By giving them a simple, short explanation ("I'm just really tired this afternoon—I had a bad night's sleep" or "I'm just a little grouchy because I haven't had lunch yet and I'm getting hungry!"), you let them know that your problems are not their fault. *Even if they are driving us crazy, you're the adult:* You're smarter and have more life experience and can figure out a way to cope whether it is by taking a break yourself, piling into the car for a drive and some nice tunes, or walking to the park or a friend's house for a change of scenery. Ordering pizza or hitting the drive-thru for dinner can be a lifesaver on crazy days! Raising children is incredibly challenging and particularly exhausting (physically and emotionally) when they are young. Do what you need to do to refill your own tank, and don't feel guilty about it!

Appendices

. . .

Appendix A

Quick Reference Guide of
Tips and Strategies

Appendix B

Early Warning Signs
of Big Problems

Throughout this book we have discussed glitches that may occur in a child's development. Usually these glitches take the form of little problems, which can be alleviated with a few specific strategies. Sometimes, however, the strategies outlined in this book aren't enough to affect a child's development in a positive way. The problem is bigger than parents and teachers can solve on their own.

If you believe a child is showing signs of a big problem, discuss your concerns with the child's pediatrician promptly. The pediatrician may refer you to a specialist who can more accurately diagnose or rule out a specific developmental problem.

Additionally, consider contacting your pediatrician or local school systems for information on services to support development of children age five and under, to access a free developmental evaluation by their professionals. An early childhood special educator, speech and language pathologist, occupational therapist, physical therapist, or pediatric registered nurse are among the professionals who may participate in a developmental evaluation through the school district or early intervention programs. If these professionals determine that a child has a significant delay in one or more areas of his development, he will be eligible for free therapeutic services to address the delay. The federal law that mandates these free services and programs is called the Individuals with Disabilities Education Act (IDEA). See appendix H for more information on IDEA.

Should a specialist ultimately place a label on a child, it is important to remember that he is still the same child he was the day before the specialist diagnosed him. To that end, it is important to remember that you, the parent, know your child best. How you manage his behavior and tailor the environment to smooth out his daily routines will probably not change just because he's got a formal diagnosis of some sort. Always see the child first and foremost as a unique individual with his own set of strengths. Find ways to help him use his strengths to offset his weaknesses. This is a formula for success, regardless of the diagnosis.

Appendix C

Is My Child Ready
for Preschool?

The current trend toward earlier schooling reflects the needs of the community, as many families need child care because of work schedules. But the question always lingers as to what is the best for the child. There is no simple answer to this question, because all children are different. They develop at different rates, have different social/emotional constitutions, and varying family situations. Additionally, all parents are different: While stepping out of the workforce for a few years to stay home with kids may be a perfect fit for one parent, the loss of income and other intangibles, such as daily intellectual and social stimulation, may be extremely stressful or even impossible for another parent.

If child care is not necessary, a couple-of-hours-a-week preschool program can still be a positive development for some, not all, two-year-olds. Separating from a parent twice a week or so for a few hours can be a healthy step for both parent and child. Learning to function in a group, rather than just one-on-one with a parent at home, is another big skill that some children may begin to develop in a twos' program; others may develop this skill much more easily (and with less frustration!) in a threes' program. Exposure to messy sensory art experiences, new toys, new songs, and new people are further benefits of an early preschool program.

Forming an attachment with an adult outside the family should be the goal of a child's introduction to preschool. Many two- and three-year-olds experience separation anxiety when they start preschool, but most get over it within a few weeks as they become comfortable with the staff and learn the routine of the classroom. If not, discuss with the teacher strategies to ease the transition. Perhaps accompanying the child would help. Perhaps having a "lovey" from home or small photo book of family members would help. If the environment continues to be too overwhelming for him (he's very upset, not playing with the toys or interacting with the staff), he may not be ready for preschool.

Similarly, if a two-year-old is biting others and acting aggressively at preschool, he may be trying to say that he's not ready for this environment. This doesn't mean he's "failed." He may be better suited, for now, to group experiences such as Mommy and Me classes, a private baby gym–type program, or an informal neighborhood playgroup. Try child-care swaps with a familiar friend: Playing with one other familiar child under the supervision of another parent may be a helpful step toward preschool.

If a child is not ready for preschool at age two, this is *not* a big problem! Use sound judgment based on the child's individual temperament, abilities, and preferences. Not going to a twos' program doesn't mean he won't go to Harvard someday!

Shopping Around for a Good Child Care or Preschool Program: What the Professionals Look For

The Obvious:

- How many children?
- Staff to student ratio?
- Staff qualifications?
- Is it a certified program?

The Subtleties of the Physical Environment:

- Does it feel crowded?
- Are the children working on (or are there displays on the wall

which reflect) "cookie-cutter" art projects that all look the same, probably because the youngsters were instructed to do exactly the same thing, or does the artwork in the room seem to reflect more open-ended instruction with ample room for children to use materials as they see fit?

- Do their projects and activities seem to be process-focused rather than product-focused?
- Is the daily schedule posted at children's eye level, with drawings or pictures depicting the various activities or is it only displayed for adult use?
- Are there multiples of toys, to reduce fights?
- Are the various areas of the room clearly defined?
- Are toys and dress-up clothes organized neatly and easily accessible to the children?
- Does the room feel inviting?
- Is there a quiet, cozy place, such as a book nook or loft?
- Is it clean? For toddler rooms, is there a designated bucket or place for toys that have been mouthed and need to be washed?
- Is there a sensory table full of rice, dry pasta, or water?

The Subtleties of the Social Environment:

- Are children encouraged to clean up after themselves, put away toys by themselves, and do other things that encourage independence?
- Do the teachers speak to the children while down at their eye level?
- Do they use gestures along with their words to help the children understand their meaning?
- Do they make a point of getting a child's attention before speaking to him?
- Do they give children specific praise as well as nonverbal cues to indicate that they like how they are behaving?
- When a child is having difficulty, how do they support him?
- Are children encouraged to interact with each other?
- Does the staff use clear, simple language that is age-appropriate for the group?

- Do the children have opportunities to play alone, with another child or two, as well as in a large group?
- Do they have ample opportunities to be self-directed in their play and interactions, or do the adults dictate this?
- Does the staff take advantage of young children's preference for sameness by setting up daily routines that are predictable and comforting for the children?
- Do they accept and respect some children's need for security objects, such as a blanket or a special toy, particularly at the beginning of the year and/or at nap time?
- Do they use information-giving responses when enforcing a rule, so that the children understand why the rule exists? "We don't build the blocks higher than our shoulders because if they fell from that height, they could hurt us."
- Do they use diversion, conversation, or novelty to diffuse tense moments and avoid power struggles?
- Do they accommodate the children's need for physical exercise every day, preferably outdoors?
- Do they give the children ample choices and opportunities to be independent?
- Do they have wide but firm boundaries for acceptable behavior, and show consistency?

Appendix D

Is My Child Ready
for Kindergarten?

When considering a child's readiness for kindergarten, his social skills and attentional skills are equally if not more important than his pre-academic skills. Does he negotiate and play well with peers? Use words to solve problems? Articulate thoughts and converse easily with adults and peers? Attend to tasks for long enough to finish them? Listen and attend well during group instruction times like circle time or morning meeting?

Socially, kindergarten is very different from preschool. The class size is typically larger and there are fewer staff. Students do not receive nearly as much individualized attention as they do in preschool. In most cases, they are expected to stay on task at a table or learning center of the teacher's choosing. At lunch and recess, they typically join with other classes and find themselves in a much, much larger group of children with very little adult interaction. Regular school-wide assemblies present even more noise and stimulation. Such settings can be quite challenging and overwhelming for a child who lacks adequate social skills.

For children, academics are really secondary to the social and emotional aspects of beginning school. For example, difficulty finding a seat on the bus or finding someone to sit with at lunch can overshadow any good experience that a child has within the classroom. A voracious early reader will not care that she's in the highest reading group if she can't sort out all the voices talking simultaneously at recess and is too shy to ask a new classmate to repeat herself. These stumbling blocks can seem insurmountable to a young child and make the school experience unappealing. Compound such issues with difficulty finishing assignments, coming up with a correct answer when asked, or understanding an instruction, and the child is now experiencing frustration or angst throughout his day. His behavior will begin to reflect this frustration. In addition to the social demands, the academic demands are much greater than they were a generation ago. Kindergarten is no longer solely comprised of play centers and introducing "Mr. A" and "Miss B"!

However, automatically holding a child back because his birthday is close to the kindergarten cut-off date is not necessarily a good thing. What will he do during the upcoming year? Will he be bored? If he is bored, he is more likely to get into trouble and mischief. If he understands that most of his friends are going on to kindergarten, he may feel badly about himself, as if he has failed in some way.

On the flip side, repeating kindergarten after a bad year can be even more demoralizing because his whole class is going on to the next grade in the same school. At least with preschool, children are typically going off to a variety of elementary schools so it isn't as obvious if a child has a second year of pre-K. Kindergarten teachers often say they rarely have a parent regret holding a child back before starting kindergarten, but they've had plenty of parents who wish they hadn't started their child because he or she ended up having such a tough year.

If a child does struggle with kindergarten, do not assume that more of the same (i.e., another year in kindergarten) is necessarily going to help. Assess the situation more carefully. Where exactly does he need extra support? Just because he reads doesn't mean he has the motor capabilities for the writing that may be required for answering questions. He may know an answer but struggle with how to express it if he has difficulty writing. Consider assessing a specific area of need: an occupational therapy evaluation for handwriting problems or a speech and language evaluation for difficulty processing complex instructions, answering open-ended questions, or speaking intelligibly, for example.

In sum, share your concerns with your child's preschool teacher, read any literature the school district provides about kindergarten readiness, and if possible have the elementary school staff meet with your child to assess his skills for themselves. Many schools have an open house in the spring at which they informally get to know the children by working on a simple art project together, for example. This is another opportunity to raise concerns about a child's kindergarten readiness. As with starting preschool, youngsters sense parents' angst: If parents are worried, their children will assume there is something that they should be worried about too, but if parents show confidence in their child, while still respecting any doubts or anxieties he shares, his belief in himself will be a little stronger, which will help ease his transition into the big new world of elementary school.

Appendix E

Using Visuals to Support Children
and Enhance Learning

When adults get busy, they pull out their daily calendars, Palm Pilots, and to-do lists to transform the chaos into a manageable daily schedule.

Children also benefit from visual strategies to help them understand where they need to be and what they are expected to do. This is particularly important for preschoolers and young school-age children who are still developing their understanding of such time concepts as yesterday, tomorrow, before, and after. The use of visuals in the form of pictures, photos, and line drawings can help a young child understand what is happening and significantly decrease frustration.

Much of the pioneering work on this topic was done by speech pathologist Linda Hodgdon. She proposes that using visual strategies helps a child delay gratification; understand what is going to happen; break tasks into smaller, more manageable steps; and begin to comprehend the concept of time.

Parents and teachers often ask why a visual message is easier to understand than a spoken one. Remember, spoken information is fleeting: It is said and then it is gone. A spoken message requires you to shift and refocus your attention. A visual message gives you time to get a child's attention before the message disappears.

Think about how hard it is for some children to transition from one activity to another or to listen in a noisier environment. Youngsters who are frustrated or upset cannot listen to a spoken message. Simply put, they shut down. Other children may have intermittent difficulty; at times, due to fluid in their middle ears, allergies, or sensory challenges, they have find it hard to pay attention. Because this is an inconsistent difficulty, it may appear to be a behavior problem.

Helping Children Use Visuals

There are many times during the day that parents can use visual strategies to help a child get through a difficult activity, deal with separation, or more successfully get through a daily routine.

The Endless Errand

Jane is an energetic three-and-a-half-year-old who eagerly gets in the car to accompany her mother to do errands on a typical Saturday morning. Jane knows that one of the errands is a stop for lunch at McDonald's, and she requests it constantly from the moment they back out of the driveway. Her mother finds it exhausting to answer over and over that they will get to McDonald's after picking up the cleaning and running to the drugstore. In the drugstore, Jane whines constantly because she wants to go to McDonald's.

VISUAL STRATEGY: PICTURE SCHEDULE

Jane's mother can use a simple picture schedule to show her what they will do that morning, including a visual reminder that she is working toward her goal (McDonald's). Her mother can take pictures of the errands they will do and paste the pictures onto a poster board or manila file folder. Before they leave the house, they can review the pictures and talk about what errands they will do before going to McDonald's. As an errand is completed, they can put a mark next to it (such as a happy face) and discuss what they will do next. Jane's mother has turned an ordeal into a pleasant outing.

What Day Is It Anyway?

*Three-year-old Tim knows that some days he goes to preschool
and some days he stays home with his mother and younger
brother. He is very confused about what he is doing each
day and is often uncooperative about getting ready for the
day ahead. On school days, once he gets to his class, he is fine.
However, he and his mother find school mornings to be chaotic
and exhausting.*

VISUAL STRATEGY: PICTURE CALENDAR

Tim's parents print out a large weekly calendar. They take him to a
craft store and buy him two rubber stamps, one depicting a home, the
other a school. Now each night, they sit with Tim and talk about the
next day in simple terms. They help Tim stamp on the next day's square
whether it will be a "home" day or a "school" day. The next day, they refer to the calendar as they get ready for school. Tim participates more

SUNDAY	MONDAY	TUESDAY	WEDNESDAY	THURSDAY	FRIDAY	SATURDAY
AUGUST	OCTOBER					1
2	3 Labor Day/ Last Quarter	4	5	6	7	8
8 Home	9 Home	10 First Day	12 Home	13	14 Home	15 Home
16 Home	17 Home	18	19 Home	20 First Quarter	21 Home	22 Home Yom Kippur
23 Autumnal Equinox / 30	24	25	26 Full Moon	27 First Day of Sukkot	28	29

actively in his morning routine and is more compliant because he knows what is expected of him.

Missing Daddy

Jamie is an exuberant four-year-old whose father has just begun a job that requires some overnight travel. This is especially hard for Jamie, who looks forward to evenings with her dad. She repeatedly asks her older siblings and mother when her father will be home, but she doesn't seem to understand the reply.

VISUAL STRATEGY: PICTURE CALENDAR

Jamie's parents also print out a large weekly calendar. They use stickers to depict her father's schedule on the calendar. They use an "airplane" sticker to designate when he has flown out on a business trip, and a "home" sticker to designate when he will be home. The calendar is placed at Jamie's eye level on the refrigerator, and she and her father put the stickers in the corresponding squares. When he is away, she and her mother draw an X on that square to mark off when another day has passed. Consequently, Jamie can see that time is passing and soon her father will be home.

In Need of a Nighttime Routine

Michael is a four-year-old who generally wakes up eager and ready for his school day. However, lately he has been going to bed later and later, and is very irritable when he wakes up to get ready for school. His parents feel that he would benefit from a more consistent bedtime routine.

VISUAL STRATEGY: NIGHTTIME PICTURE SCHEDULE

Michael's parents break his evening routine into small manageable steps. For example, in the evening he has a snack, takes a bath, puts on pajamas, brushes his teeth, reads a story, and is kissed good night. His parents use a digital camera to take pictures of each of these events. They cover a piece of poster board with transparent self-stick shelf-liner paper.

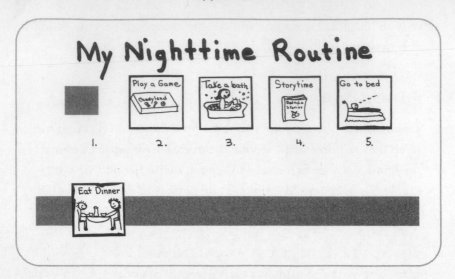

Michael's parents discuss the bedtime routine with their son and show him the pictures. Velcro is added to the back of the pictures so they can be placed on the board. In the evening as Michael goes through his routine, his father points to the next picture and helps him complete that step. As Michael finishes each sequence, he places the picture into an envelope at the bottom of the poster board and goes to the next picture. Michael is in bed by eight o'clock, and his parents are delighted!

> *Joey is a three-and-a-half-year-old who is beginning his first year in nursery school. He has been having a hard time settling in to this first year of preschool.*

VISUAL STRATEGY: PHOTO ALBUM

Joey's mother asked the teacher if she could come into the classroom to take pictures of the children and the teachers. She also took pictures of Joey participating in classroom activities and put all of these photos in a photo album. This way, Joey could look at the book with his parents and learn the names of his classmates and teachers more easily. Seeing pictures of himself and the other children having fun at school also made him more comfortable with his teachers and classmates.

The "Nuts and Bolts" of Visual Strategies

In determining what kind of visual supports to provide for children, it is important to know how well they match objects, understand categories, and understand the relationship between two-dimensional (2-D) pictures and three-dimensional (3-D) objects.

For a toddler, first set up an identical matching game with three objects. Give an identical matching item to the child and ask him to make a match. Once he can match 3-D to 3-D, try photographs of real objects and see if he can match the item to a photo of the item. When fairly confident of his matching abilities, use board books or homemade photo books of common items and ask him to touch various items. Only once he's adept at this, you should move to black-and-white (or color) sketches of items. Many toddlers or even three-year-olds do best with real photos or cutouts from product containers (such as the cracker box logo).

Older children, such as early readers, benefit from a sketch next to the printed word, so they can begin to associate the spelling of the word with the item it represents. Only fluent readers should have words without the icon drawings: these visual systems are meant to support a child at his weakest, worst moment when he is not processing much of anything too well, so the pictures are important even for early elementary school–age children.

Other points to consider include the size of the pictures and the field, or the number of pictures shown at one time. Toddlers who have no trouble identifying a 4 x 6-inch photo may have difficulty with 2 x 2-inch sketches of the same items. When choices on a board or activities posted on a schedule become too numerous, it can be difficult for a child to process and sort out all the information simultaneously. Many child-care centers may only post the first half of the day's schedule at a time so as not to overwhelm the children visually. Laminate the pictures or cover them with transparent self-stick shelf-liner paper so they will last longer. Pictures and photos, once laminated, can be stuck to a board with Velcro. Keep your use of Velcro consistent. For example, always put the smooth

Velcro on the back of the pictures and the rough side of the Velcro on your board. This will allow your picture boards to be interchangeable.

Finally, remember that visuals need to be at a child's eye level. The child should be taught how to use them successfully. Your youngster will learn most optimally from visual supports if he is more actively involved with them. So let your child stamp a calendar, add the stickers, or manipulate the pictures depicting the schedule. Incorporate some of these visual strategies and see just how much your child will learn!

Appendix F

How to Make and Use
Behavior Plans and Star Charts

This section goes into greater detail about how to make and use behavior plans and token reinforcement systems, also known as "star charts."

1. Identify a behavior you'd like to address.
   - Be sure to define this behavior clearly so that all who care for the child have the same perception of what the targeted behavior is, and can treat it consistently.
   - When identifying the behavior, be realistic and age appropriate in your expectations.
   - Aim for small, incremental changes. Build on small successes.
   - Consider timing such as upcoming holidays, family changes, and routine changes.

2. Analyze the current challenging behavior: Identify the behavior's antecedents (or triggers), its current consequences, and its function.
   - Keep a log for a few days to track what is happening when the behavior occurs and what the consequence is. Pay atten-

tion to time of day, location, and the presence of others when trying to discern the triggers and consequences of a behavior.

- Comparing the antecedent with the consequence should provide insight about the function of the undesired behavior. Remember the four main functions of behavior are:
  a. Getting attention
  b. Getting something tangible
  c. Escaping a situation
  d. Doing something because it is intrinsically motivating (it feels good).

3. Make a plan of action with the following components:
   - List environmental adjustments that may prevent the behavior from occurring.
   - Identify a more socially appropriate replacement behavior that the child can use to get his needs met (i.e., when he finds himself in a situation where he'd typically resort to the targeted behavior, what should he do instead?).
   - Describe what kind of positive reinforcement will be used to encourage the child to use the new behavior instead of the old one—social praise or a token reinforcement system, for example.
   - State what the negative consequences will be when the target behavior does occur, taking into consideration the function of the behavior, to ensure that he's not inadvertently receiving positive reinforcement from the consequence.

When in doubt, focus on the positive reinforcement for the new, replacement behavior. Positive reinforcement is so powerful! It is almost always more effective than negative reinforcement with children.

Behavior Plan

Target Behavior: _____

_____

Antecedents: _____

_____

Consequences: _____

_____

Function: _____

_____

****

Environmental Adjustments: _____

_____

Replacement Behavior: _____

_____

Positive Reinforcement Strategies: _____

_____

Consequences (Negative Reinforcement for Target Behavior):

_____

_____

Star Charts

Basically, a star chart is a system whereby a child "earns" stars (or happy faces or check marks) for good behavior. After a certain number of stars, he may earn a prize or desired privilege. At school, a child may come home daily with a chart showing a happy or sad face by each of the day's activities to inform the parents of his behavior throughout the day. If a child has a certain number of smiley faces, for example, he may earn extra play time (either at school or at home) or some other previously agreed-upon privilege. At home, a child may earn a star for playing appropriately with a sibling (i.e., without biting or hitting), completing chores without reminders, or finishing homework each night. The chart may be kept in a prominent location, such as on the refrigerator or on the child's desk, to serve as a frequent visual reminder of the expectations. Alternatively, it may be kept somewhere more discreet, such as in a child's pocket, where he can feel it during the school day (and remember what it represents) but not feel singled out among his peers for having it.

Why Does It Work?

Children may be motivated by such external reinforcement as desired foods, activities, or privileges. They may be willing to try extra hard to behave in a certain way if they believe that they can "earn" a special reward via their star chart. These children understand the concept of *delayed gratification* and they have *basic math skills* that allow them to track how close they are getting to earning a prize or reward. They also understand that the stars *represent* their behavior or actions. Mastery of such concepts are essential if a star chart is to work.

When Doesn't It Work?

When young children do not have the prerequisite cognitive skills to impart meaning to the chart, it fails to be motivating. Getting a sticker right after going potty might provide immediate positive reinforcement for a two- or three-year-old, but being expected to put that sticker on a chart and count how many other stickers have been earned and are still needed, is way over the head of such a youngster. Be sure such a system is age appropriate for the child! To ensure understanding, ask the child to explain the chart to you. **We generally don't recommend using such systems for children younger than four.**

Other reasons for a star chart's failure include: insufficient motivation, unrealistic expectations, and inconsistent usage. If the reward for earning stars or check marks doesn't seem worthwhile to the child, he may stop trying. If a child has been earning stickers for a week, he may become bored—adding stickers may not be thrilling anymore. Switching to a hand-stamp may be a more interesting alternative. Be sure he is motivated by the reward by letting him have a say in what it will be. If possible, give him a few choices and let him pick.

All the money in the world can't make most of us perform like a world-class athlete, regardless of how motivated we are. The same principle applies here: Be sure that your expectations of the child are realistic and attainable for him! Think baby steps.

When adults forget to use the star chart, or to provide whatever is necessary for its usage (like a clean sheet each day or week), it will lose its potency. Consistency and repetition are essential for lasting behavior change.

Duration

Extrinsic motivation, such as privileges, stickers, prizes, and food, are best reserved for very new or challenging skill development. Once a child becomes proficient, the skill or behavior should become *expected* rather than *rewarded*. As your children grow, you naturally raise your expectations of them. This is no different. Often, the star chart naturally falls by the wayside as the child stops relying on it and the parent stops relying on it. Social praise becomes reinforcing enough, and then eventually even that drops off. Think: How often do you hear a ten-year-old being praised for using his words instead of his teeth with his little brother?

Star Chart Variations

- For an avid reader, draw a series of dashes to represent the letters in the name of what he's earning. Each time he uses the desired behavior, he earns a letter. Once he's completed the word, he gets the reward that he has just spelled out. Examples include: V-I-D-E-O, D-E-S-S-E-R-T, B-I-K-E-R-I-D-E.
- Use a pie chart format for a child who is fuzzy on number concepts: Once the whole circle is colored in, she gets the reward.
- Draw a picture of the reward on the chart for beginning readers, rather than just writing.
- Let the child draw the star or check each time, because the kinesthetic input from doing it himself will reinforce the understanding that he's earned another mark.
- For efficiency, use a laminated chart with a dry-erase marker, which can be wiped clean and reused daily. Or, cover the chart, front and back, with clear self-adhesive shelf-liner paper that can be wiped clean with a damp paper towel.
- Before marking the chart, ask the child what he thinks he should get (happy vs. sad face) or if he thinks he has earned a star at that moment. Self-monitoring and reflection help to reinforce awareness of what he is expected to do.

Appendix G

Working with Other Professionals

If You Think Your Child Needs Therapy or Has Been Referred for Therapy

Who Might Make the Referral?

You have just had a parent conference or just come from the pediatrician where it is suggested to you that your child may benefit from an assessment in a particular developmental area. Or perhaps you had a conversation as you waited during soccer practice and another parent mentioned that her son had similar difficulties and that an occupational therapist or a speech and language therapist had helped him tremendously.

A common thread runs through all these conversations. Your child seems to be having some difficulties with coordination, fine motor skills, or language skills. This is something that you have noticed; however, you were told, by well-meaning friends and family and even in some cases your doctor, to leave him alone and he'll catch up. *However, now you feel that it is affecting his ability to function and he is getting frustrated.*

How Do You Find the Right Therapist?

Ask the person who made the referral or suggestion for therapy who they would recommend. Often, word-of-mouth referrals are the best. Some therapists will schedule a consultation meeting so you can meet the therapist and decide if you have common goals and philosophy. The therapist should specialize in pediatrics and have experience with treating children. Also, be sure that the therapist is licensed to practice in your state.

How Do You Maximize Your Chances of Insurance Approval?

Call your insurance company to check on what kind of coverage you have for the specific therapy. Be proactive! Get a letter of referral or letter of medical necessity from your pediatrician. If you must use a provider from your insurance network, get a list of providers and do your homework to see which, if any, are pediatric therapists. If you have already found a therapist see if she can become an approved provider for your insurance company.

What Do You Tell Your Child?

This varies according to the age of your child. Very young children can be told they are going to play in a therapy gym, or with a therapist. Older children may benefit from a more detailed description. Explain what skills the therapist will help them develop. For example, "Miss Jones will play games with you that help you talk more clearly" or "Mr. Bob will help you learn to write." Younger children often see this as another adventure, whereas older children may have a sense of relief that someone is going to help them.

Most children love to come to therapy because a good therapist structures activities for success. Who doesn't like to play, move, talk, and be successful?

What Happens in a Therapy Session?

A therapy session will vary, depending on the type of therapy, the therapist's style, and what kind of a facility is providing the therapy. Therapists work out of outpatient clinics, in hospitals, or in private therapy practices. They can be located in a variety of settings, including private homes, schools, or commercial locations. A first therapy session will usually include an evaluation, either formal or informal. From that evaluation the therapist will write a report, determine the need, and establish goals for therapy. There may or may not be a parent meeting. Most often, the evaluating therapist will be the treating therapist, who will then begin to work on the therapeutic goals. A typical therapy session will have three parts: warm-up activities, time to work on the basic components of targeted needs, and, finally, a closure activity to practice skills in a functional way. With young children, many of these activities are introduced through play.

How Will You Know What Is Going On?

Parents usually bring their child to therapy and, if the child is young, may actually observe the entire session. A good therapist focuses on the child and treatment, waiting until the last few minutes to translate the "what's and why's" of treatment. In cases where the child is a little older or the parent and therapist decide the parent's presence during therapy is a distraction or unnecessary, a therapist will often invite a parent to observe on a monthly or quarterly basis.

Another important way the parent receives information about the session is during those few minutes when the therapist returns the child to the parent. This is a great time to include the child in the conversation, sharing successes and accomplishments (e.g., "John can tie his shoe!" or, "Susan can follow a three-step direction!"). The therapist helps the child demonstrate a newly acquired skill and sends the family home with "homework" (ways to practice the new skill in other environments). It is a good rule of thumb to keep those end-of-session times short and child centered. By then, the child is usually tired and wants his parent's attention. Some therapists have an ongoing dialogue with parents through a notebook; others send home weekly handouts of activities for child and parent to do. E-mail and voice mail have made communication much easier for everyone as well.

To Tell or Not to Tell . . . Should You Tell Your Child's Teacher that She Is Receiving Therapy?

In our "don't ask, don't tell" world, it can be truly difficult for parents to share with child-care providers or teachers that a child is receiving therapy. Many parents worry that this will be in the child's permanent record or limit future school options. Others hope that maybe these challenges won't be so obvious to the teacher.

However, in a busy sensory rich environment such as a classroom, whatever difficulties you have seen in your home will be magnified. Your child is much more likely to experience frustration and feel less successful unless the teacher is let in on the game plan and can then help implement strategies to ensure his success. For example, if a child has difficulty making certain speech sounds, he will have more difficulty communicating in a classroom. Many children with these challenges tend to retreat into solitary activities and talk less to teachers and classmates. However, if the teacher knows about these challenges, she can implement the therapist's strategies to support communication in the classroom, and the child will feel successful. If, for example, he receives motor therapy, the teacher needs to know so she can help him safely manage stairs and playground equipment, and facilitate new skills so they generalize to a functional environment, such as the school's play yard.

When parents do not share that their child is in therapy, a lot of valuable time can be wasted. Even in a busy classroom, a teacher can ascertain that a child is struggling with communication, motor, or sensory challenges. However, if the educators do not know that the youngster is receiving therapy, they can spend the first months redundantly documenting the child's delays and waiting for the right moment to share this information with parents.

Sometimes teachers may misconstrue information about a child if his parents are not straightforward about the challenges he is facing. For example, if he has difficulty motor planning and imitating motor sequences, he may appear to be noncompliant when the teacher gives directions, when in reality he has trouble organizing and imitating movements.

How Do You Help Your Child Use the Skills He's Learning in Therapy in Real-life Situations?

For some children, one of the biggest challenges is generalizing skills. Some children need support to transfer skills they learn with a therapist to their "real life" at home or school.

Let the Right Hand Know What the Left Hand Is Doing

Make sure all of the important people in your child's life know specifically what she is working on so that they can support progress in other parts of her life. Give teachers and child-care providers copies of the child's progress reports, assessments, and goals so they know what challenges she faces and what therapeutic goals she is working on. This is the most important way a parent can work on generalizing goals to real life.

"Let's Talk"

Parents need to give permission for the therapist to talk to the teachers or child-care providers as needed. Encourage them to exchange e-mail addresses and phone numbers so that the therapists can provide specific strategies to support the youngster in real-life situations. Some therapists communicate with teachers or child-care providers by writing in a notebook that goes back and forth with the child. This form of communication can be used periodically and can help ensure success outside the therapy room.

A child in physical therapy, for example, may need very specific strategies to encourage safe exploration of the climbing equipment at the playground. A child with difficulties understanding language may experience more success if the adults communicate in a slow, normal rate of speech, pausing at punctuation and breaking down longer sentences into smaller units. A child receiving occupational therapy for sensory integration challenges may better participate in a circle if he sits in close proximity to the teacher, where he feels safe. By letting the therapist be a resource to all of the people who care for and regularly interact with the child, parents maximize his opportunities for successful interactions and experiences in his day-to-day life.

A Final Plea . . .

Enrolling your child in therapy but not telling the teachers or child-care providers in your life is like giving him a kickboard and putting weights on his legs. Share the information and all of the important real-life strategies that the therapist provides, so that your child has more opportunities to thrive in all his environments.

Appendix H

Resource Guide

All Kinds of Minds
Dr. Mel Levine: Understanding All Kinds of Learning
1450 Raleigh Road, Suite 200
Chapel Hill, NC 27517
888-956-4637
www.allkindsofminds.org/contact.aspx

American Occupational Therapy Association Inc.
P.O. Box 31220
Bethesda, MD 20824
www.aota.org/

American Speech and Language Association (ASHA)
10801 Rockville Pike
Rockville, Maryland 20852
www.asha.org/public/

Anxiety Disorders Association of America
11900 Parklawn Drive, Suite 100

Rockville, MD 20852

301-231-9350

www.adaa.org

Association for Behavioral Analysis

213 West Hall

Western Michigan University

1201 Oliver Street

Kalamazoo, MI 49008

616-387-8341

www.wmich.edu/aba/contents.html

Autism Society of America

7910 Woodmont Avenue, Suite 300

Bethesda, MD 20814-3067

301-657-0881 or 800-3AUTISM (1-800-328-8476)

www.autism-society.org/site

The Brazelton Institute

1295 Boylston Street, Suite 320

Boston, MA 02215

Tel: 617-355-4959

Fax: 617-730-0074

www.brazelton-institute.com/

Cambridge Center for Behavioral Studies

336 Baker Ave.

Concord, MA 01742

978-369-2227

www.behvior.org

Centers for Disease Control and Prevention

1600 Clifton Road

Atlanta, GA 30333

Tel: 404-639-3311

Public Inquiries: 404-639-3534 / 800-311-3435
www.cdc.gov/ncbddd/dd/ddautism.htm

Children with Attention Deficit Disorders (CHADD)

499 NW 70th Avenue, Suite 101
Plantation, FL 33317
800-233-4050
www.chad.org

The Interdisciplinary Council on Developmental and Learning Disorders

4938 Hampden Lane, Suite 800
Bethesda, Maryland 20814
301-656-2667
www.icdl.com

National Association for the Education of Young Children

Promoting excellence in early childhood education
1313 L Street NW, Suite 500
Washington, DC 20005
202-232-8777
800-424-2460
webmaster@naeyc.org

National Information Center for Children and Youth with Disabilities (NICHCY)

Box 1492
Washington, DC 20013
800-695-0285
www.nichcy.org

SPD Foundation

5655 S. Yosemite, Suite 305

Greenwood Village, CO 80111

www.SPDFoundation.org

Zero to Three: National Center for Infants, Toddlers and Families
200 M Street, Suite 200
Washington, DC 20036
202-638-1144
www.zerotothree.org

National Institute of Mental Health (NIMH)
Public Information and Communications Branch
6001 Executive Boulevard, Room 8184, MSC 9663
Bethesda, MD 20892-9663
www.nimh.nih.gov/publicat/autism.cfm

HELPFUL ONLINE RESOURCES
American Academy of Pediatrics
Dedicated to the health of all children; Web site for information, resources, parents, professional information on childhood health, and safety information
www.aap.org/

Apraxia-Kids
Provides information and articles about verbal apraxia
www.apraxia-kids.org/

Children's Disabilities Information
Articles and resources on the impact and treatment of sensory integration disorder
www.childrensdisabilities.info/sensory_integration/

Community: Sensory Integration
Excellent selection of articles on sensory integration in children.
www.comeunity.com/disability/sensory_integration/

Dr. Stanley Greenspan's Homepage

Renowned child psychiatrist is dedicated to helping children and families with information, training, and resources concerning: DIR Model, FloorTime, autism spectrum disorders, developmental disorders, and disorders of communicating and relating, and the social emotional growth of children.

www.stanleygreenspan.com/

Future Horizons

This is the largest publisher devoted to resources about autism spectrum disorders and Asperger's syndrome.

www.FutureHorizons~autism.com

Hanen Center

The Hanen Center is committed to providing parents and child-care providers with the knowledge and training they need to help the child develop language, social, and literacy skills. The center provides training seminars, resources, books, and video- and audiotapes for professionals and parents.

www.hanen.org/

Online Asperger's Syndrome Information and Support—O.A.S.I.S.

www.udel.edu/bkirby/asperger/

www.ummed.edu:8000/pub/o/ozbayrak/asperger.html

Neuro-Developmental Treatment Association

The Neuro-Developmental Treatment Association (NDTA) is a nonprofit professional organization of physical therapists, occupational therapists, and speech-language pathologists who are devoted to promoting the theory and principles of the neuro-developmental treatment approach. This is a hands-on therapy approach for children and adults who have difficulty controlling movement.

www.ndta.org/

The Prompt Institute

The Prompt Institute was founded by speech pathologist Deborah Hayden to promote a speech therapy intervention whose main focus uses tactual, sensory, auditory, and visual information to support and develop speech-motor functioning, leading to improved communication skills. It is especially useful for children with motor-speech disorders.

www.promptinstitute.com/mission.html

Selective Mutism Group—Childhood Anxiety Network

www.selectivemutism.org

Sensory Processing Disorder Network

Provides parents, occupational therapists, and physicians with articles and Internet resources

www.SPDwork.org

The Gray Center for Social Learning and Understanding

The Gray Center for Social Learning and Understanding is a nonprofit organization dedicated to helping children to improve their social interactions through the use of Social Stories. The site offers books and resources by Carol Gray, the creator of the concept of Social Stories.

www.thegraycenter.org

Touchpoints: The Brazelton Center

Touchpoints was developed by T. Barry Brazelton, the world-renowned pediatrician. This center and Web site is dedicated to a practical approach for enhancing the competence of parents and building strong family-child relationships from before birth through the earliest years, laying the vital foundation for children's healthy development.

www.touchpoints.org

EQUIPMENT, TOYS, AND MATERIALS

Achievement Products for Children

Products for home and school to help children with sensory processing problems

800-951-2804

www.specialkinkidszone.com

Beyond Play

Beyond Play focuses on a great selection of resources, toys, and equipment for young children with and without special needs and are appropriate for young children.

877-428-1244

www.beyondplay.com/index.htm

Communication Skill Builders Inc.

This company provides resources and books with an emphasis on communication.

555 Academic Ct.

San Antonio, TX 78204

800-211-8378

www.hbtpc.com

Community Playthings

A variety of toys for children with and without special needs

PO Box 901

Rifton, NY 12471-0901

800-777-4244

www.communityproducts.com

Handwriting Without Tears

This is an excellent handwriting program developed by Jan Olsen, an occupational therapist. The goal of Handwriting Without Tears is to make legible and fluent handwriting an easy and automatic skill for all students. The curriculum uses multisensory techniques and consistent habits for letter formation to teach handwriting to all students—Pre-K through Cursive. In addition, HWT provides parents and teachers with the instructional techniques and activities to help improve a child's self-confidence, pencil grip, body awareness, posture, and so much more!

301-263-2700

www.hwtears.com

Lakeshore Learning Materials
Educational products, adaptive equipment, and both outdoor and indoor equipment
800-421-5354
www.lakeshorelearning.com

Linda Hodgdon's: Use of Visual Strategies
This Web site features a speech and language pathologist who offers resources on the benefits for using visuals, and tips on how to use them. Geared for parents and professionals working with children with autism spectrum disorders, many of the tips and resources may be used for any child that is experiencing problems in communication.
248-879-2598
office@usevisualstrategies.com
http://UseVisualStrategies.com

Mayer-Johnson Co.
This company provides the communication system software for visuals known as the PECS system, and publishes books, materials and resources.
PO Box 1579
Solana Beach, CA 92075-7579
www.mayer-johnson.com

Southpaw Enterprises
This company provides a variety of toys and equipment for children with sensory processing problems.
PO Box 1047
Dayton, OH 45401
800-228-1698
therapy@southpawenterprises.com

Sportime
Equipment for fun physical activities, such as tunnels, mats, and obstacle courses
800-444-5700
www.sportime.com

Pocket Full of Therapy

Therapeutic games, books, and equipment for improving oral, fine, and gross motor skills

800-PFOT-124

www.pfot.com

PDP Products

This company publishes books, and manufactures sensory materials for fidget toys and fun toys.

PO Box 2009

Stillwater, MN 55082

651-439-8865

www.pdppro.com

Sensory Resources

This is a publisher of books and resources on sensory processing disorders. It publishes books, audiocassettes, videos, CDs, and other materials related to sensory issues and related disorders. Sensory Resources sponsors workshops for professionals and parents on topics related to sensory processing.

www.SensoryResources.com

End Notes

ONE: A CHILD IN HIS ENVIRONMENT
Chess and Thomas, *Temperament*.
Gardner, *Frames of Mind*.
Greene, *The Explosive Child*.
Neville and Johnson, *Temperament Tools*.
Rothbart, "Social Development."
Sameroff and Chandler, "Reproductive Risk."
Turecki, *The Difficult Child*.

TWO: PLAY
Bunce, *Building a Language-Focused Curriculum*.
Egan, "Just Add Drama."
Freedman, "Top Tips for a Successful Playdate."
Katz and McClellan, *Fostering Children's Social Competence*.
Sturges, "The Joy of Cooking with Children."
Weitzman, *Learning Language and Loving It*.

THREE: SOCIAL EMOTIONAL DEVELOPMENT
AND MANAGING BEHAVIOR
American Psychiatric Association, *Manual of Mental Disorders*.
Durand, *Severe Behavior Problems*.
Foxx, *Decreasing Behaviors of Persons*.
Foxx, *Increasing Behaviors of Persons*.
Harris and Weiss, *Right from the Start*.

FOUR: SPEECH AND LANGUAGE DEVELOPMENT

Children's Hospital, "Sequence of Speech and Language Development."

Genesee, Paradis, and Crago, *Dual Language Development and Disorders.*

Hall, Oyer, and Haas, *Speech, Language and Hearing Disorders.*

Hamagunchi, *Childhood Speech, Language and Listening Problems.*

Hodgdon, *Visual Strategies for Improving Communication.*

James, "Order for the Comprehension."

Marshalla, *Becoming Verbal with Childhood Apraxia.*

Furuno et al., *Hawaii Early Learning Profile.*

Tabors, *One Child, Two Languages.*

Weitzman, *Learning Language and Loving It.*

FIVE: MOTOR DEVELOPMENT

Abrash, *Hands, Wonderful Hands*

Anderson, Hiltbrand, *Moving Along*

Applebaum and Kawar, *From Eyesight to Insight.*

Balanche, Botticelli, and Hallway, *Neuro-Developmental Treatment.*

Brazelton, *Touchpoints.*

Center for Child Development, *Developmental Transitions.*

Gilfoyle and Grady, *Children Adapt.*

Gardner, *Test of Visual-Perceptual Skills Revised.*

Shevlov and Hanneman, *The American Academy of Pediatrics.*

Spock and Needleman, *Dr. Spock's Baby and Child Care.*

Semmler and Hunter, *Early Occupational Therapy Intervention.*

SIX: SENSORY PROCESSING

Abrash, "Do You Sense a Difference."

Anderson and Emmons, *Unlocking the Mysteries of Sensory Dysfunction.*

Ayres, *Sensory Integration Learning Disorders.*

———. *Sensory Integration and the Child.*

Balanche, Botticelli, Mary Hallway, *Neuro-Developmental Treatment and Sensory Integration Principle.*

Brazelton, *Touchpoints.*

Chandler, Dunn, and Rourk, *Guidelines for Occupational Therapy Services.*

DeGangi, *Pediatric Disorders of Regulation in Affect and Behavior.*

Dunn, *Sensory Profile.*

Eide, "Sensory Integration."

Fisher, Murray, and Bundy, *Sensory Integration.*

Freedman and Greenberg, "Let's Talk, Run, Rattle and Roll . . . Infants to 12-Month-Olds."

———. "Let's Talk, Run, Rattle and Roll . . . Toddler and Preschooler Development."

Greene, *The Explosive Child.*

Greenberg and Freedman, "Summer Sensory Fun."

Greenspan, Wieder, and Simons, *The Child with Special Needs.*

Klass and Costello, *Quirky Kids.*

Koomar et al., *Answers to Questions Teachers Ask About Sensory Integration.*

Kranowitz, *101 Activities for Kids in Tight Spaces.*

————. *The Out of Sync Child.*

————. *The Out of Sync Child Has Fun.*

Kurcinka, *Raising Your Spirited Child.*

Lande, Wiz, and Hickman, *Song Games for Sensory Integration.*

Levine, *All Kinds of Minds.*

Miller and Fuller, *Sensational Kids.*

Myles et al., *Asperger Syndrome and Sensory Issues.*

Nelson, "Sensory Integration Dysfunction."

Richter, Oetter, and Frick, *MORE.*

Silver, *The Misunderstood Child.*

Stephens, "Sensory Integrative Dysfunction in Young Children."

Trott, Laurel, and Windeck, *SenseAbilities.*

Williams and Shallenberger, Introduction to *How Does Your Engine Run?*

————. *How Does Your Engine Run?*

Williamson and Anzalone, *Sensory Integration and Self-Regulation.*

Wilbarger and Wilbarger, *Sensory Defensiveness in Children Aged 2–12.*

Wilbarger, Patricia, "The Sensory Diet."

————. "Planning an Adequate 'Sensory Diet.'"

APPENDIX E: USING VISUALS TO SUPPORT CHILDREN AND ENHANCE LEARNING

Hodgdon, *Visual Strategies for Improving Communication.*

Bibliography

Abrash, Alice. "Do You Sense a Difference." *Clinical Connection* 9, no. 3 (1998), 15–17.

———. "Hands, Wonderful Hands." *Washington Parent Magazine,* 1998.

American Psychiatric Association. *American Psychiatric Association Diagnostic and Statistical Manual of Mental Disorders.* 4th ed. Washington, D.C.: 1994.

American Speech and Language Association. "Selective Mutism," http://www.asha.org/public/speech/disorders/Selective-Mutism.htm

Anderson, E., and P. Emmons. *Unlocking the Mysteries of Sensory Dysfunction.* Arlington, TX: Future Horizons, 2004.

Anderson, Sharon, and Nancy Hiltbrand. "Moving Along—Ten Tips for Enhancing Your Preschooler's Motor Development." *Washington Parent Magazine,* April 2001.

Appelbaum, Stanley, and Mary Kawar. Lecture, "From Eyesight to Insight," presented at conference "From Eyesight to Insight: Visual/Vestibular Assessment and Treatment," Baltimore, February 11–12, 2005.

Ayres, A. J. *Sensory Integration Learning Disorders.* Los Angeles: Western Psychological Services, 1972.

———. *Sensory Integration and the Child.* Los Angeles: Western Psychological Services, 1979, revised 2005.

Balanche, Erna, Tina Botticelli, and Mary Hallway. *Neuro-Developmental Treatment and Sensory Integration Principle.* Tucson: Therapy Skill Builders, 1995.

Brazelton, T. Berry. *Touchpoints—The Essential Reference: Your Child's Emotional and Behavioral Development.* Reading, MA: Addison-Wesley, 1992.

———. *Touchpoints: Your Child's Emotional and Behavioral Development.* Cambridge: Da Capo Press, 1994.

Brown, Laurie Krasny, and Marc Brown. *How to Be a Friend.* Boston: Little Brown and Company, 1998.

Bunce, Betty. *Building a Language-Focused Curriculum for the Preschool Classroom*, Vol. 2. Baltimore, Maryland: Paul Brookes Publishing Co., 1995.

Carey, William B., and Martha Jablow, Children's Hospital of Philadelphia. *Understanding Your Child's Temperament*. New York: Macmillan Publishing Company, 1999.

Center for Child Development, Department of Nursing; Children's National Medical Center; and George Washington University Medical Center. Syllabus from conference "Developmental Transitions in Toddlers and Preschoolers," Children's National Medical Center, Washington, D.C., 1996.

Chandler, B., Dunn, W., and J. Rourk. *Guidelines for Occupational Therapy Services in the School System*. 2nd ed., Bethesda: American Occupational Therapy Association, (AOTA), 1989.

Chess, Stella, and Alexander Thomas. *Temperament: Theory & Practice*. New York: Brunner/Mazel, 1996.

_____. *The Goodness of Fit*. Philadelphia, PA: Brunner/Mazel, 1999.

Children's Hospital National Medical Center's Hearing and Speech Center. *Sequence of Speech and Language Development, Two-to-Six Years*. Washington, D.C.: CHNMC.

Cohen, Lucy. "Play and Language: A Developmental Complement." *Washington Parent,* Spring 1998.

DeGangi, Georgia. *Pediatric Disorders of Regulation in Affect and Behavior*. San Diego: Academic Press, 2000.

Dunn, Winnie. *Sensory Profile: Caregiver Questionnaire*. Los Angeles: The Psychological Corporation, 1999.

Durand, V. Mark. *Severe Behavior Problems*. New York: The Guilford Press, 1990.

Egan, Amy Wusterbarth. "The ABCs of Dealing with Behavior Problems." *Washington Parent,* February 2002.

_____. "Changing Your Child's Behavior, One Step at a Time." *Washington Parent Magazine*, November 2002.

_____. "Just Add Drama—Prop Boxes for Dramatic Play." *Washington Parent Magazine,* September 2005.

_____. "Preschool Separation Anxiety: Theirs and Yours." *Washington Parent,* September 2002.

_____. "Ten Tips for Clean-up Time." *Washington Parent,* September 2003.

_____. "Turning Sibling Rivalry into Sibling Revelry." *Washington Parent,* April 2004.

Eide, Fernette F., MD. "Sensory Integration: Current Concepts and Practical Implications." *Sensory Integration Special Interest Quarterly* (American Occupational Therapy Association) 26, no. 3 (2003).

Evans, I. M., and L. H. Meyer. *An Educative Approach to Behavior* Problems. Baltimore: Paul H. Brooks, 1985.

Faber, Adele, and Elaine Mazlish. *How to Talk So Kids Will Listen and Listen So Kids Will Talk*. New York: Avon Books, 1999.

Fisher, Anne, Elizabeth Murray, and Anita Bundy. *Sensory Integration: Theory and Practice*. Philadelphia: F. A. Davis. 1991, revised 2002.

Flipek, P. A., et al. "The Screening and Diagnosis of Autism Spectrum." *Journal of Autism and Developmental Disorders* 29, no. 2 (1999), 439–84.

Foxx, Richard M. *Decreasing Behaviors of Persons with Severe Retardation and Autism.* Ottawa, Canada: Research Press, 1982.

———. *Increasing Behaviors of Persons with Severe Retardation and Autism.* Ottawa, Canada: Research Press, 1982.

Freedman, Amy. "Do You Hear What I Hear? Strategies to Develop Auditory Processing Abilities." *Washington Parent Magazine,* March 2002.

———. "Preschool Peer Relationships: Tips to Facilitate Socialization and Play." *Washington Parent Magazine,* October 2004.

———. "Stuttering and Your Preschool Child: Top Tips to Support Fluent Speech." *Washington Parent Magazine,* March 2004.

———. "Talking Tips: Developing Early Social Language Skills." *Washington Parent Magazine,* March 2000.

———. "Talking Tips: Using Books and Pictures to Promote Speech and Language." *Washington Parent Magazine,* November 1999.

———. "Top Tips for a Successful Play Date." *Washington Parent Magazine,* October 2002.

Freedman, Amy, and Judith Greenberg. "Let's Talk, Run, Rattle and Roll: An Integrated Look at the Infants to 12-Month-Olds." *Washington Parent Magazine,* September 2001.

———. "Let's Talk, Run, Rattle and Roll—An Integrated Look at Toddler and Preschooler Development." *Washington Parent Magazine,* October 2001.

———. "Let's Talk, Run, Rattle and Roll—An Integrated Look at Toddler and Preschooler Development," Part 2. *Washington Parent Magazine,* November 2001.

———. "Putting in the Pieces: Top Tips for a Successful Preschool Experience." *Washington Parent Magazine,* November 2003.

———. "Smoothing the Bumpy Road to Pre-School: Strategies for Success." *Washington Parent Magazine,* September 2000.

———. "Visuals Support and Enhance Learning." *Washington Parent Magazine,* April 2003.

———. "When Producing New Speech and Motor Movements Is So Darn Hard! Tips to Help the Apraxic Child." *Washington Parent Magazine,* October 2005.

Freedman, Amy, Judith Greenberg, and Sharon Anderson. "More Top Tips to Promote Playground Play." *Washington Parent Magazine,* June 2002.

———. "Top Tips to Promote Playground Play." *Washington Parent Magazine,* May 2002.

Freedman, Amy, Sharon Anderson, Amy Egan, and Judi Greenberg. "Top Tips for Success in Preschool." *Washington Parent Magazine,* September 2006.

Furuno, S., Katherine O'Reilly, Carol Hosaka, Takayo Inatsuka, Barbara Zeisloft-Falbey and Toney Allman. *Hawaii Early Learning Profile.* Palto Alto: VORT Corporation, 1988.

Gardner, H. *Frames of Mind: The Theory of Multiple Intelligences.* New York: Basic Books, 1993.

Gardner, Morrison F. *Test of Visual-Perceptual Skills Revised.* Hydesville, CA: Psychological and Educational Publications, Inc., 1996.

Genesee, F., J. Paradis, and M. B. Crago. *Dual Language Development and Disorders.* Baltimore: Paul Brookes, 2004.

Gilfoyle, Elnora, and Ann Grady. *Children Adapt.* Thorofare, NJ: Charles B. Slack, Inc., 1981.

Greenberg, Judi, and Amy Freedman. "Summer Sensory Fun." *Washington Parent Magazine,* June 2003.

Greene, R. W. *The Explosive Child: A New Approach for Understanding and Parenting Easily Frustrated, Chronically Inflexible Children.* 2nd ed. New York: Harper-Collins, 2001.

Greenspan, S. I., and N. T. Greenspan. *First Feelings: Milestones in the Emotional Development of Your Baby and Child.* Reprint, New York: Penguin USA, 1994.

Greenspan, S. I., Serena Wieder, and R. Simons. *The Child with Special Needs: Encouraging Intellectual and Emotional Growth.* Cambridge, MA: Perseus, 1998.

Hall, Barbara, Oyer Herbert, and Haas William. *Speech, Language and Hearing Disorders: A Guide for the Teacher.* Needham Heights: Allyn and Bacon, 2001.

Hallowell, E. M., and J. J. Ratey. *Driven to Distraction: Recognizing and Coping with Attention Deficit Disorder from Childhood through Adulthood.* New York: Simon and Schuster, 1995.

Hamagunchi, Patricia. *Childhood Speech, Language and Listening Problems: What Every Parent Should Know.* New York: John Wiley and Sons, Inc., 2001.

Harris, S. L., and M. J. Weiss. *Right from the Start: Behavioral Intervention for Young Children with Autism.* Bethesda, MD: Woodbine House, Inc., 1998.

Hodgdon, Linda. *Visual Strategies for Improving Communication.* Troy Michigan: QuirkRoberts Publishing, 1996.

Horowitz, F. D., ed. *Caretaking Casualty: Review of Child Development Research,* Vol. 4. Chicago: University of Chicago Press.1999, 187–244.

James, Sherry. "Order for the Comprehension of Questions in Children between 2 and 5.5 Years of Age." Adapted from "Children's Answers to Wh-Questions" by R. S. Chapman, in *Assessing Language Comprehension in Children,* edited by J. Miller. Baltimore: University Park Press, 1984.

Katz, Lillian, and Diane McClellan. *Fostering Children's Social Competence.* Washington, D.C.: National Association for the Education of Young Children, 1997.

Keogh, Barbara K. *Temperament in the Classroom: Understanding Individual Differences,* Baltimore: Brookes Publishing Company, 2003.

Klass, Perri, and Eileen Costello. *Quirky Kids.* New York: Ballantine Books, 2003.

Koomar, Jane, C. S. Kranowitz, Stacey Szkut, Lynn Balzer-Martin, Elizabeth Haber, and Deanna Sava. *Answers to Questions Teachers Ask About Sensory Integration* (audiotape and booklet). Las Vegas, NV: Sensory Resources, 2004.

Kranowitz, C. S. *101 Activities for Kids in Tight Spaces.* New York: St. Martin's Press, 1995.

———. *The Out-of-Sync Child: Recognizing and Coping with Sensory Integration Dysfunction.* New York: Perigee, 1998, revised 2005.

———. *The Out-of-Sync Child Has Fun.* New York: Perigee, 2003, revised 2006.

Krystal, J. *The Temperament Perspective.* Baltimore: Brookes Publishing Company, 2005.

Kurcinka, M. S. *Raising Your Spirited Child: A Guide for Parents Whose Child Is More Intense, Sensitive, Perceptive, Persistent, Energetic.* New York: Harper Perennial, 1991.

Lande, A., B. Wiz, and L. Hickman. *Song Games for Sensory Integration* (audiotape and booklet). Las Vegas, NV: Sensory Resources, 1999.

Levine, Mel. *All Kinds of Minds: A Young Student's Book about Learning Abilities and Learning Disorders*. Cambridge, MA: Educators Publishing Service, 1992.

———. *A Mind at a Time: America's Top Learning Expert Shows How Every Child Can Succeed*. New York: Touchstone Books, 2003.

Marder, Tammy. "Early Signs of Autism." *Washington Parent Magazine*, Spring/Summer 2005.

Marshalla, Pam. *Becoming Verbal with Childhood Apraxia*. Kirkland, Washington: 2003.

Maurice, C. Green, and G. Luce. *Behavioral Intervention for Young Children with Autism: A Manual for Parents and Professionals*. Austin, Texas: Pro-ed. 1994.

Miller, Lucy Jane, and A. Doris Fuller. *Sensational Kids: Hope and Help for Children with Sensory Processing Disorders*. New York, Putnam. 2006.

Myles, Brenda Smith, Katherine Cook, Nancy Miller, Louann Rinner, and Lisa Robbins. *Asperger Syndrome and Sensory Issues, Practical Solutions for Making Sense of the World*. Shawnee Mission, Kansas: Autism Asperger Publishing Co., 2000.

Nelson, Sandra. "Sensory Integration Dysfunction." The Misunderstood, Misdiagnosed and Unseen Disability. http://mywebpages.comcast.net/momtofive/SID WEBPAGE2.htm.

Neville, Helen, and Diane Clark Johnson. *Child's Temperament Tools: Working with Your Child's Inborn Traits*. Seattle: Parenting Press, 1998.

Niehues, A. N., A. C. Bundy, C. F. Mattingly, and M. C. Lawler. "Making a Difference: Occupational Therapy in the Public Schools." *Occupational Therapy J Res*. 11 (1991), 195–212.

Phelan, Thomas. *1-2-3 Magic*. Glen Ellyn, Illinois: Child Management, Inc., 1995.

Richter, E., P. Oetter, and S. Frick. *MORE: Integrating the Mouth with Sensory and Postural Functions*. Hugo, MN: Professional Development Press, 1993.

Rothbart, M. K., and M. J. Hanson, ed., *Social Development Atypical Infant Development*, chap 8. Austin, TX: Pro-Ed, 1996.

Sameroff, A. J., and M. J. Chandler. "Reproductive Risk and the Continuum of Caretaking Casualty. In *Review of Child Development Research*. Chicago: University Press, 1975.

Selective Mutism Group—Childhood Anxiety Network Web site. http://www.selectivemutism.org

Semmler, Caryl, and Jan Hunter. *Early Occupational Therapy Intervention*. Gaithersburg, MD: Aspen Publishers, Inc., 1990.

Setsu, Furuno, et al. *Hawaii Early Learning Profile (HELP)*. Palo Alto, CA: VORT, 1984.

Shevlov, Steven, and Robert Hanneman. *The American Academy of Pediatrics: Caring for Your Baby and Young Child Birth to Age 5*. New York: Bantam Books, 2004.

Shick, Lyndall. *Understanding Temperament: Strategies for Creating Family Harmony*. Seattle: Press Inc., 1998.

Silver, L. B. *The Misunderstood Child: A Guide for Parents of Children with Learning Disabilities*. 3rd ed. Blue Ridge Summit, PA: TAB Books, 1992.

Spock, Benjamin, and Robert Needleman (rev. ed.). *Dr. Spock's Baby and Child Care*. 8th ed. New York: Pocket Books, Simon and Schuster, Inc., 2004.

Stephens, Linda C. "Sensory Integrative Dysfunction in Young Children." *SEE/Hear*, Fall 1997 and *AAHBEI News Exchange* 2, no. 1 (Winter 1997). http://www.tsbvi.edu/Outreach/seehear/fall97/sensory.htm.

Sturges, Lina. "Kids in the Kitchen—Cooking Up Creativity," *Washington Parent Magazine,* January 2002.

Sturges, Lina Lewis. "Understanding Learning Styles—The Key to Developing Your Child's Talents and Gifts." *Washington Parent Magazine,* January 2001.

Tabors, P. O. *One Child, two languages: A guide for preschool educators of children learning English as a second language.* Baltimore: Paul H. Brookes Publishing Co., 1997.

Thomas, A., and Stella Chess, *Temperament and Development.* New York: Brunner/Mazel, 1977.

Trott, M. C., M. Laurel, and S. L. Windeck, *SenseAbilities: Understanding Sensory Integration.* San Antonio, TX: Therapy Skill Builders, 1993.

Turecki, Stanley. *The Difficult Child.* New York: Bantam Books, 1989.

Turecki, Stanley, and Leslie Tonner. *The Difficult Child: Expanded and Revised Ed.,* N.Y.: Bantam Books, 2000.

Weitzman, Elaine. *Learning Language and Loving It.* Toronto: Hanen Publication, 1992.

Wilbarger, Patricia. "The Sensory Diet: Activity Programs Based on Sensory Processing Theory." *Sensory Integration Special-Interest Section Newsletter* 18, no. 2 (1995).

———. "Planning an Adequate 'Sensory diet'—Application of Sensory Processing Theory During the First Year of Life." *"Zero to Three"* 5, no.1, 1984, 7–12.

Wilbarger, Patricia, and Julia Wilbarger. *Sensory Defensiveness in Children Aged 2–12: An Intervention Guide for Parents and Other Caretakers.* Santa Barbara, CA: Avanti Educational Programs, 1991.

Williams, M. S., and S. Shallenberger. Introduction to *"How Does Your Engine Run?" The Alert Program for Self-Regulation.* Albuquerque: Therapy Works, 1992.

———. *How Does Your Engine Run? A Leader's Guide to the Alert Program for Self-Regulation.* Albuquerque: Therapy Works, 1994.

Williamson, G. Gordon, and Marie Anzalone. *Sensory Integration and Self-Regulation in Infants and Toddlers.* Washington, D.C.: Zero to Three, 2001.

Selected Reading

SPEECH AND LANGUAGE

Agin, Marilyn, MD, et al. *The Late Talker*. New York: St. Martin's Press, 2003.

Hall, Barbara, Oyer Herbert, and Haas William. *Speech, Language and Hearing Disorders: A Guide for the Teacher*. Needham Heights: Allyn and Bacon, 2001.

Hamagunchi, Patricia. *Childhood Speech, Language and Listening Problems: What Every Parent Should Know*. New York: John Wiley and Sons, Inc., 2001.

Hodgdon, Linda. *Visual Strategies for Improving Communication*. Troy, Michigan: QuirkRoberts Publishing, 1996.

Manolson, Ayala. *It Takes Two to Talk*. Toronto: Hanen Publication, 1992.

Marshalla, Pam. *Becoming Verbal with Childhood Apraxia*. Kirkland, Washington, 2003.

Weitzman, Elaine. *Learning Language and Loving It*. Toronto: Hanen Publication, 1992.

SENSORY INTEGRATION/SENSORY PROCESSING

Biel, Lindsey, and Nancy Peske. *Raising a Sensory Smart Child: The Definite Handbook for Helping Your Child with Sensory Integration Issues*. New York, Penguin Books. 2005.

Eide, Brock, and Fernette Eide. *The Mislabeled Child: How Understanding Your Child's Unique Learning Style Can Open the Door to Success*. New York: Hyperion, 2006.

Emmons, Polly Godwin, and Liz McKendry Anderson. *Understanding Sensory Dysfunction: Learning, Development and Sensory Dysfunction in Autism Spectrum Disorders ADHD, Learning Disabilities and Bipolar Disorder*. London: Jessica Kingsley Publishing, 2005.

Heller, Sharon. *Too Loud Too Bright Too Fast Too Tight: What to Do if You Are Sensory Defensive in an Over-stimulating World.* New York: Quill. 2003.

Kranowitz, C. S. *The Goodenoughs Get in Sync.* Las Vegas, NV: Sensory Resources, 2004.

Smith, Karen A., and Karen R. Gouze. *The Sensory-Sensitive Child.* New York, HarperCollins, 2004.

Index